Religious Education Encounters
Liberation Theology

Religious Education Encounters Liberation Theology

DANIEL S. SCHIPANI

Religious Education Press
Birmingham, Alabama

Library of Congress Cataloging-in-Publication Data
Schipani, Daniel S., 1943-
   Religious education encounters liberation theology/Daniel S. Schipani.
   Includes bibliographies and indexes.
   ISBN 0-89135-059-4
   1. Christian education—Philosophy. 2. Liberation theology.
I. Title.
BV1464.S335 1988
268'.01—dc19   88-13093
                                                                                CIP

Religious Education Press, Inc.
5316 Meadow Brook Road
Birmingham, Alabama 35243
10 9 8 7 6 5 4 3 2

Religious Education Press publishes books exclusively in religious education and in areas closely related to religious education. It is committed to enhancing and professionalizing religious education through the publication of serious, significant, and scholarly works.

PUBLISHER TO THE PROFESSION

To PAULO FREIRE

Christian Educator
Liberation Theologian
Mentor and Friend

Contents

Preface

The title of this book is meant to evoke the two related images of meeting and confronting. The first image is that of liberation theology and religious education meeting each other "face to face" so that a direct "interfacing" may occur. *Encounter* in this case denotes interaction by way of juxtaposing those two fields. The second image is that of confrontation as "standing firmly (and even defiantly) in front of." Confrontation suggests a challenge, at least in the fashion of a mutually critical engagement, a kind of theoretical and ideological wrestling, as it were, between religious education and liberation theology. This specific connotation of the title and theme of the book is facilitated, of course, by the inherently confrontational character of liberation theologies, especially the Latin American contributions on which we will concentrate. This chosen focus is not only due to the author's historicocultural context of life and work but also because that theology is the most systematically articulated and developed and widely translated and read among current liberation theologies.[1]

Several additional comments may be appended parenthetically in regard to the relevance of our topic, beginning with the fact that the Latin American community in North America, including of course the refugees, is already larger than the entire population of Central America. In connection with that, the peculiar nature of relations between the United States and Latin America must be acknowledged, involving critical issues such as economic policies and foreign debt and the perennial political and military interventionism. Further, one must reckon with the liberationist assumption of a certain correlation between the impressive concentration of power and resources (i.e., "development") of the rich nations and the widening gap with the so-called "underdeveloped" countries, including the associated evils of militarism and repression, grinding hunger and poverty, and related indicators of dependence, marginalization, and exploitation. Together with the bankruptcy of the paradigm of dependent capitalism, the collapse of the Christendom model of Roman Catholicism is another factor to take into account.

By interest, purpose, design, and effect, liberation theologies

1

foster nonconformity, critique, and alternative perspectives and corrective social action in light of the contexts of oppression and alienation from which they have emerged. In this connection, religious education often becomes the target of the liberationists' indictment to the point of Christian education being considered "the great failure of contemporary Judeo-Christian life" for having failed to produce an American nation of equality and justice.[2]

Liberation theology is undoubtedly a leading, well-established school of thought, as C. Ellis Nelson has indicated,[3] and religious education must encounter it both critically and constructively. In other words, we are not dealing with just another theological fad but with an approach and a movement that will continue to develop and to exert a significant influence in the foreseeable future. The major reason for this assertion is that liberation theology is not founded on any fashionable philosophy but on the very geopolitical and socioeconomic configuration of our world which elicits a longing for freedom, peace, and justice.

Finally, we must indicate that Latin American liberation theology presents a *pedagogical* structure and orientation which has not been duly recognized and evaluated. Yet that is apparent in a number of tenets and emphases held by liberationists, such as those concerning the normative import of the teachings of Jesus, the view of the Bible as the text of the church and the book for the people, the dynamics of faith as discipleship (i.e., the committed following of Jesus Christ) and doing theology as—essentially— church education for the ministry and mission of the ecclesial community. This pedagogical structure and orientation, which will become more apparent in our discussion throughout the book, actually calls for and facilitates this project.

Since 1970, several religious educators and educationists have attempted to deal with liberation thought.[4] However, those efforts have been far too tentative, schematic, and inconclusive, with the exception of Thomas H. Groome's *Christian Religious Education: Sharing Our Story and Vision*, and my own study, *Conscientization and Creativity*.[5] Given the very apparent impact of liberation theology during the last few years,[6] our aim is to provide a broad and critical overview of liberation thought from the unique vantage point of religious education. Rather than an exhaustive treatment of liberation theology as such, we are interested in underscoring and incorporating its major insights in light of the overall liberation thrust and spirit. This task is to be accomplished by way of a direct interfacing with religious education. Simply stated, it is our thesis that in the encounter between religious education and liberation theology—while the integrity of both is respected—mutual enlightenment will take place and the two fields will be advanced in their own terms. This being the case, the book is also intended to contribute to the larger ongoing conversation on the relationship between theology and religious education and the germane question of theory and practice. The subject of the interplay between religious education and theology, as such, will be addressed throughout the book. It is helpful and relevant for us to keep in mind several key questions that have been raised in this regard as follows: succinctly put by Randolph Crump Miller—"What theology can provide the background for religious education? What should be the relation between theology and education?";[7] skeptically asked by Iris V. Cully—"Can any theology be pivotal for religious education theory today? . . . Can there be a theological restatement that would make an acceptable basis for religious education theory?";[8] inquiringly phrased by Norma H. Thompson—"Does theology determine (or influence) decisions regarding the content of religious education? How does theology affect methodology, objectives, curriculum, and administration in religious education? . . . Does the educational process itself have a creative role to play in religious education; that is, as the process goes forward, is reconstruction and reinterpretation of the basic concepts of that faith a natural outcome of that process? What is the result of the interaction of theology and the educational process?"[9] We assume that our discussion will contribute to illumine those questions and will provide some pertinent answers.

Because of personal commitment, academic and professional experience, and theological preference and bias, it is *Christian* religious education that is meant here. Therefore, in a sense the specific context and orientation of the following discussion are those of the Christian faith community even though, to be sure, the concern for liberation is shared in many ways by religious educators in other faith communities and religious and theological traditions.

The body of the book consists of five chapters each centering around a major liberation motif (conscientization, kingdom of God, praxis knowing, critical interpretation, and base community). After a brief overview of the topic, the perspectives of the liberationists are presented as specifically related to religious education. Then follow analysis and critique in which strengths and contributions as well as weaknesses and limitations are indicated from a religious education standpoint. The discussion leads also to constructive restatements of principles for the practice and theory of religious education. The idea is to maintain the "*encounter*" throughout the essay rather than considering implications for religious education in a merely reactive manner. For reasons that will become clear early in the discussion, the work and thought of Paulo Freire serves as a centerpiece of the book.

The brief gospel reference at the beginning of each chapter symbolizes the normative character that the person and the teaching model of Jesus assume for both Christian religious education as well as Latin American liberation theology. The accompanying parallel quotations selected represent both an anticipation of the focal thrust of each chapter and samples of the rich and diverse contributions available from both fields. The conclusion brings together a summary of our findings in light of the stated purposes and some basic issues that will be addressed along the way as well as implications for futher reflection and dialogue.

The substance of this book emanates from several years of work and reflection in divers sociohistorical settings in South, Central, and North America, and the Caribbean. I have had the privilege of participating in a number of projects and dialogues with friends, colleagues, teachers, and students as well as other people struggling with the questions of justice, faith nurture, and transformation. In different ways I am indebted to all of them. I appreciate especially the guidance of my former teachers at Princeton Theological Seminary—James E. Loder, Richard Shaull, and D. Campbell Wyckoff—who initially oriented my academic work in the areas discussed in this book and the encouragement of Paulo Freire to pursue the critical reflection and the dialogue here registered. Special thanks are due to the Seminario Evangélico de Puerto Rico where I started to design the project and to the Associated Mennonite Biblical Seminaries that facilitated its completion. I also want to acknowledge with grateful appreciation the counsel and support received from my publisher, James Michael Lee, the skillful secretarial assistance of Sue DeLeon and, most especially, the unfailing company of my life partner, Margaret Anne, and our two children, David and Marisa.

D.S.

Elkhart, Indiana

Notes

1. It can also be argued that other liberation theologies, such as black or feminist, share some basic analogous concerns and methodologies and provide similarly meaningful contributions in certain areas. The following works are helpful for an interpretive consideration of liberation theologies: Frederick Herzog, *Liberation Theology: Liberation in the Light of the Fourth Gospel* (New York: Seabury, 1972); Rosemary Redford Ruether, *Liberation Theology: Human Hope Confronts Christian History and American Power* (New York: Paulist, 1972); World Council of Churches, "Theological Symposium with James H. Cone, Paulo Freire, and others," in *Risk* 9:2 (1973); Letty M. Russell, *Human Liberation in a Feminist Perspective* (Philadelphia: Westminster, 1975); James H. Cone, *God of the Oppressed* (New York: Seabury, 1975) and "From Geneva to Sao Paulo: A Dialogue Between Black Theology and Latin American Liberation Theology," in *The Challenge of Basic Christian Communities*, ed. Sergio Torres and John Eagleson (Maryknoll, N.Y.: Orbis, 1981), pp. 265-281, also *For My People: Black Theology and the Black Church* (Maryknoll, N.Y.: Orbis, 1984), chap. 3, and *My Soul Looks Back* (Maryknoll, N.Y.: Orbis, 1986), chaps. 4, 5; Robert McAfee Brown, *Theology in a New Key: Responding to Liberation Themes* (Philadelphia: Westminster, 1978); Gerald H. Anderson and Thomas F. Stransky, eds., *Mission Trends No. 4: Liberation Theologies in North America and Europe* (New York: Paulist/Grand Rapids, Mich.: Eerdmans, 1979); Brian Mahan and L. Dale Richesin, eds., *The Challenge of Liberation Theology: A First World Response* (Maryknoll, N.Y.: Orbis, 1981); Harvey M. Conn, "Theologies of Liberation: An Overview" and "Theologies of Liberation: Toward a Common View," in *Tensions in Contemporary Theology*, 2nd ed., ed. Stanley N. Gundry and Alan F. Johnson (Grand Rapids, Mich.: Baker, 1983), pp. 325-434; Georges Casalis, *Correct Ideas Don't Fall From the Skies: Elements of an Inductive Theology*, trans. Jeanne Marie Lyons and Michael John (Maryknoll, N.Y.: Orbis, 1984); Roger Haight, *An Alternative Vision: An Interpretation of Liberation Theology* (New York: Paulist, 1985); Dean William Ferm, *Third World Liberation Theologies: An Introductory Survey* (Maryknoll, N.Y.: Orbis, 1986); and *Third World Liberation Theologies: A Reader* (Maryknoll, N.Y.: Orbis, 1986).

2. Olivia Pearl Stokes, "Black Theology: A Challenge to Religious Education," in *Religious Education and Theology*, ed. Norma H. Thompson (Birmingham, Ala.: Religious Education Press, 1982), pp. 90-93.

3. "Theological Foundations for Religious Education," in *Changing Patterns of Religious Education*, ed. Marvin J. Taylor (Nashville: Abingdon, 1984) p. 21.

4. The first North American articles and essays on or directly related to liberation theology began to appear in 1970. At the risk of arbitrariness, it is hereby suggested that we consider Boardman W. Kathan's call for active engagement in the struggle for liberation, social change, and justice ("Religious Education in the 70's: Human Liberation in an Uptight Age," *Religious Education* 66:1 [January-February 1971], pp. 5-13) as a starting point in the succession of specific references to liberation in religious education. Those references are to a certain extent correlated with the ongoing theological discussion on the matter. Some noticeable examples are the following: Miriam Clasby, "Education as a Tool for Humanization and the Work of Paulo Freire," *Living Light* (Spring 1971), pp. 48-59; Marcel van Caster, "A Catechesis for Liberation," *Lumen Vitae* 27:2 (June 1972), pp. 281-303; Bruce O. Boston, "Conscientization and Christian Education," *Learning for Living* 13:3 (January 1974), pp. 100-105; William B. Kennedy, "Education for Liberation and Community," *Religious Education* 70:1 (January-February 1975), pp. 5-44; John L. Elias, "Paulo Freire: Religious Educator," *Religious Education* 71:1 (January-February 1976), pp. 40-56 and "Education for Power and Liberation," *Living Light* 13:1 (Spring 1976), pp. 56-69; Grant S. Shockley, "Liberation Theology, Black Theology, and Religious Education," in *Foundations for Christian Education in an Era of Change*, ed. Marvin J. Taylor (Nashville: Abingdon, 1976), pp. 80-95; Malcolm L. Warford, "Between the Plumbing and the Saving: Education, Theology and Liberation," *Living Light* 11:1 (Spring 1974), pp. 60-77 and *The Necessary Illusion: Church, Culture and Educational Change* (Philadelphia: United Church Press, 1976); John H. Westerhoff III, *Will Our Children Have Faith?* (New York: Seabury, 1976), chap. 2; John Charles Wynn, *Christian Education for Liberation* (Nashville: Abingdon, 1977), chap. 3; Stephen A. Schmidt, "Religious Education Toward a Prophetic Word," *Religious Education* 72:1 (January-February 1977), pp. 5-17; Brian Wren, *Education for Justice* (Maryknoll, N.Y.: Orbis, 1977); Thomas H. Groome, "The Critical Principle in Christian Education and the Task of Prophecy," Religious Education 72:3 (May-June 1977), pp. 262-272, and *Christian Religious Education: Sharing Our Story and Vision* (San Francisco: Harper & Row, 1980), especially chaps. 3, 5, and 8; Maurice Monette, "Paulo Freire and Other Unheard Voices," *Religious Education* 74:5 (September-October 1979), pp. 543-554 and "Justice, Peace, and the Pedagogy of Grass Roots Christian Community," in *Education for Peace and Justice*, ed. Padraic O'Hare (San Francisco: Harper & Row, 1983), pp.83-93; Kenneth R. Barker, *Religious Education, Catechesis, and Freedom* (Birmingham, Ala.: Religious Education Press, 1981), chap. 4; Allen J. Moore, "Liberation and the Future of Christian Education," in *Contemporary Approaches to Christian Education*, ed. Jack L. Seymour and Donald E. Miller (Nashville: Abingdon, 1982), pp. 103-122; Stokes, "Black Theology: A Challenge to Religious Education"; William B. Kennedy, "Conversation with Paulo Freire" and "Education for a Just and Peaceful World," *Religious Education* 79:4 (Fall 1984), pp. 511-557 and "Ideology and Education: A Fresh Approach for Religious Education," *Religious Education* 80:3 (Summer 1985), pp. 331-

344; John L. Elias, *Studies in Theology and Education* (Malabar, Fla.: Krieger, 1986), part III; Alice Frazer Evans, Robert A. Evans, and William Bean Kennedy, *Pedagogies for the Non-Poor* (Maryknoll, N.Y.: Orbis, 1987).

5. Daniel S. Schipani, *Conscientization and Creativity: Paulo Freire and Christian Education* (Lanham, Md.: University Press of America, 1984). This book includes the first thorough reinterpretation of Freire's contribution, with focus on the epistemological and theological foundations and dimensions of his work and thought.

6. Any serious attempt to examine and assess the influence of Latin American liberation theology on recent theological reflection in the North American scene should take into account at least the following categories, with representative examples supplied: 1) general interpretive appraisals such as Brown's *Theology in a New Key* and Haight's *An Alternative Vision.* 2) Critical assessments such as Carl E. Armerding, ed., *Evangelicals and Liberation* (Nutley, N.J.: Presbyterian and Reformed Publishing House, 1977); Ronald H. Nash, ed. *Liberation Theology* (Milford, Mich.: Mott Media, 1984); Shubert M. Ogden, *Faith and Freedom: Toward a Theology of Liberation* (Nashville: Abingdon, 1979); Sacred Congregation for the Doctrine of the Faith, "Instruction on Certain Aspects of the 'Theology of Liberation,'" appendix in Haight, *An Alternative Vision.* (For a comprehensive evaluation and response to the Vatican document see Juan L. Segundo, *Theology and the Church: A Response to Cardinal Ratzinger and a Warning to the Whole Church,* trans. John W. Diercksmeier [Minneapolis: Winston, 1985]. The subsequent Vatican's document, "Instruction on Christian Freedom and Liberation," in *National Catholic Reporter* [April 25, 1986], pp. 9-44, does not engage liberation theology explicitly. As an essay in Catholic social doctrine, it attempts to present an alternative approach.) Michael Novak, *Will It Liberate?: Questions About Liberation Theology* (New York: Paulist, 1986). 3) Studies of a single theme or figure: Alfred T. Hennelly, *Theologies in Conflict: The Challenge of Juan Luis Segundo* (Maryknoll, N.Y.: Orbis, 1979). 4) Evaluative comparisons between theological perspectives: Dennis P. McCann, *Christian Realism and Liberation Theology* (Maryknoll, N.Y.: Orbis, 1981); Daniel S. Schipani, ed., *Freedom and Discipleship: Liberation Theology in Anabaptist Perspective* (Maryknoll, N.Y.: Orbis, forthcoming). 5) Partial adoption of the liberation perspective in the discussion of classical themes: Daniel L. Migliore, *Called to Freedom: Liberation Theology and the Future of Christian Doctrine* (Philadelphia: Westminster, 1980). 6) Critico-constructive development of liberation theologies in the North American situation: Frederick Herzog, *Justice Church: The New Function of the Church in North American Christianity* (Maryknoll, N.Y.: Orbis, 1981); Richard Shaull, *Heralds of a New Reformation: The Poor of South and North America* (Maryknoll, N.Y.: Orbis, 1984). 7) Joint writing/publication projects on special areas: Norman K. Gottwald, ed., *The Bible and Liberation: Political and Social Hermeneutics* (Maryknoll, N.Y.: Orbis, 1983); Sergio Torres and John Eagleson, eds., *The Challenge of Basic Christian Communities.* 8) Significant appropriation of liberation thought in reshaping certain theological traditions: Nicholas Wolterstorff, *Until Justice and Peace Embrace* (Grand Rapids, Mich.: Eerdmans, 1983).

7. Randolph Crump Miller, "Theology in the Background," in *Religious Education and Theology*, p. 30.
8. Iris V. Cully, "The Problem and the Clue," in *Process and Relationship: Issues in Theology, Philosophy, and Religious Education*, ed. Iris V. Cully (Birmingham, Ala.: Religious Education Press, 1978), p. 3.
9. Norma H. Thompson, "The Role of Theology in Religious Education: An Introduction," in *Religious Education and Theology*, p. 14.

Chapter 1

Conscientization, Liberation, and Creativity

"You will know the truth, and the truth will make you free."[1]

JESUS

"The church, education, and the role of the churches in education, can only be discussed historically. . . .

"The prophetic church, like Christ, must move forward constantly, forever dying and being reborn. In order to be, it must always be in a state of becoming. The prophetic church must also accept an existence which is in dramatic tension between past and future, staying and going, speaking the Word and keeping silence, being and not being. There is no prophecy without risk. This prophetic attitude is accompanied by a rich and very necessary theological reflection . . . the theology of liberation—a prophetic, utopian theology, full of hope.

"Thus . . . education must be an instrument of transforming action, as a political praxis at the service of permanent human liberation. This does not happen only in the consciousness of people but presupposes a radical change of structures in which process consciousness will itself be transformed."[2]

PAULO FREIRE

"One of the fundamental dimensions of religious education is its prophetic role. . . .

"Religious education by its nature pushes back the frontiers of an individual's or a culture's way of knowing, feeling, and living. Religious education is an activity by which the individual or society is helped to put on the new human, to be propelled more and more into actualizing the pleroma. If it is to fulfill its mission, religious education must not so much bring the now into the future as to bring the future into the now. This is true because the educational experience is not one of preparing the learner to live in the future but rather of helping the learner to live the future right now."[3]

JAMES MICHAEL LEE

INTRODUCTION

The gospel reference of John 8:32 illumines the discussion of conscientization, liberation, and creativity by juxtaposing the questions of *knowing the truth* and *becoming free*. The Jerusalem setting of oppression and confrontation in which Jesus finds himself is very apparent in the context of the whole passage[4] in which verse 31 provides an important clue: "If you hold to my teaching [or, "if you abide in my word"] you are really my disciples." In other words, Jesus establishes parallel equations in typical rabbinic fashion: abiding in his teaching—knowing the truth, becoming his disciples—being made free. Thus, truth and freedom are also correlated with obedience in terms of the dynamic and transforming processes of teaching-learning and discipleship.[5] Further, the disciples must be enabled to become faithful bearers of liberating truth and empowered to serve as agents of liberation, like Jesus himself: "As the Father has sent me, I am sending you" (John 20:21). This is, then, a divine summons which requires that the church, religious education, and theology assume a corresponding prophetic stance consistent with the gospel of liberation. It is a prophetic stance that the quotations from Paulo Freire and James Michael Lee highlight for us in the title page.

Knowing the truth and *becoming free* are also essential in Freire's understanding of education. For him, education is an act of knowing and an exercise of freedom, a critical approach to reality.[6] Further, we have a glimpse of the religious inspiration and theological base of his work and thought in a rather informal reference to the Johannine motifs of truth and the Word become flesh: Christ was not the processor of a truth to be transferred to or imposed on others. He was himself the Truth, the Word that became flesh. And the meaning of Christ's word can be learned if it is grasped when his word becomes also incarnate in us. This is the basis of the invitation that Christ makes to us, that we come to know the truth of his message through faithfully practicing it. His word is a whole way of learning.[7]

Two fundamental observations concerning the significance of Paulo Freire need to be made at this point, since much more than personal or sentimental reasons led us to dedicate this present volume to him. In the first place, his work and thought have helped to reshape pedagogical practice and to reformulate educational philosophy on a wide international scale. Second, Freire's own praxis-engaging action and reflection has stimulated the emergence and development of liberation theology in Latin America and elsewhere. This twofold contribution is in turn especially significant for Christian religious education because of the key foundational role that pedagogical practice, educational philosophy, and theology play in regard to our field.

Therefore any proper overview of liberation theology from the standpoint of religious education must begin with the work and thought of Paulo Freire. This is so because of historical reasons and also due to the very pedagogical character and orientation of liberation theology as a praxis-centered methodological process of critical reflection. Furthermore, it is noteworthy that the rich and complex material presented by Freire and liberation theology stem from the struggle for justice, freedom, and peace in Latin America. It is a circumstance that facilitates as well as conditions the dialogical interplay engaging liberation theology and religious education. It provides a clear focus of reflection for a thorough treatment of the main issues involved in the critical dialogue between the two fields.

In the first part of the chapter we will refer to Freire's contribution in terms of his approach to "education for liberation" or "cultural action for freedom." We will then consider the connection and mutual stimulation between conscientization and liberation theology. Finally, we will illustrate the reformulation of conscientization as creativity that informs uniquely the process of religious education.

This chapter will help us to set the agenda for the rest of the book. In a certain sense, the subsequent reflection will further unfold, expand, and deepen the treatment of the key liberationist motifs vis à vis the main theoretical categories of religious education. Those motifs are: the prophetic-utopian vision and the political-eschatological dimensions of the gospel (chapter 2); the praxis way of knowing and the epistemology of obedience and doing justice (chapter 3); critical reflection and understanding for transformation (chapter 4); and the privileged situation of the oppressed and the context of the base ecclesial community (chapter 5).

EDUCATION FOR LIBERATION

To couple the words "education" and "liberation" tends to evoke immediately the work and thought of Paulo Freire, whose contribution can be appreciated most keenly in the field of religious education. This is so, primarily, because his approach demonstrates critically the close relationship and the harmony that should exist between practice and theory. Freire presents the connections between philosophical foundations and principles of educational practice in a consistent and explicit manner. Further, he understands the relationship of practice and theory, not in terms of opposition or superiority of one over the other, but as a dialectical association that underscores the tension and critical correlation between the two as well as their unity, in the tradition of George Hegel and Karl Marx.[8]

This chapter includes only a brief statement of Freire's educational philosophy in the context of our interest in liberation theology in dialogue with religious education. We will discuss the essence of his contribution, major strengths and weaknesses, and a restatement of the conscientization approach in terms of creativity.

Conscientization and Human Emergence

Paulo Freire designed and developed his educational model and his philosophy of education during several years of direct and active involvement in Brazil and Chile. He worked first among the rural poor in a highly successful literacy and conscientization program, which was to be implemented eventually throughout Brazil but was truncated by the military coup of 1964.[9] While in exile in Chile Freire worked for five years in adult education with rural and urban illiterates and also with the educational facet of the Christian Democratic government's plan of agrarian reform. This was an opportunity to make adaptations and to test, develop, and promote his educational ideas. Freire's work and thought evolved further during his decade-long assignment as a Special

Educational Consultant to the World Council of Churches, Office of Education, and at the Institut d'Action Culturelle (IDAC) in Geneva. No other major philosopher of education has ever been personally involved in so many different kinds of projects. It would also be noted that his wife, Elza, herself an educator, was Freire's indispensable partner and loving critic for over forty years.[10]

Freire's pedagogy and educational philosophy centers on the human potential for freedom and creativity in the midst of the historical reality of cultural and political-economic oppression. It aims at discovering and implementing liberating alternatives in human interaction and structural transformation through a *radical sociopolitical approach*,[11] originally identified as *conscientização*.[12] In the following paragraphs we will discuss succinctly this key liberationist motif in an overview of Freire's philosophy which will be supplemented later.[13]

Conscientization, Praxis, and Utopia. Conscientization is a process of cultural action in which women and men are awakened to their sociocultural reality, move beyond the constraints and alienations to which they are subjected, and affirm themselves as conscious subjects and co-creators of their historical future. Together with the deepening awareness of that socioculture reality that shapes their lives, persons actually realize their capacity and potential to transform reality, including themselves. In other words, conscientization connotes more than consciousness raising by underscoring two additional dimensions. First, it must be seen as a disciplined or intentional action-education process which Freire discusses as *cultural action,* i.e., "the way we culturally attack culture. It means to see culture always as a problem and not to let it become static, becoming a myth and mystifying us."[14] Second, conscientization must be viewed as a continuing process which involves *praxis* understood as the dialectic relationship of action and reflection. That is, Freire's praxis approach affirms critically reflective action and critical reflection informed by and validated in practice. In his terms, the interrelation of self-awareness and action constitutes a "permanent, constant dynamic of our attitude toward culture itself."[15]

It is at the level of praxis that conscientization occurs in the Freirean sense because conscientization implies "a critical insertion into history," i.e., a willful personal involvement or historical commitment and awareness in order to remake the world. And that critical awareness leads not only to analysis and understanding but also to the means for transformation together with others who assume the role of subjects, "to fashion their existence out of the material that life offers them."[16] Freire puts it plainly: Conscientization implies that when people realize that they are oppressed they also know they can liberate themselves if they transform the concrete situation where they find themselves oppressed.[17]

That critical insertion into a historical process and commitment to transformation is dynamized by a utopian attitude toward the world. Freire uses *utopia* in the positive sense of a realistic and hopeful vision of a future, possible, "good place" in terms of welfare for all, freedom and community, justice and peace. Conscientization calls for the dual utopian movements of denouncing dehumanization, oppression, and alienation, and announcing alternative structures for humanization and liberation. The language of protest, resistance, and critique is coupled to the language of possibility and hope.[18] Thus conscientization fosters a prophetic and hopeful stance which keeps the future open for those involved in the process of transformation. This is a utopian stance which inspires further praxis and is in turn reshaped by praxis.

We should notice finally that the meaning of *transformation* associated with conscientization, praxis, and utopia, relates to the epistemological shift that led Freire to embrace a radical pedagogy.[19] Because of that, Freire began to focus more sharply on the questions of education and politics in concrete historical situations, class struggle, and the ideological undergirding of pedagogy and education as a form of revolutionary praxis in the context of commitment to and with the oppressed. In light of the epistemological reformulation, Freire redefined conscientization by stressing more the dialectical relationship of knowing reality and the work to transform it, put in terms of action-reflection, and the necessity of a prior ideological option toward radical social change for liberation and justice.[20] Thus, Freire's contribution becomes, at least partially, an attempt to articulate the pedagogy implicit in Karl Marx's *Theses on Feuerbach* and the focus for exploring the dynamics of knowing, action, and power.[21]

Education as Conscientization. One of the great intuitions of Paulo Freire is to have perceived the association and the structural continuity between his literacy method on the linguistic-symbolic dimension, on the one hand, and the conscientization process on the level of self and social interaction, on the other hand. He has highlighted the interconnections engaging language, politics, and consciousness by appraising the way language forms our perceptions of the world and our intentions toward it. Thus Freire asserts that conscientization must occur simultaneously with the literacy or postliteracy process because the word is not something static or disconnected from the people's existential experience but a dimension of their thought-language about the world. Through critical participation in the educational process the learners rediscover their own words and expand their capacity for self expression by the development of their creative imagination.[22]

Freire's vision of education and society must be seen in the context of his involvement in the struggle for enabling the submerged masses of population to emerge and effectively "speak the word." He believes that modern society does not encourage authentic freedom and does not promote the development of critical consciousness. Further, he claims that people must liberate themselves in order to fulfill their human potential in light of their *ontological vocation* as history makers. That twofold assumption inspires his trenchant critique of the traditional "banking" concept of education as a "necrophilic" instrument of oppression and domestication.[23] Freire unveils the fundamental presuppositions of the banking model, and exposes its distortions, such as the dichotomizing consciousness-world, the teacher-learner contradiction, and the lack of dialogue and mutuality in the educational process and context.

Freire proposes a liberating, "biophilic" education defined by the conscientization approach. In it, the participants essentially are engaged together in the teaching-learning phases of investigation, thematization, and problematization emanating from and leading to actual praxis in given existential situations. Freire's pedagogy is a problem-posing and dialogical political cultural action that fosters critical consciousness, transforming action, and cultural synthesis.[24] Although this characterization applies basically to all kinds of educational projects, Freire reminds us of the literacy-conscientization paradigm by using the metaphor of "political literacy" to describe education for liberation:[25] We must learn to "read" (critically interpreting and understanding) reality in such a way that oppressive limit situations are confronted and transcended in the process of "speaking our word" and "rewriting" (transforming action) the story and the destiny of our world.

Conscientization and Emergence. Freire has identified the lack of critical consciousness—rather than mere "ignorance" as such—as the cause of marginality, cultural submersion, and historical oppression of the popular masses. He assumes that how we know depends on the manner in which we experience reality mediated through thought-language. Hence, oppressed states of consciousness constitute a historical epistemological problem.

Crucial to understanding conscientization is the notion of the various levels of consciousness. For Freire, there are several identifiable ways of viewing one's relationship with reality. These are the historically conditioned levels of consciousness which must be perceived in light of historical-cultural reality as a superstructure in relation to an infrastructure.[26] In that context, he has proposed the overcoming of diverse forms of "magical" and "naive" consciousness and the development of critical consciousness as a fundamental goal of the conscientization approach, especially at the cognitive and linguistic registers of behavior. That kind of learning which is truly liberating and transforming is seen as the movement to higher levels of consciousness. And the content of consciousness includes the view that people have of their own existence in the social reality and the power that they possess to determine their destiny and future. The learning process starts with the present level of consciousness as it is reflected in the language, living conditions, self-concept, and worldview.

The magical or "*semi-intransitive*"[27] consciousness is typical of closed societies with a "culture of silence." It is characterized by a "quasi-immersion" or "quasi-adherence" in objective reality as a dominated and conformed conscience with no sufficient distance to objectify reality in order to know it in a critical manner.[28] Due to a certain obliteration imposed by objective conditions (e.g., extreme privation) the only data grasped by this dominated consciousness are the data that lie within the range of its lived experience. The lack of a "structural perception" of reality—i.e., understanding problem situations in terms of institutions and other social factors—makes people search for some super-reality or to something within themselves. Action is not directed toward social change but rather to those falsely assumed agents or to their own, self-imposed, incapacity. Their social action tends to have the features of defensive or therapeutic magic.

The development toward a *naive-transitive* consciousness is assumed to correlate with the changing socioeconomic pattern of modernization such as urbanization and technological development. For Freire, "simplism" in the interpretation of problematic situations is the main characteristic of this mode of consciousness. It tends to be seduced by massification; it is not permeable for investigation and its argumentation is fragile, with strong emotional overtones; it prefers arguments over dialogue and tends to see the cultural situations as determined by other people. At this level, the masses can be manipulated and exploited by populist leaders and programs who seem to give people a sense of worth and power. However, Freire also argues that under certain circumstances populism may become a factor in democratic mobilization.[29]

Critical transitivity is the highest level of consciousness and it involves the capacity to perceive reality structurally. In Freire's words, this mode of consciousness corresponds to interrogative, highly permeable, restless, and dialogical forms of life.[30] Critical consciousness is active intentionality in the examination and questioning of reality, with self-confidence and a sense of human interdependence. Therefore, a key educational task is to sponsor the achievement and exercise of critical transitivity.

Freire supplements those considerations on the levels of consciousness by focusing on the dynamics of self and class. In terms of these dynamics, the movement of human emergence is from the oppressed false consciousness to a liberating consciousness of oppression.[31] Freire thus appropriates the Hegelian motif of the dialectic master-slave and the question of subordination to and incorporation of the oppressor's consciousness. In fact, here we have the clue for understanding the *pedagogy of the oppressed* becoming a pedagogy for the whole human being.[32] For Freire, the great humanistic and historical task of the oppressed is to liberate themselves and their oppressors as well. Further, true solidarity with the oppressed involves struggling at their side for the transformation of the objective reality that makes them beings for another. This pedagogy of the oppressed and, therefore, of human emergence has two distinct stages. In the first, the oppressed unmask the world of oppression and, through praxis, commit themselves to its transformation. In the second stage, when the reality of oppression is being transformed, that pedagogy becomes a pedagogy of all human beings in the process of permanent liberation.[33]

Our study of the word and thought of Paulo Freire concludes that his approach contains a developmental structure and that it makes a contribution to our understanding of human development. We have also established that Freire's pedagogy is truly liberating to the extent that the developmental process is reactivated by way of a recapitulation of the stage transition movement.[34] Together with that, we must reiterate that conscientization and critical consciousness are not ends in themselves. The goal par excellence is human emergence or humanization through the liberating process of cultural action for societal transformation that enables and empowers persons as well as communities in the search for freedom, justice, and peace.

Liberating Conscientization

The subheading is deliberately ambiguous. Freire's conscientization approach can be affirmed as authentic education for liberation with numerous implications for religious education. Yet it is itself in need of "liberation" from certain contradictions and limitations, and for inspiring greater freedom and creativity. With that challenge in mind, we will discuss some pertinent issues in light of our twofold interest in religious education and liberation theology.

Strengths and Contributions. We have underscored already several aspects of Freire's work and thought that can provide foundation and orientation for the educational ministry. Several other dimensions will be discussed below and, especially, in the last section of this chapter. At this point we will indicate some specific insights and principles stemming from Freire's epistemological perspective. Conscientization, as a theory of knowing put into practice, has a developmental structure that fosters human emergence, especially in terms of a liberating process of learning as knowing. At least the five following interrelated areas must be recognized in this regard.

First, the conscientization approach includes a helpful methodological paradigm for religious education as a process of *awakening* that eschews instructional manipulation and ideological propaganda. The approach is rooted in the Socratic tradition of the dialectical process of indirect communication between teachers and learners, especially as that tradition is mediated by Kierkegaard.[35] The idea is that authentic appropriation of truth, deepening self-reflection, and the emerging power for self and societal transformation necessitate that "maieutic" teachers thrust backwards, as it were, thus making space for awakening as repossession and reinvention of learning, as Freire would say.[36] This pedagogical principle is essential for enhancing creativity and for informing a liberating instructional practice in religious education as discussed later. It is especially conducive to the transformation of personal frames of reference—or, "meaning perspectives" as indicated below—in fostering personal and social change.

Second, Freire has devised an approach that promotes radical learning in the fashion of *vision* or *paradigm transformation*. Jack Mezirow's definition of *perspective* transformation in fact fits well this dimension of conscientization as a way of knowing: It is the praxis or the emancipatory process of "becoming critically aware of how and why the structure of psychocultural assumptions has come to constrain the way we see ourselves and our relationships, reconstituting this structure to permit a more inclusive and discriminating integration of experience and acting upon these new understandings."[37] A true re-vision takes place including a major reordering of reality as previously experienced and the reassessment of possibilities within that reality as well as action decision. "Perspective" and "paradigm" stand for restructuring new frames of reference or, as McKenzie puts it, the development of a new theory of life and one's place in life.[38] Conscientization facilitates learning about "meaning perspectives" defined as integrated psychological structures with dimensions of thought, feeling, and will. More than just a way of seeing in the narrow sense, meaning perspectives are proposals to experience one's life which involve a choice to take action. Further moving to a new perspective and sustaining the actions dictated by it depend on the communal association with others who share the new perspective and support and reinforce the whole process. Actually the process described by Mezirow as a crucial developmental task of maturity is strikingly analogous to a creative process.[39] In light of this approach, a conscientization-inspired teaching-learning process will aim to identify, precipitate, facilitate, and reinforce the transformation of the learners' meaning perspectives as well as the implementation of corresponding action strategies.

Third, the developmental base and structure of conscientization appears to enhance the *formal-operational* level of cognitive development, i.e., the optimal structure of the human mind according to Jean Piaget.[40] The Freire approach stimulates the emergence and manifestation of formal thought as inferred in the following expressions of human intelligence: 1) The *ability to utilize a second symbol system,* or to think about thinking, so to speak, which is essential for introspection and reflection on one's personal and social situation, for instance in the process of discerning the dynamics of self-consciousness and alienation. 2) The *capacity for combinatorial thought,* as required, for example, when taking diverse factors and alternatives into account in the tasks of problematizing and critical reflection. It facilitates, among other things, structural perception of reality and recognition of new dilemmas or conflict situations. 3) The *capacity to construct ideals or utopias,* or conceiving that the world could have a different shape and could be run in a different way. This capacity is necessary, together with the other two, for overcoming accommodation and conformity, for confronting limit-situations with confidence, and for creatively devising "untested feasibilities" and "limit acts." To the extent that conscientization helps actualize and exercise those possibilities, it makes it possible to experience real liberation of thought-language structures within a wider personal picture engaging diverse registers of behavior. In the conscientization process, an arrested state of personal growth is thus overcome and new possibilities and "power" indeed become available for the participants. The following two paragraphs suggest other dimensions of human emergence fostered by conscientization in terms of moral and faith development.

Fourth, it can be claimed that conscientization *challenges radically conventional* (i.e., pro-establishment) *morality* as described by Lawrence Kohlberg from a structuralist, cognitive-developmental perspective.[41] It does that to the extent that it confronts conformity and mere social adjustment or resignation while stimulating problematizing and discernment of new alternatives ("untested feasibilities") in a critical, dialogical, and democratic educational context. Conscientization seems to provide a nice illustration of how to foster moral development as a transforming learning process that includes the "dislodging" of oppressive structures and identification with oppressors as well as transformational role-taking. The very conscientizing pedagogical approach contains a message of liberation[42] from restrictive patterns of moral reasoning and for higher and better forms of understanding and solving moral dilemmas in the quest for justice. Further research could ascertain, for example, the actual impact of conscientization in the face of the stage 3 moral reasoning mentality, defined by Kohlberg in terms of mutual interpersonal expectations, relationships, and conformity, for which the "right" is playing a good (nice) role, being concerned about the other people and their feelings, keeping loyalty and trust with partners, and being motivated to follow rules and expectations.[43]

Fifth, and in the same line of discussion, it can be argued that Freire's conscientization fosters *faith development* as conceptualized by James W. Fowler in his structural-developmental theory.[44] For instance, Fowler has indicated that the movement toward stage 4—the "demythologizing" stage of individuative-reflective faith—is particularly critical, for it is in this transition that late adolescents or adults must begin to take seriously the burden of responsibility for their own beliefs and attitudes, commitments and lifestyles. In discussing developmental criteria for theological adequacy, Fowler argues for the desirability of theologies that call for reflective awareness over against the embeddedness of synthetic-conventional faith. In that context he refers to Freire as having proposed a method and an educational theology, as it were, which are designed to assist persons to break out of mass-consciousness into critical awareness of who they are and who they are called to be.[45] This would be analogous to what must happen in any real transition from stage 3 to stage 4. Again, this suggests promising further insights related to new research endeavors such as those undertaken in the area of faith development in the adult life cycle.[46]

Weaknesses and Limitations. From the vantage of religious education we can make several critical observations which point to needed correctives in Freire's approach for the sake of consistency with its stated aim of promoting genuine liberation. It can be noticed that, in a sense, the strengths of the pedagogy and philosophy of conscientization at some points tend to become liabilities. Further, it can also be said that the critique articulated in the following four areas should be kept in the background of any assessment of liberation theology.

First, we must indicate an unfortunate *absence of a critical stance* toward the philosophical foundations of conscientization. The lack of a deliberate, discerning examination of presuppositions and ideologies that inform Freirean thought is striking in light of the very hermeneutical structure and dynamics of the conscientization process which dictate problematizing and critical reflection and interpretation, not to mention the dialectical unity and correlation of theory and praxis by Freire. A major case in point is the uncritical assimilation of Marxism starting with *Pedagogy of the Oppressed.*[47] Freire simply affirms those foundations with strong conviction and fails to evaluate them critically. Ironically, this is the kind of lack of discernment that Freire himself denounces emphatically in the case of the "banking" traditional educational model. To this we must add the risk of falling into reactionary, fatalistic sectarianism, in his words, that promotes a false view of history and generates forms of action which negate freedom, ending up "without the people—which is another way of being against them."[48]

Second, we must realize the potential problem of *ethnocentrism* when analyzing language and consciousness structures in groups of people assumed to need emergence, humanization, via conscientization programs. Actually, the whole question of levels of consciousness and awareness raising in particular can be critiqued in principle, as Peter Berger does, in terms of "philosophical error" and "political irony."[49] The claims concerning a hierarchical view of consciousness may contain a philosophical error. Cognitively superior people are supposed to be at a higher level of freedom and, hence, humanity, by virtue of their heightened consciousness. However, there is no empirical evidence to substantiate the ontological hierarchy assumed in those claims. The political irony lies in the attitude of *messianic paternalism* and *elitism* often betrayed by would-be "conscientizers." In connection with this, we must mention that the notions of "humanization" and "full humanity" include the assumption that there is an underlying human nature—a lost humanity—that must be recovered, actualized, or restored. The problem arises whenever it is implied that some enlightened'persons possess the key to open the door of comprehension and transformation so that human actualization and re-creation may take place.

Third, it is clear that acquiring and developing critical consciousness is a necessary but not a sufficient condition for liberation and humanization. In his conscientization proposal, Freire does not appraise well enough the involvement of the total person in social interaction. The pain, dreams, and longings of the people are indeed taken into account in terms of oppressive situations as felt by them. Yet what really counts is critical reflection, transitivity, and consciousness as such. Noncognitive registers of behavior tend to be underestimated. Manifestations such as affect and imagination do not share the privileged status of reasoning and thought processes in the crucial concept of praxis. The conscientization approach thus overemphasizes cognitive, verbal rationality and becomes vulnerable to the charge of ultracognitivism.[50] An alternative understanding could be suggested, for instance, in terms of Gabriel Moran's notion of *intelligence* as the synthesis of the rational and nonrational within integrated adults, on both the personal and communal levels.[51]

Fourth, the conscientization approach presents the risk of defeating the very purpose of education for liberation because of a creeping mesh of *revolutionary optimism, determinism,* and *dogmatism* in Freire's philosophy. In fact, by demanding a previous ideological option to be eventually justified and validated a posteriori in the conscientization process, Freire appears to adopt a position which easily turns into indoctrination. Human freedom cannot be cultivated if people are induced or conditioned to assume the political option of pedagogical facilitators. The educational process may be seriously compromised when its validity is predicated on the prior commitment to a certain kind of radical or revolutionary change. The dynamics of alienation are believed to be so strong, and the resistance of the oppressors so insidious and powerful, that conscientization should necessarily lead most people to revolutionary involvement and praxis. Social reality is often cast in simplistic terms, with generalizations and dichotomizing, opposing poles, and the struggle between oppressed and oppressors presented as a picture of good and evil. These are all expressions of mythic thinking.[52] Further, there is the assumption that those are almost self-evident, revealed truths which, eventually, everybody should be willing to grasp. And, once awareness has occurred, the only fitting alternative is to join in the stuggle by participating on the side of the oppressed. It is also assumed that this grand liberation movement is ultimately consistent with the tide of history and with the advancement of the reign of God.

Unfortunately, this position can easily generate messianic and authoritarian educational patterns which violently frustrate the creative and liberating process of conscientization. That accounts for, among other things, the frequent failure to recognize and tolerate ambiguity and ambivalence, and for what Freire himself calls "absence of doubt" and the closing of oneself into "circles of certainty."[53] Yet, in Freire's approach we often miss the reference to the difficult negotiations—both internal and interpersonal and among groups—involved in the teaching-learning process, the painful struggling with diverse and even differing or conflicting views and the need to compromise and revise, to name a few, to say nothing of the nuanced complexity, dynamism, and precariousness of a given social reality per se. We are also struck by the contradiction of justifying the curtailment of dialogue and freedom for the sake of advancing the cause of liberation.[54]

Having discussed strengths and weaknesses in Freire's approach, we must move forward to suggest how the contributions of conscientization can be furthered while minimizing or correcting its limitations.

Conscientization as Creativity

We have demonstrated that, in light of Christian religious education, the basic orientation of Freire's educational approach should be perceived in terms both of liberation for creativity and of creativity for liberation.[55] Conscientization fosters a special form of human emergence consistent with the pattern of the creative process, with a structural integrity of its own. It confronts the external and internal structures that frustrate the movement toward freedom, wholeness, and community by powerful socialization forces that impose adaptation and conformity upon people's creative spirit. The dynamics of conscientization engage in that fashion various dimensions, such as thought-language and the self and the levels of communal interaction—institutional and sociocultural and politicoeconomic structures. We claim that this perspective in fact provides the most fruitful appraisal of conscientization and that it accounts for its effectiveness and for the basic integrity of Freire's contribution, including the blending of its epistemological and theological foundations.

Learning, Freedom, and Creativity. When we look at Freire's adult literacy method as paradigmatic of education as the practice of freedom and social change, we realize that, as an educational critic, Freire responded creatively against the suppression and repression of creativity. We find an explicit and clear articulation of the dimensions of freedom and creativity built in the conscientization approach already in Freire's first educational manifesto, "Education as the Practice of Freedom." Freire and his colleagues were interested in designing an educational project as an introduction to the democratization of culture, a program with people as "subjects rather than as mere recipients, a program which itself would be an act of creation, capable of releasing other creative acts, one in which students would develop the impatience of vivacity which characterizes search and invention."[56] The idea was to foster the discovery of oneself as maker of culture with a creative and re-creative impulse.[57] As we know, the project was very successful—adults learned to read and write in a matter of weeks—because participants actually experienced their potential to create and transform. Freire and others won the interest of the poor who began to hope that they could start "saying their word" in an active fashion, in the face of the larger social, economic, and political issues of the Brazilian society. Constructive participation in the political process was presented as a desirable outcome and attainable goal of the educational process.[58] Creativity was encouraged and nurtured in the context of the dialogical teaching-learning process carried out in the circles of culture.

Conscientization consists of a problem-posing and conflict-facing educational approach which affirms the person's initiative in the search for humanizing alternatives while confronting situations of privation, oppression, and marginalization characteristic of limit situations. It is no wonder that the conscientization approach soon included postliteracy education and a broader pedagogical philosophy with a strong epistemological base. It is in that epistemological context, where education is defined as a theory of knowing put into practice, that conscientization must be seen as fostering creativity. Freire believes that there is a creative drive in every human that stems from our inconclusive nature. He asserts that the more education develops that ontological drive to create—especially as critical consciousness for societal transformation—the more authentic education is. That is, it is an education that sponsors history making, the response to the challenges of the world within a given society, and implies the self-affirmation of persons and communities.[59]

From Story Telling to History Making. In conscientization, dialogue and critical reflection flow from the very stuff of everyday life, especially in the face of oppression and suffering. The approach contains an implicit conception of the "narrative quality of experience"[60] in the context of a prophetic stance involving resistance and hope, critique and possibility. The concrete challenges experienced and processed in any particular sociohistorical situation represent a specific segment and a contextualized version, as it were, of the grand human-divine struggle for liberation. The "mundane stories" shared by the people involved in conscientization programs ultimately point to the underlying and undergirding "sacred story" or "sacred script" of the overall, human-divine liberation project. In light of our comprehensive assessment of Freire's work and thought, we have suggested that he assumes a certain reading of that Story which could be rendered approximately in these terms:

Human beings are unfinished, open beings involved in a continuous process of representation, interpretation, and fashioning of reality. Yet historically, alienation has been a condition that undermines and tarnishes humanity and is a constant threat to humanization. God is engaged in the liberating and recreating enterprise in this word, particularly by enabling human beings to participate in the struggle for liberation from oppression and by empowering them to shape their lives and destiny and the human community. The Exodus of Israel and Jesus Christ's Easter Resurrection are paradigmatic of such an enablement and empowerment.[61]

In other words, conscientization allows for the existential movement from story telling to history making. The dialogical learning process of critical reflection leads people to become "authors." By telling their stories and sharing their hopes and dreams, it becomes possible to realize the vocation to "make history." By indwelling this story, people actually assume "authorship" as active learners and co-creators, and willing agents of social transformation. This happens because conscientization has a structure that is parallel to the movements of the creative process. To the extent that its fundamental integrity is sustained, conscientization promotes the experience of actual liberation, not just as emancipation (freedom from) but as enablement and empowerment (freedom for) as well.

Conscientization as Creative Process. Freire's educational approach proposes a teaching-learning process that may be seen as a variation of the creativity model. We have made explicit its latent epistemology and have also restated conscientization in terms analogous to the pattern of the creative process. The coordinators of the cultural circles aim to facilitate the occurrence of that very process in all the participants, including themselves. What happens, in short, is that a special developmental sequence is raised to the level of critical awareness, and a latent or arrested state of development is called forth or reconstructed in the educational setting. In the conscientization design, the creative process is expected to unfold both cooperatively and individually within the context of a *creativogenic* social milieu.[62] Different dimensions (linguistic-symbolic, self) and levels (ego, group process, sociocultural structures) may become engaged simultaneously as new alternatives and power do become available to individuals and groups. The approach thus makes accessible the experience of actual liberation for creativity and creativity for liberation in the educational project. For the individual participants, the ego and the coping consciousness become subject to creative transformation. The cultural circles function as "hermeneutic" and "praxis" communities who may become themselves paradigms or living models of the efficacious vision of a revitalized society and a reconstructed culture. Further, by example and by direct intervention, the larger social structures may also become subject to radical change.

Conscientization seeks to elicit the movements of the creative process as usually conceptualized,[63] beginning with 1) a conflict situation, or *baffled struggle in a context of rapport*.[64] In fact, objective and subjective situations of privation or lack, marginalization, or oppression may become curriculum material, so to say, in the supporting and encouraging setting of the circles of culture. 2) The movement of *interlude for scanning* occurs when attention is no longer focused directly on the problem situations being confronted, as initially formulated. Participants engage in sharing, dialogue, and critical reflection in a search for alternative ways of perceiving and dealing with reality in what amounts to the "incubation stage" in the typical creative sequence. 3) Resolution arrives eventually in the form of new ideas, *insights*, or *intuitions* concerning the problems faced with new realization of personal and communal worth and power often unsuspected before. 4) In connection with the occurrence of insight, there is a more affective and conative movement, consisting of *release of tension* and *discharge and transformation of energy*, invariably reported. Indeed, Freire himself provides dramatic examples of redirected energies that can be invested in further action and reflection, leading to the next movement. 5) *Interpretation* and *verification* take place in terms of the praxis—action-reflection— dialectic. Critical understandings and appropriate action will refer back to the problem or conflict situations engaged by the participants (such as correcting injustices or improving living conditions) and forward (such as organizing communal or political action). Obviously this entails the need for further discernment, verification, testing and trying, in an ongoing process of action and reflection which elicits other creative movements along the way.

Creativity provides a fundamental framework to understand the diverse dimensions and levels of conscientization as creative process, including its possible ramifications in cultural reconstruction and revitalization.[65] In this light, conscientization is seen as a powerful, potentially liberating process but ambiguous in principle because it can be used in a way that leads to further alienation, even by those committed to overcome oppressive situations.[66] This perspective, then, is essential not only to account for the effectiveness of conscientization but also to perceive and avoid possible shortcomings and contradictions and distortions, as those already indicated in the previous section. In sum, the focus on creativity is crucial for conscientization to maintain its integrity on both epistemological and ethical grounds.

It should also be noticed that Freire's contribution helps to illumine creativity itself, especially by defining the character of the dialogical context and process of conscientization. Further, the scope of creativity is expanded in light of the participation of the "common people" and, especially, the oppressed and marginal (usually considered as "underachievers," "underprivileged," and "underdeveloped" by society at large). Freire has demonstrated that creativity is not the exclusive privilege of enlightened minds or social groups such as scientists, philosophers, and artists and that it is possible and in fact imperative to "democratize" creativity. He has also helped us see that the experience and practice of the human creative potential is tantamount to freedom and health. Indeed, the liberating potential of creativity as manifest in conscientization suggests how to operationalize a creative thrust in terms of an educational project and approach.

By way of conclusion, we can indicate that Freire's approach is potentially conducive to human emergence in terms of greater freedom and wholeness, especially when reinterpreted in the light of the Christian Story and Vision from the perspective of religious education. Thus conscientization may indeed provide a specific way of actualizing the God-given capacity to participate in the struggle for liberation from oppression and alienation and to creatively fashion human life and destiny in this world.

The epistemological foundation of Freire's work and thought converges with its religious inspiration and theological base which we will discuss now. Actually, an adequate understanding and appreciation of Freire's contribution highlight the complementarity and integration of his theory of knowing and truth and his view and articulation of the Christian faith. And that realization is also essential in the case of liberation theology.

CONSCIENTIZATION AND DOING THEOLOGY

In this section we will address the question of the mutual influence affecting the conscientization approach and liberation theology. Freire inspired liberation theologians decisively and, in turn, the liberationist theological perspective provided further support for his own work and philosophy. Hence, we will refer first to the religious and theological dimensions of Freire's work and thought followed by a discussion of the appropriation of conscientization on the part of liberation theology. Finally, we will comment on Freire's own reflection on the prophetic church.

A Religious Vocation and Witness

The educational philosophy of Paulo Freire does not emanate from a well-developed, carefully articulated, and rigorous theoretical approach. Rather, he has tended to follow the flow and movement of his own thought and intuitions. This fact complicates the assessment of Freire's contribution, including his own theologizing, and makes it necessary to explore both the implicit theological foundation or infrastructure of his pedagogy as well as the explicit theological formulations in his educational philosophy. Instead of a precisely crafted conceptual framework, we look for the inspirational meaning of the religious and theological foundations undergirding conscientization. And the place to start is the convergence and blending of Freire's religious and vocational experience. Only then can we appreciate the specifically theological dimension of his contribution.

From a personal vantage point, Freire must be seen as a Brazilian Catholic who grew up in a poverty-stricken region of the country and whose mother led him lovingly in the first steps of faith. Freire speaks fondly of those early religious experiences and he adds that he once left the church deliberately for conscience's sake. He tells us that he was particularly disturbed by the contradiction between the Sunday language of piety and the lack of Christian commitment in daily life.[67] According to his testimony, Freire has since then struggled to realize the biblical imperative to love in concrete fashion. There is no question for him that the understanding of the gospels implies that we actually experience them, and in them to experience ourselves through personal social practice, in history, with other human beings. Speaking as a religious educator, Freire adds that from that religious experience proceeds the risky adventure of learning and teaching the gospels as one continuous act: "To know the gospels through seeking to practice them within the limits imposed by my own finitude is, thus, the best way I have of teaching them."[68] And that involves assuming the humble posture of a perennial learner of the Word whose faithful practice confers the authority, in the act of learning the Word, to teach it as well.

Explicit personal references to owned and confessed Christian faith appear scattered in Freire's writings and speeches, especially in response to hostile confrontation. Thus, in the face of right-wing accusations of being merely a Communist in disguise, Freire responds that he has never ceased being a Christian or, rather, daily becoming one, and he also gives testimony of holding firmly his religious convictions. In fact, Freire associates explicitly his understanding and practice of the Christian faith with his revolutionary and utopian stance.[69]

In order to comprehend Freire and his contribution to both educational philosophy and liberation theology, one must also see the connection between his religious experience and witness and the formative influence received from a number of religious thinkers such as Jacques Maritain, Gabriel Marcel, Emmanuel Mounier, Karl Jaspers, and Martin Buber. These influences provided strong foundations for Freire's anthropology and epistemology, which later included a strong Marxist humanist component that reinforced Freire's radical humanism. In this picture the special influence of a distinctively Catholic heritage must also be recognized, including elements of Thomistic philosophy and theology in his view of humans and nature and the thought of Teilhard de Chardin concerning the evolutionary character of the humanization process and indeed the entire basic course of human evolution.[70] Furthermore, religious and theological trends in Latin America, which highlight the church's vocation for justice and freedom in the midst of sociocultural and politicoeconomic oppression, have left an indelible imprint on Freire's work and thought.

In sum, in order to understand Freire's social and educational approach and contribution, it is essential to appreciate the religious nature of his vocation and witness and the religious dimension of his philosophy. On this point we agree with John L. Elias, who has shown that at all major junctures the religious dimension becomes apparent and decisively influential.[71] That observation is helpful to keep in mind before looking into the specifically theological foundation of conscientization, which we will address succinctly below.

The Implicit Theology of Conscientization. The theological structure of Freire's pedagogical practice and philosophy includes a number of Pauline motifs beginning with the triad of virtues—faith, love, and hope (1 Corinthians 13:13). The conscientization approach calls for a strong affirmation of *faith* in humanity in the sense of the potential for freedom and creativity; it requires a deep *love* toward the world, and especially the oppressed and dehumanized people; and it seeks to elicit unfailing *hope* in the realization of the dream of liberation and humanization for all. Freire asserts that without faith liberating dialogue cannot take place; without love there is no chance for authentic transformation and revolution; and without hope it is not possible to struggle for a better world. Further, as in St. Paul, love is the greatest, especially as *agape*, love concretely enfleshed in humility and solidarity.[72] In fact, trust in the people leads to a kind of conversion and to being "born-again," as it were, so that actual communion and community may be realized and nurtured. Especially the leadership must undergo an "incarnation" and must experience and practice effective solidarity as an act of self-giving analogous to the *kenotic* Christology of Philippians 2:58 ("Christ Jesus . . . made himself nothing, taking the very nature of a servant."). Religious educators authentically committed to liberation will participate in a kind of Easter process of dying (e.g., to privilege, superiority fantasies, ideological illusions) and being resurrected to new life to be shared with the lives of the oppressed. Actually Freire meshes the Exodus liberationist motif with the metaphor of Easter: liberation and redemption must be seen as two dimensions of the same process of human emergence and full humanization. "Easter" as a corporate dimension is sometimes called "class suicide"[73] on the part of those who would adhere to the cause of liberation: willingness to renounce anything that contradicts the interests of the oppressed who themselves will need to die as an oppressed class, in order to be reborn as a class that liberates itself.[74] In this way Freire identifies in principle "incarnation" and "Easter" in his implicit Christology. They are operationalized in terms of the utopian and prophetic stance involving denunciation and announcement.

The theological component of Freire's philosophy is also latent in the very articulation of conscientization which is cloaked in religious and theological language. Conscientization is the process of unveiling and "revealing" historical reality. People are to discover their own sense of worth and personhood and their potential to be subjects or co-creators through their work for transformation and their social interaction. A movement must take place from what Freire calls the domain of prevailing *doxa* (opinions, beliefs, information which fosters false consciousness) to transforming *logos* (probing and creative knowledge for humanization).[75] The movement is expected to generate a work of re-creation while encouraging the development of critical consciousness. Further, for this "revealing" task Freire implicitly adopts a biblical conception of word as instrumental for human dialogue as well as for community formation and social transformation; a word, therefore, that is praxis with the twofold dimension of action and reflection. This praxis-word is like a creative act in which people are re-created as they themselves re-create the world. That is why it is imperative to make it possible for people to effectively pronounce their word, because to exist as a human being is to express the world and to transform it. And the world, in turn, re-presents itself with new problematic images inviting further expression and transformation.[76] In other words, liberating praxis involves a kind of *creatio continua*, and creation and revelation appear intimately related in this conception of the word. Those who pronounce the conscientizing word reveal both oppressive structures and more humanizing alternatives, thus changing in fact the world with a new creation. The process is truly liberating to the extent that it is assumed by the oppressed themselves in redeeming, transforming praxis. It presupposes a position of nonconformity leading to transformation and creativity, as suggested, again, in the Pauline dictum: "Do not conform any longer to the pattern of this world, but be transformed by the renewing of your mind" (Romans 12:2).

Freire's pedagogy proposes humanization by presupposing a theological understanding which stems from a certain Christological stance. Conscientization purports to witness to the incarnate presence of God in the midst of the reality of liberating struggle. Theology as such can then clarify further and articulate that which is implicit in education for liberation, provided of course that theology itself is transformed in the light of the pedagogy of the oppressed, especially by turning toward sociohistorical reality in transforming praxis, which is precisely the orientation assumed by liberation theology.[77]

Freire's Theological Views. The religious experience and convictions of Paulo Freire are the major source not only of the theological structure of conscientization but of his own theologizing as well. Freire believes in the biblical God of the Judeo-Christian tradition, that is, God as interested in human welfare and passionately involved in the course of history. The divine liberating will finds a definitive expression in the person and mission of Jesus Christ. Freire perceives Christ to be the radical transformer and authentic liberator who calls people to realize human life in a community of freedom, peace, and love in light of God's coming reign. That faith claim ultimately inspires the hope-filled confrontation of all alienation and oppression.

Freire views the history of humankind as the starting point for theological reflection. He asserts that just as the Word became flesh in the historical Jesus, so God's Word can be approached only through human beings. Theology has to take its starting point from anthropology.[78] But there is an essential qualification when it comes to that kind of privileged theological reflection that is truly creative and at the service of liberation and humanization. Freire contends that it is in the context of the Third World—in the sense of a world that is marginated, dominated, dependent, voiceless, even within the North Atlantic nations—that a faithful theology can emerge.[79] The basic reason for this assertion is that only in those situations of massive human suffering can there be openness and capacity to receive the liberating Word of God. In contrast, theologies serving the ruling classes or the bourgeoisie cannot be utopian, prophetic, and hopeful because they fail to inspire cultural action for freedom and tend to legitimize the status quo. In light of his Latin American experience, Freire adds that those status-quo theologies and the religious education they inform present a dichotomized world and tend to nurture passive, adjusted individuals waiting for a better life in the hereafter. Prophetic and utopian liberation theologies, on the other hand, stimulate "cultural action for freedom" in Freire's terms, conscientization being their centerpiece.[80]

In Freire's own theological reflection, God is a real presence in history who invites men and women to become engaged in "history making" which is to say active participants in the historical process of liberation and salvation. The certainty that "God does not go back on his promises" does not warrant neutrality or inaction on the part of the Christian whenever people are prevented from being human. Says Freire: "My waiting (*espera*) makes sense only if I struggle and seek with hope (*esperanza*). A theology in which hope would be a waiting but not a searching would be profoundly alienating."[81] The idea is that salvation is a divine gift yet it has to be achieved as well as hoped for.

Furthermore, human beings are created in the image and likeness of God. Therefore, the more fully human we become, the more we resemble the divine. Human emergence involves growing into deeper participation in the freedom of God. Hence the liberationist claim that human freedom is the outcome of authentic human emergence, which is itself a longing and a quest that is ultimately satisfied in God.

Related to those notions, for Freire the relationship between God as creator and liberator and human beings sets the foundation and paradigm for human relationships. He states that our transcendence is based on the root of our finitude and the awareness of this finitude, of being fulfilled in union with our Creator. Our relationship with God by its very nature can never involve domestication or domination but is always a relationship of liberation. "Religion" embodies also this transcendent meaning of interhuman relationships and should never become an instrument of alienation.[82] Normatively speaking, oppression must not take place because it negates the very nature of human beings in light of their relationship with the creating and liberating God. In other words, the image and the concept of God are intimately related to what it means to be human. We are to emerge as the persons we were created to be—and essentially already are—in relationship with God and among ourselves. We are incomplete human beings, but the striving for fulfillment is the occasion for realizing our "ontological vocation" to be subjects who create and make history and community, including the elimination of external oppression such as poverty and disenfranchisement and internal bondage such as arrested, truncated, or corrupted structures of the mind and the moral conscience.

Freire thus reflects on his religious intuitions and metaphysical assumptions about what it means to be human in the face of a creating and liberating God. On this basis he speaks prophetically by denouncing oppression and announcing a liberation gospel with radical hope. His criticism of distorted images and false concepts of God is especially noteworthy, for instance, while castigating conformity and fatalism on the part of the oppressed. Thus, when presented as a distant, inaccessible, and domineering being, God appears to be ultimately responsible for a given situation and the sustainer of oppression.[83] Therefore the response is little more than resignation to fate. Attempts to subvert a given oppressive reality are often taught (and subjectively felt) to be acts of rebellion against God's will. This is the kind of situation that must be confronted in the name of the creating and liberating God, including religious structures and religious education.

The prophetic stance is apparent also in the style of Freire's statements which include appeals and exhortations in sermon-like fashion and with prescriptive force. They display the fervor, certainty, and conviction typical of the religious crusader. Unfortunately, we must recognize that Freire's gospel of liberation is far more precise in its critique (the "denouncing") than in its constructive proposals (the "announcing") concerning the character of the utopian community and the specific function of the church and its educational ministry.

Freire's overall contribution, its theological meaning, and its stance regarding the involvement of the ecclesial community in liberation projects for societal transformation must be seen in light of his personal, religious, and vocational experiences. They reflect the manner in which his work and thought have been decisively shaped by Latin American Roman Catholic Christianity in that social and historical context.[84] The liberationist theological base can be appraised in terms of a *millenialist* worldview which interprets revelation as an ongoing event in human history and perceives the just ordering of society as the unfolding project of the reign of God.[85] This is indeed an essential claim of Latin American liberation theology that Paulo Freire has contributed to inspire and which, in turn, has oriented his own reflection and action.

From Liberation Praxis to Liberation Theology

Before the systematic formulation of liberation theology began to take place there had been a multifaceted "praxis of liberation," including prominently Freire's pedagogical action and reflection on education and social transformation. Thus it is not surprising that several years before the publication of Gustavo Gutiérrez's classic *A Theology of Liberation* (the Spanish language original— *Teología de la Liberación Perspectivas*—appeared in 1971)[86] another classic essay had already made a major impact, Freire's *Education as the Practice for Freedom* (1965), followed by the better known *Pedagogy of the Oppressed* (1968).

Interestingly enough, Paulo Freire figures prominently in Gutiérrez's book in the discussion of the liberation process in Latin America, eschatology and politics, and utopia and political action. This is a good illustration of liberationist appropriation of Freirean thought. Gutiérrez perceives Freire's contribution in light of the search for a *new humanity* which is seen as an essential driving force in liberation endeavors in Latin America. Further, he underscores the goal of fostering critical awareness by means of an unalienating and liberating "cultural action" as a clear case of a creative and fruitful effort toward a cultural revolution undertaken by the oppressed themselves.[87] The essential features of the new emerging human beings include the capacities to critically analyze the present, to fashion their human destiny, and to be oriented toward the future in hope. These new human beings whose actions are directed toward a new society yet to be built are more of a motivating ideal than a reality already realized and generalized in full accord with the spirit and the letter of the church's teachings.[88]

Gutiérrez also finds Freire's work and thought foundational when discussing the meaning of *utopia* in light of biblical faith and political action. For Gutiérrez, the notion of "utopia" is to be characterized by three features—its relationship to historical reality, its verification in praxis, and its rational nature. Freire's emphases on the inseparable dimensions of *denunciation* (of the existing order) and *annunciation* (of what is not yet, but will be), and the place of historical *praxis* between (retrospective) denunciation and (prospective) annunciation, are particularly illuminating in this regard.[89]

It is possible to provide many other examples of theological appropriation of Freire's conscientization approach, including the field of biblical hermeneutics[90] and the case of theologians reflecting in other sociohistorical settings.[91] The point to underscore in light of our agenda is that liberation theologians welcomed the contribution of the Brazilian educational philosopher and theorist of pedagogical revolution, not only because of its impressive effectiveness in terms of actual "praxis of liberation," but also because it provided a crucial foundation for the distinctive method of liberation theology. In fact, in devising his pedagogical approach and the corresponding philosophy of conscientization, Paulo Freire contributed the key methodological principle for liberation theology. Actual involvement in programs of liberating education and "cultural action for freedom," together with his reflections and writings, produced a significant influence in terms of process as well as ecclesial context of doing theology. Thus the ongoing involvement of the church on the side of the poor and oppressed was further stimulated, including the grassroots education movement (Base Education Movement) which, in turn, helped to encourage the emergence of the base Christian communities in Brazil.[92] Marginalized and "submerged" people became more aware of their rights and dignity as human beings and of their creative potential for transformation. Furthermore, the work and thought of Paulo Freire stimulated insights into

Christian praxis which became essential in the methodological formulations of liberation theology, as we will indicate in detail in chapters 3, 4, and 5. The notion of *praxis* is indeed central to Freire's approach. Genuine liberation for him can only be realized through human beings effectively committed to making their own history.[93] By praxis, Freire understands historical, practical activity essential to transforming the world in the direction of justice. Praxis builds on theory and, in turn, continuously calls for the rebuilding of theory. In other words, praxis always involves a dialectic of action and reflection. In articulating his own understanding of liberation from a Christian perspective, which affirms the primacy of praxis, Freire helped to lay the groundwork for the method adopted by liberation theologians. That method builds on solidarity with the oppressed and commitment to them in a praxis of suffering, resistance, and liberation.

In his pedagogical practice, Freire advanced some key motifs which are also central in liberation theology, such as the revealing of ideologies and false perceptions of the world, the centrality of political-economic domination in the Latin American setting, the structural dimensions of violence as initiated and maintained by the oppressors, and liberation as growth in humanness for all, including the oppressors. In fact, the background of Freire's contribution is very helpful for understanding the significance of liberation theology as proposed, for example, by José Míguez Bonino in terms of the following five theses:[94]

First, a new Christian consciousness has emerged in Latin America as a growing number of Christians become involved in the struggle for liberation. (The point of departure for liberation theology is the sociopolitical fact that faith and obedience are interpreted in terms of a committed participation in a historical-cultural process involving critical analysis and action in the name of Christian love.)

Second, that the struggle for liberation is a total historical project presupposing a sociopolitical analysis of Latin America in terms of domination and dependence and proposing a revolutionary change in the direction of a socialist society. (The terms of this analysis come from the social sciences rather than from theology; further, liberationists do not necessarily equate revolutionary change with bloodshed and destruction—as the liberal ideology, which itself evolved through bloodshed and destruction, tends to do—but with basic economic and social transformation.)

Third, the Christian consciousness related to liberation presents a qualitative change in the relation of Christianity to the Latin American society; it is an attempt to overcome a Christianity projected into purely mythical and subjective dimensions and to move toward a projection in historical and political dimensions. (Cultic and religious practices as well as individual piety are incorporated into a larger historical framework; and the key question for Christian ethics is how love can best become fruitful and effective within the conditions of reality in which we live.)

Fourth, this new Christian consciousness requires a new form of theologizing which assumes historical praxis as the matrix of theological reflection. (Christian truth is a vision and an invitation to transform the world in the direction of God's reign; and theological formulations must be understood in light of the form of historical action which they encourage, support, or perhaps disguise.)

Fifth, this theology attempts the repossession and reconception of the biblical and historical tradition from the perspective of theology's relation to the struggle for liberation. (Latin American liberation theology seeks to deal with the agenda of the whole Christian tradition worldwide and to assess and restate it in light of its self-understanding and its own basic commitment.)

Method is the clue to understanding liberation theology as a purported "new way of doing theology" which highlights the process of consciousness raising. The main characteristics of theological method in the liberationist perspective are discussed in detail in chapter 4 in terms of Gutiérrez's definition of "critical reflection on Christian praxis in the light of the Word."[95] Constructive theologizing flows from the adoption of the conscientization methodology, an observation discussed by Dennis McCann in theological perspective and by James Michael Lee from the standpoint of religious education. McCann asserts too neatly that liberation theologians *first* adopted a method, and *then* began to construct a theology from it.[96] However, he is right in indicating that there is a correspondence or correlation linking Freire's pedagogy of the oppressed with liberation theology at three levels: 1) the proposal for institutionalizing the dialogical action of conscientization provides a rationale for the base ecclesial communities; 2) Freire's revolutionary educational theory confirms the centrality of the "generative themes" of oppression/liberation and gives them conceptual definition; 3) Freire's "dialectical vision" that pictures the whole of history as a struggle for liberation is embraced in the liberationist strategy and tactics of "conscientizing evangelization" as the liberating God of the Bible is identified with the struggle of the oppressed.[97]

The connection between Paulo Freire's work and thought and the emergence of liberation theology has been observed by James Michael Lee from the vantage point of religious education. In the context of his rejection of religious instruction as "messenger-boy" and "translator" of theology, Lee points out that liberation theology "arose as a theological reaction, and not as a proaction, to the sociology of Marx, the political activity of Latin American revolutionaries, and the instructional practices of Paulo Freire."[98] This reference is interesting in light of our overall discussion of the interface engaging religious education and liberation theology.[99]

Consistent with the conscientization approach, liberationists propose *critical reflection on [Christian] praxis*. That is, while traditional theology has emphasized understanding the truths of revelation, liberation theology underscores "doing the truth," i.e., being actively engaged in living out biblical faith, the gospel of the reign of God. Reflection upon the gospel and faith—or "faith seeking understanding"—is to happen in light of that experience. In other words, obedience, or doing the truth (orthopraxis), becomes more important than assenting to and articulating truth correctly (orthodoxy). Further, commitment to praxis assumes a fairly specific direction in the sense of identification with the plight and the cause of the poor and the oppressed and joining their struggle for liberation and reconstruction of society. Therefore, theology can never be independent of praxis but—as a second, or derivative, act—theology is, precisely, critical reflection *on* praxis. To the question of praxis and knowing we will return in chapter 3.

As in the case of Freire, critical reflection is perceived as a conscientizing communal process with a three-dimensional focus: It leads people to look for the fundamental causes of alienation and marginalization, poverty and oppression by engaging the analytical memory in search for root causes and understandings; it attends to present reality in order to "problematize" it and to question the prevailing social system and its supporting ideology; it also envisions future consequences and possibilities in terms of "utopia" by engaging the creative imagination.[100] Needless to say, critical reflection also leads to a reassessment of the church's own trajectory and witness for freedom and justice in light of its theology, its social teachings, and its pastoral ministry. In other words, a new understanding of faith and theology includes a new comprehension of the church and its mission in the midst of the historical situation. This is a concern that Freire himself has articulated as we will indicate in the following section.

The Case for the Prophetic Church

Our exploration of the mutual influence affecting conscientization and liberation theology reveals that Freire's personal and vocational experience is paradigmatic of the dialectics of praxis and theological reflection. The logic and the integrity of that ongoing dialectical process finds a remarkable expression in his work and thought.

Paulo Freire does not claim to be a theologian in the traditional sense of the word, nor is he interested in presenting a systematic theological statement on education. Rather, he declares himself to be a committed Christian who also considers that theology has a vital function to perform. The genius of what Freire has accomplished, theologically, is working out the meaning and implications of his own faith in regard to education for liberation and the way in which he has done it. He entered into the challenge and allowed his religious experience and theological orientation to decisively shape his whole pedagogical perspective and philosophy. It is in that sense that Freire has provided a paradigm of what it means to reflect theologically today in the midst of concrete sociohistorical situations and to let that theology inform both the process and content of action and thought. Therefore, with that realization in mind, we will focus on his understanding of the church as particularly relevant from the standpoint of religious education.

The Church Takes Sides. In his approach to the church, Freire begins as an educationist. That is, he applies to the faith community the kind of sociological analysis that has illumined for him the political meaning, dimension, and potential of educational institutions, structures, and processes. He concludes that, if education cannot be neutral, the political partiality or nonneutrality of the church must, by the same token, never be underestimated. For Freire, to proclaim the neutrality of the faith community is either to be naive in the view of church and history, or—shrewdly enough—to conceal a real option on the side of the status quo. Those who are "naive" can eventually appropriate the ideology of domination thus transforming their "innocence" into "shrewdness." But they can also discover and reject their idealistic illusion of impartiality in a conversion process involving a certain death and resurrection (Easter). This renunciation implies the negation of many myths cherished by respectable religious people such as their assumed moral superiority or purity of soul, the illusion of possessing a higher knowledge and wisdom, the paternalistic mission to "save" the oppressed, the myth of the neutrality of the church, theology, and education as well as their own assumed impartiality.[101]

There is a logic in Freire's critique of the illusion of impartiality. For him, the defense of the Christian religion—but actually the religiously sanctioned ideology supporting the present order—amounts to the defense of class interests. In attempting the impossible posture of neutrality regarding economic and political structures, the church undertakes the task of reconciling the irreconcilable for the sake of stability and "peace." Thus the prophetic mission of the church is suppressed and its call to witness for life, freedom, and justice is curtailed due to an incapacity to risk and the fear of transformation in the face of an unjust world. The Christian faith community then becomes merely "religious" in the sense of reactionary and content with self-preservation.[102] Freire contends that true visionaries and revolutionaries, Christian or not, cannot accept a church allied with oppressive classes, either "naively" or "shrewdly."[103]

Freire affirms the faithful Christians who take sides in solidarity with the marginal, the poor and oppressed, and often suffer persecution or even death for confronting the destructive power of imperialism, neocolonialism, and local manifestations of alienation, exploitation, and poverty. For Freire, this is a crude illustration that the "necrophilic" (death loving) cannot tolerate the witness of the "biophilic" (life loving).[104] There is a call, then, for the affirmation of the prophetic task of the church: the denunciation of all manifestations of injustice and the annunciation of a better world for all, to be fashioned in the historical praxis of the oppressed and their strategic allies. This is the vision that inspires the approach of conscientization. The transformation of societal structures correlates with the transformation of consciousness in the process of human emergence in which faith communities have a unique role to play.

Social Structures and Consciousness. Freire establishes a number of correlations between sociocultural structures and levels of consciousness understood in light of historical conditioning as indicated before: *magical,* semi-intransitive consciousness corresponds to relatively closed societies and "cultures of silence"; *naive* or semitransitive consciousness is typically promoted by populist political systems in modernization processes. The influence of Marxist thought is again apparent in Freire's reference to the typology of church and religion insofar as the historicocultural reality is seen as a superstructure in relationship to an infrastructure, the faith community.[105] The first two levels of consciousness—the magical and *conformed* and the naive and *reformed*—are expressions of *false consciousness* in the Marxian analysis, and they correlate with the two types of unfaithful church and religiosity that Freire describes—the traditionalist and modernizing varieties. Hence, there is a convergence of epistemological and theological foundations in Freire's reflection as well as complementarity between them. Language, worldview, self-image, and objective living conditions manifest themselves more or less consistently within the different levels of consciousness. The actual consciousness context in each of those three levels includes basically two closely related phenomena—self-understanding as the personal view of one's existence in the social world and the power one possesses to determine or fashion one's own future. That is why Freire insists that education must be an instrument of transforming action as a political praxis at the service of human liberation. This "does not happen only in the consciousness of people, but presupposes a radical change of structures, in which process consciousness will itself be transformed."[106] Therefore the most important educational task is to sponsor the emergence and expression of critical transitivity or reflectivity, i.e., criticopolitical consciousness. That is also the essential task of the educational ministry in the prophetic church.

The Prophetic Church. "Traditionalist churches alienate the oppressed social classes by encouraging them to view the world as evil. The modernizing churches alienate them . . . by defending the reforms that maintain the status quo," writes Freire.[107] The ecclesial community that is faithful to the gospel is hope-filled, utopian, and prophetic. Instead of the accommodating and patronizing stances of the "traditionalist" and "modernizing" models, the prophetic church is committed to the oppressed and to the transformation of the social order. It does not claim to be neutral nor does it conceal its nonconformed, politically subversive or even revolutionary option. It searches for complementarity and integration between the "secular" and "religious" domains, while rejecting the dichotomy separating (this) worldliness and other-worldliness or transcendence, liberation and salvation, and related beliefs and practices pertaining to worship, discipleship, service, and mission. The prophetic church encourages a critical understanding of faith and promotes communal and social responsibility such as are manifest in the emerging grassroots Christian communities throughout Latin America. Freire has in mind this ecclesial movement of the popular church in his description of faithful communities constantly moving forward, "forever dying and forever being reborn . . . always in a state of *becoming.*"[108] This is precisely the experience of the prophetic church which has inspired a theological reflection that is also prophetic, hopeful, and utopian—the theology of liberation.

The affirmation of utopian hope for a classless society and full humanization for all is the corollary of Freire's view of the gospel. The call for solidarity with the oppressed includes the summons to reveal and confront injustice and to challenge the powerful. The main proof of love to show the oppressors is trying to take away from them the objective conditions that make oppression possible. It is a political and revolutionary task that includes the right to rebellion in light of the institutionalized or structural violence of unjust systems.[109] Freire goes as far as to declare that true revolutionaries must perceive the revolution, "because of its creative and liberating nature," as an act of love.[110] Needless to say, liberationists have to labor hard in order to provide inspiration for the call to revolution as "an act of love" on the basis of the Exodus and Easter biblical motifs. The attempt is to find theological support and religious sanction to a "revolutionary love" that necessitates the annihilation or the subsequent repression of the former oppressors.[111]

In the prophetic church the educational ministry consists of an approach of transforming action, political praxis at the service of liberation and humanization. The key propositions of church education in light of Freire's conscientization approach include, in short, the following tenets: 1) *solidarity* with the poor and oppressed as the starting point, including the commitment to confront the situation of unjustice; 2) multifaceted *conversion* as educational goal, involving both teachers and learners and diverse dimensions (self, relationships, community, social structures); 3) consciousness raising as appropriation of *critical* and *praxis knowing* for liberation and community building; 4) deliberate release and encouragement of human *creativity* in cooperation with the ongoing work of God in the midst of history. Interestingly enough, we can find very analogous proposals in the search for revitalizing religious education in light of the liberationist contribution in quite different sociocultural contexts.[112]

In our discussion so far two general observations stand out as pertinent for the theory and practice of religious education. First, there is the challenge to analyze and critique our historical-cultural situation in terms of the nature and mission of the church and, especially, the function of the educational ministry. Assessment of instructional patterns and awareness of the sociology of knowledge are crucial for religious education to become a means for discernment, criticism, and reconstruction of the sociocultural reality. Second, Freire's contribution is especially helpful in highlighting the interrelationship of practice and theory or the dialogical synapse of action and reflection (praxis) in the creative process of conscientization for human emergence.

CONSCIENTIZATION AND CREATIVITY
IN RELIGIOUS EDUCATION

The question of liberating truth—or, knowing the truth and being made free, as highlighted in the gospel reference of John

8:31-32—presents a privileged place of intersection for religious education and theology. And that place has been revisited by Freire and other liberationists in a way that encourages further critical dialogue at the very intersection. As indicated in the Preface, it is our thesis that in the encounter between religious education and liberation theology—if the integrity of both is respected—mutual enlightenment takes place and the two fields are advanced in their own terms. A major underlying assumption here is that conscientization is indeed foundational for enhancing diverse facets of religious education, provided that its liberating potential is processed critically and creatively. In fact, self-critical consciousness is a central tenet of liberation theology. Thus when "critical reflection" is lacking, the wholesale assimilation of liberation thought into religious education simply becomes an ironic contradiction and a failure to do justice to either field. It is indeed ironic that neither liberation theologians nor religious education-ists by and large have exercised the self-critical discipline inher-ently mandated by the pedagogy and theology of liberation that they embrace.[113]

On the basis of that major assumption, we have critiqued and reformulated the conscientization approach from the standpoint of religious education. The process of conscientization is analo-gous to the creative process. Now we can provide an illustration of the constructive restatement of religious education resulting from the confrontation with the liberationist witness and thought. This discussion will be supplemented in subsequent chapters in terms of other dimensions and theoretical categories of religious education.

We will focus now on the questions of process and develop-ment as suggested by Freire's contribution on *conscientization for human emergence.* Thus we must underscore the integrity and unity of process and content.[114] The rich and complex dynamics of learning and teaching (structural content) are perceived as intimately related to the scope of Christian religious education, that is, the substantive content or subject matter. And those ma-jor questions, of course, are inseparable from the other dimen-sions of the practice and theory of religious education, especially those pertaining to purpose and goals (discussed in chapter 2) and persons in context (chapter 5).

In the discussion of Freire's conscientization approach and process, we indicated that significant human learning is perceived as the process in which a person moves from one level of consciousness to another. We also pointed out that the content of consciousness includes the view persons have of their own existence in the social world and the power they have to fashion their own future. Learning takes place starting with the present level of consciousness as manifest in current living conditions as well as the language, self-concept, and worldview of the people involved. In this context, transforming learning implies awaring and awakening, especially becoming aware of the contingency of social reality. It is precisely in the face of such contingency that the human will and power to create and to transform must be nurtured. Hence, Freire's work and thought challenges much of the church's educational ministry, particularly in regard to the questions of content and methodology. For one thing, diverse problems with prevailing practices can be identified more pointedly, such as the "banking" reliance on mere memorization or the lack of relevance in light of sociohistorical reality. Also, we can indicate several alternatives, especially in line with the emphasis that learners must be considered as subjects invited to "say their word" and to participate in the re-creation of their world. Freire's contribution inspires a religious education approach that is *dialogical* in spirit, *prophetic-eschatological* in vision, *praxis* oriented, *hermeneutical* in character, and *communal* in shape. Such an inspiration, however, must be made explicit on the basis of our critical appraisal of that contribution. We can thus suggest a number of principles regarding the profile of the Christian religious educator, questions of subject matter or scope, and a special paradigm involving learning sequence and tasks.

Principles of Liberating Teaching

Religious educators whose ministry is illumined by our discussion will take seriously into account a number of considerations in the form of guidelines or dependable guides to practice.

First of all, there is the challenge for religious educators to engage themselves in a thorough search into the life situation of the people they serve, with acceptance, respect, and hope. Genuine closeness and communion, as proposed by Freire's pedagogy, require a movement of *immersion* at every stage of the teaching-learning process. Therefore, religious educators must find ways in which to meet people wherever they happen to be, with the twofold attitude of gently making themselves available and welcoming the learners—especially the oppressed, marginal, strangers—for a joint educational journey.

The multifaceted content of Christian religious education is to be focused in terms of the real life struggles and conflicts of the people: their needs and concerns, their longings and dreams. Teachers should be willing to consider and discern, together with the learners, outstanding themes for reflection and action, selected from the existential situation of those who share in the church's educational program and process.

A special teaching concern and objective will be the facilitation of *dialogue* as encounter between and among subjects. This involves making space for sharing personal stories and visions as well as reflecting critically upon them. Rather than just an educational strategy or a method, this dialogical process is to be fostered as a *style*[115] and an attitude that will decisively shape the whole learning context. Paulo Freire has described in detail and illustrated the requirements for such a dialogical spirit and pedagogical stance in terms of profound love for people, humility, and intense faith in the human potential to create and transform, an orientation of hope, and the will to question critically present reality as it appears to be.[116]

Dialogical religious education promotes listening and open conversation. It is potentially freeing and empowering for both teachers and learners, by facilitating the kinds of experiences and processes briefly discussed in terms of awakening, perspective transformation, and intellectual, moral, and faith development. It can also foster mutual caring and community building.

Appropriate resources and activities that will facilitate the discussion of the "generative themes" pertaining to lived-out faith may be adapted or invented, such as printed materials, graphic representations, drama, video, and so on. Diverse methods and techniques can be utilized in a manner analogous to that of the "codification" phase in the conscientization process. In other words, far from being passive observers, teachers are expected to develop their ingenuity in order to enhance the learning process and consciousness raising for transforming action in particular.

Educators will also explore ways in which God's Word and Spirit will be allowed to inform and transform the discussion and reflection, the very subject matter under consideration and the lives of the participants. Biblical input as well as the church's teachings and understandings will be made available but not in an authoritarian and indoctrinating fashion. Also, active participation and involvement on the part of all will be sought.

As indicated before, the role of the teacher is informed by the function of the coordinators of "culture circles" as described by Freire. This calls for both a "democratic" (i.e., fostering equality and mutual responsibility) orientation to leadership as well as personal involvement in reflection and action, *praxis*, in the face of the agreed-upon agenda of the group. Hence, commitment to responsible faith decisions and concrete responses on the part of all is to be elicited in consistency with the very demands and expectations of the gospel. Procedure and substantive content are thus integrated in the same creative and liberating educational dynamics.

The whole field of human relationships, history, and nature is potentially the subject of conscientization and religious education. Freire's contribution suggests clues and explicit directions for a critical analysis leading to the choice of more humanizing alternatives in the face of the situation in which people find themselves. However, it is also possible to address another fundamental question, namely, how can Christian faith itself be further nurtured and enhanced? In light of the liberationist perspective, one of the major tasks of Christian religious education concerns the "purification" of faith, or freeing Christian faith from ideological captivity with a particular historical situation. This is the frequent case of the gospel becoming but a pallid and distorted version of the Christian faith which thus necessitates critical analysis and reformulation.[117] Also, the dialogical conscientization approach involving critical reflection can help to "decodify" theological symbols, liturgical expressions, and sacraments as well as religious behavior and practices. The objective is to recapture anew the transcendent meaning and the liberating and humanizing potential of those and other manifestations of faith in terms of the actual historical context of the ecclesial community.

These considerations obviously reject the model of faith as a finished product, or as a "deposit" of sacred, static beliefs and actions to be carefully transmitted as a parcel of truth. This is not what "abiding" in Jesus' word (John 8:31) is about. Actually, religious language is always subject to transformation which is in itself a condition of its own transforming power. In other words, the religious educator must embrace the opportunity and the invitation to re-create the very language of faith. We thus underscore a special dimension of "authorship" so intentionally fostered by Freire in his conscientization approach and philosophy. A new language of Christian faith can always evolve in a context of freedom to create. The faithful can reappropriate and communicate the gospel in their own terms, in their own words, with a praxis-oriented language, i.e., a language which spells commitment to God and neighbor and which is efficacious for consistent interpretation and transformation of reality. Christian religious education can also facilitate discovering and sharing new ways of expressing faith in a teaching-learning process in which dynamics and method intentionally become part of the content and the message of liberation and creativity, as we will indicate below.

Principles of Liberating Learning

We have demonstrated that conscientization is essentially a form of the creative process transposed into an intentional endeavor to deal with existential and social conflict. It is the process employed so that the conflict situation becomes an occasion for new insight and the heightening of consciousness in liberating and creative praxis. Essentially, then, the process of religious education inspired by Paulo Freire and liberation theology will reflect the learning sequence that reproduces the pattern of creativity, or "grammar of transformation," in the terms of James E. Loder.[118] Further, we can identify specific *learning tasks* in connection with the different movements of that transformational pattern. Those intentionally fostered forms of learning must be seen as interrelated, completing and supplementing each other. An integral part of the scope of Christian religious education, learning tasks become, therefore, special forms of "substantive process product" engaging a wide variety of registers of behavior, as we will indicate briefly in the following description.

The typical learning sequence begins with the *identification and focus on given social and existential conflict situations.* The prophetic church that sponsors conscientizing evangelization will regard conflict engagement and complexity as occasions for human emergence and growth of faith. Religious educators will be especially sensitive to the real life challenges of the people, particularly situations of oppression and suffering. Hence, apparent "limit situations" and the "generative themes" challenging Christian life will be identified and processed as problems to be communally confronted although personally borne. This movement corresponds to "baffled struggle in a context of rapport" in the creativity paradigm.[119] In our own experience the question of family economy and finances represents a recurring "limit situation" often compounded by inflation, unemployment, and other social and economic ills. This theme is promptly associated with critical issues such as work, values and priorities, consumerism, and stewardship. The task immediately associated with this movement in the transformational sequence is *learning to discern, face, and embrace conflict* with perseverance and care. As Loder indicates, however, learners must move beyond the sole concern with human struggles on different levels in order that the consciousness of God's action in the world may also be heightened.[120] This realization will decisively inform the rest of the learning sequence in a distinctly Christian religious education setting, thereby allaying potential humanistic reductionism, Marxist or otherwise.

In prophetic religious education, "problematizing" takes the place of traditional transmission-of-information pedagogicaal approaches. That stance makes room for an *interlude for scanning* in the creativity paradigm. In actual practice, the formulation of critical problems and conflict situations is followed by dialogue and discussion in search for new realizations, associations, and meanings. This may take a variety of expressions in terms of methodological procedures and group dynamics, including of course the component of "critical reflection *in light of the Word*," i.e., the explicit inclusion of the biblical and Christian message— or the Story and Vision of the faith community, as Groome proposes—explicitly made available to the participants. In the case of our example, the learners will receive that message concerning the problem considered and critically reflected upon—

economics, alienation, and oppression, dealing with finances and related questions.

In the creative-liberating educational sequence, *learning to search and to explore with expectance and hope* is the task to be intentionally fostered. Negatively speaking, it involves learning, not to take for granted reality as it is, or what is normally presented as "reality," but rather to question, criticize, discern, and search for alternatives. This is especially challenging in the face of the tendency to arrive too soon at easy or simplistic answers and to get emotionally involved in arguments about religious and financial-economic matters. Thus this major learning task involves also the development of communication skills, such as sensitive listening to external as well as internal messages.

Religious education for freedom and creativity will lead to fitting discoveries connected with the initial conflicts and quests of the people. This is the movement characterized by *intuition and insight* in the creativity paradigm. Actually, resolution may arrive rather suddenly, for instance in the form of new clues for enhancing the sense of vocation, fostering stewardship, prophetic witness, or the illuminating relevance of a certain biblical text or motif (e.g., compassion, nonconformity, mutual care, and sharing). Insights and intuitions often may take the shape of heightened awareness of hidden assumptions or contradictions as well as alternatives for transformation in terms of the issues at hand. Resolution usually involves not merely an appropriate response to the conflict situation faced, but also a new way of perceiving the problem (e.g., no more as a genuine "limit" situation in the sense of closed and hopeless) or a new set of questions. In other words, in the religious education version of conscientization, the "raising of awareness" may assume a variety of meanings and directions which cannot and should not be figured out in advance.

Religious education for freedom and creativity will intentionally foster the inclination to attend to, value, and trust those intuitions and insights emerging in the process on conscientization. It will also encourage the disposition to actually learn from those new realizations and to share them in the context of the learning ecclesial community. Hence this learning task of *receiving hospitably one's own insights* will be closely related to the learning to search and explore with expectance and hope.

In the creativity paradigm, insights experienced with intuitive and convincing force are normally associated with or followed by release and redirection of energy bound up with the original existential or social conflict situation. This is the movement of *release of tension and transformation of energy.* Tensions related to the problem being confronted tend to be dissolved with a pleasant sense of freedom and transformation already happening—for instance, in connection with realizing ways to be freed from the economic "rat race" and envisioning alternatives of fulfillment and wholeness consistent with a life of service even in the midst of a materialistic and alienating social milieu.

The celebration of learning and awareness that tends to take place spontaneously can be affirmed and further refocused in terms of *learning to celebrate.* This is particularly fitting due to the clear association that exists between liberation and celebration and the liberationist emphasis on the struggle for justice in the context of Christian spirituality.[121] In a profound sense, that association also enlightens the political meaning of worship as response to God's re-creating and liberating grace. It is political because of the very nature of the lordship of the liberating Christ and the reign of God confessed by the prophetic ecclesial community.

Interpretation and verification take place in the final movement of the transformational sequence of creativity. Critical interpretation is necessary for understanding the connection between insights and conflict situations and for probing their correspondence with the public context of those conflicts. The conscientization approach and process illumines the dialectic of action and reflection in terms of praxis learning and transformation. Critical reflection engaging reason, memory, and imagination correlate with concrete faith responses in light of the gospel. In the case of our example, the participants may develop, for instance, a more clear appraisal of the dynamics of their economic situation together with new tangible expressions of faithful and voluntary discipleship (e.g., sharing of resources, changes in the practices of buying, budgeting, administering, or working for economic justice). Thus the religious education process affirms the mutually informing relationship between reflection and action ("praxis") so consistently underscored by Freire and liberation theologians.[122]

The corresponding learning task that religious education for freedom and creativity fosters is that of *interpretation and responsible action* as expressing the hermeneutic nature of the prophetic ecclesial community. That learning task is promoted in the ongoing process of reflection and action aimed not merely at the immediate personal benefit of the participants but also at preparing them to account for the Christian hope that they hold, both in word—sound doctrine, or "theory"—and in deed—relevant witness, or "practice."

Further questions and conflicts will elicit new engagements in this transformational (i.e., freeing and creating) learning process attuned to the vision of the reign of God. This is the prophetic and utopian vision that highlights the *political and eschatological* dimension of the gospel. It is a second key liberationist motif that defines the mission of the church and informs the guiding principle of religious education. To that we will turn our attention in the following chapter.

Notes

1. John 8:32.
2. Paulo Freire, "Education, Liberation and the Church," *Religious Education* 79:4 (Fall 1984), pp. 524, 544-545.
3. James Michael Lee, "Introduction," in *The Religious Education We Need*, ed. James Michael Lee (Birmingham, Ala.: Religious Education Press, 1977), p.1.
4. See Raymond E. Brown, *The Gospel According to John (I-XII)* (Garden City, N.Y.: Doubleday, 1966), pp. 352 ff. For a liberationist commentary, see Jose P. Miranda, *Being and the Messiah: The Message of St. John*, trans. John Eagleson (Maryknoll, N.Y.: Orbis, 1977).
5. For a lucid and inspiring discussion of "obedience to truth" which builds on the Johannine texts, see Parker J. Palmer, *To Know as We Are Known: A Spirituality of Education* (San Francisco: Harper & Row, 1983), pp. 43 ff. and chap. 4.
6. Paulo Freire, "Conscientization," *Cross Currents* 24:1 (Spring, 1974), p. 23.
7. Paulo Freire, "Know, Practice and Teach the Gospels," *Religious Education* 79:4 (Fall 1984), pp. 547-548.
8. For a discussion of the dialectic between theory and practice in religious education, see John L. Elias, *Studies in Theology and Education* (Malabar, Fla.: Krieger, 1986), chap. 1. Elias discussed a critical correlation concerning four elements that characterize that relationship: mutual explanation

or interpretation; interdependent directiveness; reciprocal criticism or evaluation; and two-way imagination (pp. 6-12).

9. For an introduction to Freire's pedagogy see Paulo Freire, *Education for Critical Consciousness* (New York: Seabury, 1973), especially his discussion of education and conscientization in the essay "Education as the Practice of Freedom." See also Paulo Freire, *The Politics of Education*, trans. Donaldo Maceado (South Hadley, Mass.: Bergin & Garney, 1985), chaps. 2,3,6,8. A good exposition of Freire's literacy method is included in Cynthia Brown, "Literacy in Thirty Hours, Paulo Freire's Process in Northeast Brazil," *Social Policy* (July-August 1974), pp. 25-32. One of the best introductions to Freire, in English, is Denis Collins, *Paulo Freire: His Life, Works and Thought* (New York: Paulist Press, 1977). See also Robert Mackie, ed., *Literacy and Revolution: The Pedagogy of Paulo Freire* (New York: Continuum, 1981).

10. On November 20, 1983, the Religious Education Association William Rainey Harper Award was fittingly presented to both Paulo and Elza Freire, with the citation "Educators and Prophets of the Pedagogy of the Oppressed, Champions of Justice and Peace."

11. Freire's pedagogy and philosophy of education can be seen in terms of *reconstructionism* or, more specifically, a *radical* adult education approach in that it aims to utilize education to bring about profound social, political, and economic changes in society. The term reconstructionism was first used on a popular scale by Theodore Brameld to denote and espouse an educational philosophy which builds on Deweyian progressivism but goes beyond it. Freire's philosophy of education gains a somewhat broader perspective when viewed through the lens of reconstructionism. Theodore Brameld, *Patterns of Educational Philosophy* (Yonkers, N.Y.: Word, 1950), pp. 389-652. On adult religious education as a proactive force in society, see John L. Elias and Sharan Merriam, *Philosophical Foundations of Adult Education* (Malabar, Fla.: Krieger, 1980), chap. 6. According to Kenneth Barker's typology, Freire inspires the *political* approach to religious education for freedom, *Religious Education, Catechesis, and Freedom* (Birmingham, Ala.: Religious Education Press, 1981), introduction and chap. 4. Barker studies three typical approaches taken implicitly or explicitly by contemporary theorists—the psychological, the political, and the cultural. The political approach is taken by those critical of a privatized arena of human freedom who emphasize freedom's sociopolitical dimensions. It is freedom *from* cultural oppression and *for* the power to work together to change existing conditions and participate in building the reign of justice and peace (*shalom*). Also, John L. Elias includes Freire's contribution in the category of *sociopolitical* adult religious education, *The Foundations and Practice of Adult Religious Education* (Malabar, Fla.: Krieger, 1982), pp. 171-175. These discussions are very useful except that they do not fully account for the dynamics and effectiveness nor the limitations of Freire's work and thought, including further ramifications of his potential contribution.

12. According to Freire, the term *conscientização* was popularized and given currency by another outstanding Brazilian prophet, Dom Helder Camara. Concerned about the misuse of the term, Freire also indicated in that context that the word should probably be used in its Brazilian form and

spelled that way, "Conscientization," *Cross Currents*, pp. 23-24. Following the advice of Elza Freire, he later announced that since 1974 he has preferred not to use the word because of the frequent distortions in the understanding and the use of the concept, especially the idealistic interpretations: "Consciousness is neither the creator of reality, nor is it merely the reflection of reality. On the one hand we cannot therefore interpret conscientization as something that happens simply inside you, but also we can't interpret it without understanding it as something which happens without critical reflection." ("Conversation with Paulo Freire," *Religious Education*, 79:4 [Fall 1984], p. 514.) Actually, Freire points out two kinds of misuses of his pedagogical approach: *methodizing*, or reducing conscientization to any one single small-group technique, that is, without concern for change in the social structure and thus without involving risk; and *mythologizing*, or idealization of praxis so that conscientization becomes a subjective idealism (see Freire, "Education, Liberation, and the Church," *Religious Education*, pp. 526ff.). Freire stresses the interdependence of action and reflection: consciousness transformation, a major change of mind, necessitates some ongoing action aimed at changing the social reality. Conversely, major structural change cannot take place while the old mentality persists on the part of the persons involved. Obviously, we have chosen to keep using the term in its English adaptation while endeavoring to affirm the meaning and connotations intended by Freire.

13. For a full treatment of these and related areas of Freire's pedagogy and educational philosophy, see Daniel S. Schipani, *Conscientization and Creativity: Paulo Freire and Christian Education* (Lanham, Md.: University Press of America, 1984).

14. Paulo Freire, "Conscientizing as a Way of Liberating" (Washington D.C.: LADOC II), p. 29. For a comprehensive discussion, see Paulo Freire, *Cultural Action for Freedom* (Cambridge: Harvard Educational Review and Center for the Study of Development and Social Change, 1970).

15. Freire, "Conscientizing as a Way of Liberating," p. 5. The concept of conscientization is founded upon a *phenomenological* and *dialectical* conception of consciousness and the world: It involves intentionality, the affirmation of the subjective-objective dialectic, and consciousness and the world dialectically constituting each other.

16. Freire, "Conscientization," *Cross Currents*, p. 25.

17. Ibid.

18. This reference to the language of critique and possibility is employed by Henry A. Giroux to characterize Freire's overall contribution to a critical theory of pedagogy, in his Introduction to Freire, *The Politics of Education*, pp. xiff. Giroux rightly states that Freire's discourse stands between two radical traditions: the language of critique embodies many of the analyses of the new sociology of education; and Freire's philosophy of hope and struggle is rooted in a language of possibility that draws extensively from the tradition of liberation theology: "By combining the dynamics of critique and collective struggle with a philosophy of hope, Freire has created a language of possibility that is rooted in what he calls a permanent prophetic vision" (p. xvii).

19. Since *Pedagogy of the Oppressed*, the theoretical tools of historical materialism define Freire's analysis of reality as well as the main propositions

concerning the program and process of conscientization (Marx had presented a concrete phenomenology of economic relations and had underscored the dialectical character of reality and history and the purpose of philosophy in the praxis of social transformation). Freire eventually adopted the Marxist interpretation of the theory of ideology as foundational for his pedagogical approach, including important claims in the area of sociology of knowledge. Thus, for instance, the notion that the oppressed are bearers of "pragmatic truth" is reflected in Freire's reiterated assertion of the need to approach the common people, especially the marginal, as the genuine source of knowing and truth. This is of course consistent with the proposal that people must educate themselves. Among other implications, truth is now conditioned to a class situation, and the ultimate educational goal becomes the facilitation of radical transformation of the social structure. Marxism provides mainly a key epistemological and ideological base in terms of Freire's notion of dialectics. From Marxian dialectics he appropriates such ideas as the necessity of class struggle, the unity of action and reflection, human work as praxis, the function of ideology, and the structure and dynamics of alienation. See my detailed analysis in Schipani, *Conscientization and Creativity*, pp. 15-20, 21ff., 61ff, 162-164.

20. Ibid., pp. 16-17.
21. On this topic, see the essay by Michael Matthews, "Knowledge, Action and Power," in *Literacy and Revolution: The Pedagogy of Paulo Freire*, ed. Robert Mackie, pp. 82-92.
22. Freire, *Cultural Action for Freedom*, p. 22.
23. Paulo Freire, *Pedagogy of the Oppressed*, trans. Myra Bergman Ramos (New York: Seabury, 1970), chap. 2.
24. Ibid., chap. 4.
25. Freire, "The Process of Political Literacy," in *The Politics of Education*.
26. Freire, *Cultural Action for Freedom*, p. 32.
27. The reference to "transitivity" denotes an analogy from grammar and linguistics.
28. Freire, *Cultural Action for Freedom*, p. 36.
29. Ibid., p. 40.
30. Ibid., p. 46.
31. The description of the levels of consciousness in the context of Freire's educational approach appears in his major essays starting with "Education as the Practice of Freedom," in *Education for Critical Consciousness*, pp. 17ff. It is clear that Freire never repudiates that understanding but, rather, he reinterprets it in light of his epistemological reformulation.
32. Freire, *Pedagogy of the Oppressed*, pp. 28ff.
33. Ibid., p. 40.
34. Schipani, *Conscientization and Creativity*, p. 15.
35. For this way of posing the question I am indebted to James O'Donnell, "Education as Awakening," *Religious Education* 76:5 (September-October 1981), pp. 517-524. O'Donnell compares the contributions of Freire, Illich, and Kozol in a perceptive discussion of education as a method of awakening. The method calls for a Kierkegaard inspired "repellent effect" on the part of the teachers who prize learning as an awakening and promote existential appropriation of truth by the learners.
36. Freire, *Education for Critical Consciousness*, p. 6.

37. Jack Mezirow, "A Critical Theory of Adult Learning and Education," in *Selected Writings on Philosophy and Adult Education*, ed. Sharan Merriam (Malabar, Fla.: Krieger, 1984), p. 124.
38. Leon McKenzie, *The Religious Education of Adults* (Birmingham, Ala.: Religious Education Press, 1982), p. 123.
39. See Jack Mezirow, "Perspective Transformation," *Adult Education* 28:2 (1978), pp. 104 ff. A question arises, however, with regard to Mezirow's assertion that people must take the perspective of others who have a more critical awareness, rather than leaving the transformational process open. It seems that the risk of collapsing creativity and fostering subtle manipulation might otherwise reemerge.
40. See Barbel Inhelder and Jean Piaget, *The Growth of Logical Thinking from Childhood to Adolescence*, trans. Anne Parsons and Stanley Milgram (New York: Basic Books, 1958). Thomas H. Groome's discussion of "shared praxis" from a Piagetian perspective is also relevant for our topic. *Christian Religious Education: Sharing Our Story and Vision* (San Francisco: Harper & Row, 1980), chap. 11.
41. Lawrence Kohlberg, *The Philosophy of Moral Development: Moral Stages and the Idea of Justice: Essays on Moral Development*, Vol. I (San Francisco: Harper & Row, 1981) and *The Psychology of Moral Development: The Nature and Validity of Moral Stages; Essays on Moral Development*, Vol II (San Francisco: Harper & Row, 1984). For an examination of the Kohlbergian approach from a variety of complementary perspectives, see Brenda Munsey, ed., *Moral Development, Moral Education, and Kohlberg* (Birmingham, Ala.: Religious Education Press, 1980), especially chaps. 1,2,3,11,16.
42. On the question of method as message, see Robert E. Carter, *Dimensions of Moral Education*, (Toronto: University of Toronto Press, 1984), pp. 12ff. Carter presents the methodology and justification for the critical or philosophical approach in moral education, with an exposition of the Socratic method.
43. Kohlberg, *The Philosophy of Moral Development*, p. 410.
44. James W. Fowler, *Stages of Faith: The Psychology of Human Development and the Quest for Meaning* (San Francisco: Harper & Row, 1981). See also the excellent collection edited by Craig Dykstra and Sharon Parks, *Faith Development and Fowler* (Birmingham, Ala.: Religious Education Press, 1986).
45. James W. Fowler, "Black Theologies of Liberation: A Structural Analysis," in *The Challenge of Liberation Theology: A First World Response*, ed. Brian Mahan and L. Dale Richesin (Maryknoll, N.Y.: Orbis, 1981), pp. 69-90.
46. See Kenneth Stokes, ed. *Faith Development in the Adult Life* (New York: Sadlier, 1982). The FD/ALC Project, 1981-1986, was sponsored by the Religious Education Association and several religious organizations. The research reports from "Module 1" (quantitative survey methodology) and "Module 2" (qualitative, in-depth interview and analysis) offer supporting data concerning two of the Project hypotheses that could be associated specifically with conscientization programs and processes: *Faith development is positively related to one's involvement in social issues and concerns*, and *Faith development is positively related to one's involvement in*

educational experiences. The observations and analyses reported highlight the issues of the expanding "bounds of awareness," the enhancement of meaning-making processes, the role of involvement in community and political action projects, and dialogical and critical exposure to people and ideas outside one's social context. *Faith Development and Your Ministry*, Report based on a Gallup Survey Conducted for the Religious Education Association of the United States and Canada (Princeton, N.J.: Princeton Religion Research Center, undated), pp. 48, 50-52; Constance Leean, "Faith Development in the Adult Life Cycle," Research Report of Module 2, Religious Education Association, 1985 (unpublished), pp. 33, 37-40.

47. See note no. 19.

48. Freire, *Pedagogy of the Oppressed*, pp. 22-23.

49. Peter L. Berger, *Pyramids of Sacrifice* (New York: Basic Books, 1975), pp. 111-132. Berger develops a methodological critique against the "false consciousness" of consciousness raisers who assume that they know better than the people they claim to serve and who tend to define reality for others. He argues that, rather than "consciousness raising," this is a case of *conversion* from one worldview to another (perhaps as a case of alienating "meaning perspective transformation," we would add). Berger emphasizes the stance of "cognitive respect" based on the assumption of the equality of the worlds of consciousness. We must notice, however, that Berger seems to assess conscientization as a mere technique for consciousness raising. Further, he seems to ignore or disregard, among other things, Freire's call for conversion toward the oppressed as well as his awareness of the risks of collapsing dialogue and mutual teaching-learning on the part of educators in traditional roles.

50. On the question of "ultracognitivism" in religious education, see James Michael Lee, *The Content of Religious Instruction* (Birmingham, Ala.: Religious Education Press, 1985), pp. 612-613, 702-703.

51. Gabriel Moran, *Religious Body: Design for a New Reformation* (New York: Seabury, 1974), pp. 93ff., 169ff. Writes Moran: "The aim of education . . . is to keep open and growing a wider spectrum of feeling, a greater imagination, a heightened consciousness—in short, an intelligent life" (p. 170). For a helpful discussion of Moran's contribution from the perspective of the *political type* of religious education for freedom, see Barker, *Religious Education, Cathechesis, and Freedom.*

52. This is analogous to the critique of Marx's mythic mode of thought as helpfully presented by Robert Tucker, *Philosophy and Myth in Karl Marx*, 2nd ed. (Cambridge, Mass.: University Press, 1972), chap. 15.

53. Freire, *Pedagogy of the Oppressed*, p. 23.

54. Ibid., pp. 134, 160, 170-171.

55. See Schipani, *Conscientization and Creativity*, chap. 2.

56. Freire, *Education for Critical Consciousness*, p. 43.

57. Ibid., p. 47.

58. For a comprehensive account and evaluation of a Freire-inspired literacy-conscientization program aimed at cultural reconstruction and politicization, see Valerie Miller, *Between Struggle and Hope: The Nicaraguan Literacy Crusade* (Boulder: Westview, 1985).

59. Paulo Freire, *Educación y Cambio* (Buenos Aires: Búsqueda, 1976), pp. 27, 74.

60. This expression is borrowed from Stephen Crites, "The Narrative Quality of Experience," *Journal of the American Academy of Religion* 39 (September 1971), pp. 291-311.

61. Schipani, *Conscientization and Creativity*, pp. 26-27.

62. The special character and dynamics of "creativogenic" social settings are discussed in Silvano Arieti, *Creativity: The Magic Synthesis* (New York: Basic Books, 1976), chaps. 13 and 14.

63. The principal source for the study of creativity in light of Christian religious education is the work of James E. Loder. See especially *Religious Pathology and Christian Faith* (Philadelphia: Westminster, 1966); "Creativity in and Beyond Human Development," in *Aesthetic Dimensions of Religious Education*, ed. Gloria Durka and Joanmarie Smith, (New York: Paulist, 1979), pp. 219-235; "Negation and Transformation: A Study in Theology and Human Development," in *Towards Moral and Religious Maturity*, ed. James Fowler and Antoine Vergote (Morristown, N.J.: Silver Burdett, 1980), pp. 165-192; "Transformation in Christian Education," in *Religious Education* 76:2 (March-April 1981), pp. 204-221; and *The Transforming Moment: Understanding Convictional Experiences* (New York: Harper & Row, 1981). Other valuable sources are: Silvano Arieti, *Creativity: The Magic Synthesis*; Arthur Koestler, *The Act of Creation: A Study of the Conscious and Unconscious in Science and Art* (New York: Macmillan, 1964); Rollo May, *The Courage to Create* (New York: Norton, 1975); and Harold Rugg, *Imagination: An Inquiry Into the Sources and Conditions that Stimulate Creativity* (New York: Harper & Row, 1963).

64. The creative sequence may actually start at any point (e.g., insights—phase 3 and/or interpretations—phase 5 often move us back to focus on assessing original conflicts). However, the completion of the process necessitates the recognition of an original problem situation or baffled struggle. Further, it should be noticed that this five-movement paradigm resembles John Dewey's five steps of reflective thinking as a problem-solving process: 1) Thinking begins with a *felt* sense of the problem; 2) the problem is *formulated* ("intellectualized") in a conceptually clear, concise way; 3) then follows *exploration* of available *hypotheses* which have a significant bearing on the solution of the problem; 4) thinking about the hypotheses which have suggested themselves, *analyzing* and *elaborating* them; and 5) bringing the product of the previous steps to a testable form and proceeding with the *test*. See John Dewey, *How We Think*, (Boston: Heath, 1933), p. 107. Dewey's description of the thinking process is a general paradigm for inquiry and also a view of how we learn through solving problems. As a conceptualization of the cognitive process, however, it underestimates affect as well as the role of the unconscious. That is a major difference with regard to the creativity paradigm that we are discussing. It can also be added in the context of this observation that Dewey influenced Freire as recognized, especially, in *Education as the Practice of Freedom*. However, Freire's "problem posing" in the context of conscientization represents a significant step forward beyond Dewey's position, especially in that it fosters the development of perception in a structural perspective (cf. Danilo R. Streck, "John Dewey's and Paulo Freire's Views on the Political Function of Education with Special Emphasis on the Problem of Method," Ed.D. dissertation, Rutgers University, 1977).

65. The connection between creativity and revitalization (as proposed for instance by Freire in terms of "cultural revolution") has been established by Loder when discussing the transposition of the paradigm of the creative process into revitalization of a social milieu (Schipani, *Conscientization and Creativity*, pp. 46-49).

66. Here we can mention for example the risk and temptation to inject supposedly normative political-ideological analyses in the attempt to promote the development of "political consciousness" on the part of the "experts" in a given conscientization endeavor. Obviously, that violates the very educational process aimed at greater freedom and creativity.

67. Paulo Freire, *El Mensaje de Paulo Freire* (Madrid: Marsiega, 1976), p. 20.

68. Freire, "Know, Practice, and Teach the Gospels," p. 548.

69. Paulo Freire, "Conscientizar para Liberar," *Contacto* 8:1 (1971), pp. 43-51.

70. For a thorough discussion of the main sources of Freire's philosophy of education and how they are integrated in his own reflection and conscientization approach, see Schipani, *Conscientization and Creativity*, chaps. 1 and 3.

71. John L. Elias, *Conscientization and Deschooling: Freire's and Illich's Proposals for Reshaping Society* (Philadelphia: Westminster, 1976). For an overall assessment of Freire, from the standpoint of religious education, see Elias' "Paulo Freire: Adult Religious Educator," chap. 9 of *Studies in Theology and Education*.

72. These and other virtues associated with Christian discipleship and apostolicity appear in all the major essays by Freire, especially *Education as the Practice of Freedom, Pedagogy of the Oppressed*, and *Cultural Action for Freedom*.

73. This notion is well illustrated in the case of Freire's cooperation with the educational endeavors in former Portuguese colonies in Africa. See *Pedagogy in Process, The Letters of Guinea-Bissau*, trans. Carmen St. John Hunter (New York: Seabury, 1978).

74. Paulo Freire, *Las Iglesias, la Educación, y el Proceso de Liberación Humana en la Historia* (Buenos Aires: La Aurora, 1974), p. 20.

75. Paulo Freire, "Conscientizing as a Way of Liberating" (Washington, D.C.: LADOC) 2 (1972), pp. 2-3.

76. Freire, *Pedagogy of the Oppressed*, pp. 75 ff.

77. Hermann Brandt perceptively appraises the Latin American contribution to theology stemming from Freire's pedagogy and philosophy, "In der Nachfolge der Inkarnation, oder: Das 'Auftauchen Gottes' in Lateinamerika. Zum Verhaltnis von Befreiungspädagogik und Befreingstheologie," *Zeitschrift für Theologie und Kirche*, 78 (1981), pp. 367-389.

78. Paulo Freire, "A Letter to a Theology Student," *Catholic Mind* 70 (1972), p. 1265.

79. Ibid.

80. Ibid.

81. Paulo Freire, "Tercer Mundo y Teología," *Fichas Latinoamericanas* 1 (Diciembre 1974), p. 54.

82. Paulo Freire, *La Educación como Práctica de la Libertad*, (Montevideo: Tierra Nueva, 1972), p. 15. Freire's critique of religion essentially restates Marx's discussion of the matter which has been popularized with the phrase "opium of the people." The reason is that Freire is also interested in

the negation of alienating idolatry and the transformation of false consciousness. Freire moves beyond Marx, however, with his Christian prophetic affirmation of the creating and liberating God of biblical faith. Dialectically speaking, this affirmation negates the negation (i.e., the oppressive power of alienating idolatry and false consciousness).

83. Freire, *Pedagogy of the Oppressed*, p. 48.

84. It should be noticed that Freire and most Roman Catholic liberationists in Latin America have reacted against a predominantly "priestly" ecclesiology and practice in their tradition—which tended to canonize the marriage of altar and throne and the status quo (i.e., the church's support of the political establishment)—by adopting a strong "prophetic" stance.

85. This point is also made by Malcolm Warford, "Between the Plumbing and the Saving: Education, Theology, and Liberation," *Living Light* 11:1 (Spring 1974), pp. 60-77.

86. Gustavo Gutiérrez, *A Theology of Liberation*, trans. Caridad Inda and John Eagleson (Maryknoll, N.Y.: Orbis, 1973).

87. Ibid., pp. 91-92.

88. Ibid., pp. 213-214.

89. Ibid., pp. 233-234.

90. Among Latin Americans, another good illustration is J. Severino Croatto in the area of liberationist hermeneutics. In his important book, *Exodus: A Hermeneutics of Freedom*, trans. Salvator Attanasio (Maryknoll, N.Y.: Orbis, 1981), Croatto offers a reading of the principal moments of the Bible—creation, the prophets, Jesus, and Paul—from the liberation key provided by the Exodus event and story. Extensive use of Freire's contribution is reflected in the discussion of several issues and dynamics, including conscientization as such, ontological vocation "to be more human," freedom and creativity, fear of freedom, the internalization of the oppressor, closed and a critical consciousness, saying one's word, and a liberating pedagogy.

91. An explicit correlation of Freire and theology appears in Letty Russell, *Human Liberation in a Feminist Perspective* (Philadelphia: Westminster, 1974). Russell states that conscientization is parallel to the Christian experience of conversion and that a formal analogy exists between conversion and conscientization in the way they happen in human experience. The difference is one of emphasis: "In conversion, stress is placed on God's action while in conscientization stress is placed on human initiative . . . the process is similar and the Holy Spirit can and does work through both. . . . In classical reformation theology faith was spelled out under three interrelated rubrics. . . . These same elements are clear in Freire's typology of the process of conscientization: *logos*, or critical awareness, corresponds to *notitia*; *praxis*, or commitment to action-reflection, is similar to *assensus*; and *utopia*, self and world, correspond to *fiducia*. Together they make up the same important whole in the process of life" (pp. 122-125). The formal analogy that Russell describes is assumed to include also content or substance; the power or energy for transformation is seen as essentially the same, God's Spirit being somehow engaged in the two processes (conversion and conscientization). They are practically identified since the difference is supposed to be basically a matter of emphasis and perspective. See also Russell's later works such as *Growth in Partnership* (Philadelphia:

Westminster, 1981), especially chap. 3—"Education as Exodus"—and 5—"Pedagogy for Oppressors."

92. For a discussion of grassroots movements in Brazil, see Guillermo Cook, *The Expectation of the Poor: Latin American Basic Ecclesial Communities in Protestant Perspective* (Maryknoll, N.Y.: Orbis, 1985), pp. 62ff. In chap. 5, we will discuss the question of the place of the poor and oppressed, and the ecclesial community context.

93. Freire, *Pedagogy of the Oppressed*, p. 119.

94. José Míguez Bonino, "Five Theses Towards an Understanding of the 'Theology of Liberation,' " *The Expository Times* 87:7 (April 1976), pp. 196-200. For a good introduction to liberation theology, see José Míguez Bonino, *Doing Theology in a Revolutionary Situation* (Philadelphia: Fortress, 1975). Also, Leonardo Boff and Clodovis Boff, *Liberation Theology: From Confrontation to Dialogue,* trans. Robert R. Barr (San Francisco: Harper & Row, 1986), and *Introducing Liberation Theology* (Maryknoll, N.Y.: Orbis, 1987). One of the most complete and succinct descriptions of suppositions, experiences, and principles that together help to define the "world" of liberation theology, appears in Roger Haight, *An Alternative Vision: An Interpretation of Liberation Theology* (New York: Paulist Press, 1985), chap. 1.

95. Gutiérrez, *A Theology of Liberation*, p. 13.

96. Dennis McCann, *Christian Realism and Liberation Theology: Practical Theologies in Conflict* (Maryknoll, N.Y.: Orbis, 1981), p. 176.

97. Ibid., pp. 157-172. Some practical implications of the established correlation between the process of conscientization and the strategy and tactics of liberationist evangelization become readily apparent, such as these: 1) Liberation theologians and pastoral agents in the base ecclesial communities will function in a manner similar to the role of the coordinators in the circles of culture of the base education projects; 2) doing liberation theology will mean primarily the "problematizing" of the community's experience by way of codifying and decodifying it according to the "generative theme" of oppression/liberation; 3) the liberating God of the Bible and the epistemological privilege of the poor and oppressed become key hermeneutical principles. These and related issues are considered in detail in chaps. 4 and 5.

98. James Michael Lee, "The Authentic Source of Religious Instruction," in *Religious Education and Theology*, ed. Norma H. Thompson (Birmingham, Ala.: Religious Education Press, 1982), pp. 164-165.

99. Lee contends that "the messenger-boy and translation positions tend to rob religious instruction of its prophetic role. Religious instruction has as one of its cardinal tasks that of hastening the future, of directly generating advances in the cognitive and affective and lifestyle activities of persons and societies. . . . Religious instruction loses its unique prophetic character and force when persons attempt to transmogrify it into theology" (Ibid., p. 164). Latin American liberationists would agree with that statement on the basis of the witness of Paulo Freire and their emphasis on theology as "second act." Indeed, Lee quotes Gutierrez that theology arises at sundown, namely after activity of an ecclesial and nonecclesial nature has ceased.

100. On this point, see Thomas H. Groome, *Christian Religious Education:*

Sharing Our Story and Vision (San Francisco: Harper & Row, 1980), pp. 185-188. Building on Paulo Freire, Groome underscores the participation of reason, memory, and imagination in *critical reflection* as a major component of his "shared praxis" approach.

101. Freire, "Education, Liberation, and the Church," pp. 525-531.

102. Ibid., pp. 529-531.

103. Ibid., p. 532.

104. Freire adopts the terms "necrophilic" and "biophilic" from Erich Fromm. See Fromm's *The Heart of Man* (New York: Harper & Row, 1973) and *Anatomy of Human Destructiveness* (Greenwich, Conn.: Fawcett, 1973).

105. Freire's criticism of institutional religion became more pointed in his later writings where his Marxist orientation is more apparent. The same observation can be made concerning explicit references to Freire's religious and theological views that inspire his social philosophy. This combination is not surprising given two interrelated phenomena: the quasi-theological structure and religion-like character of Marxism itself and the agenda of Latin American liberation theology, including its selective use of Marxist analysis.

106. Freire, "Education, Liberation, and the Church," p. 545.

107. Ibid., p. 540.

108. Ibid., p. 544.

109. Freire, "Tercer Mundo y Teología," p. 55.

110. Freire, *Pedagogy of the Oppressed*, p. 77. It appears that Freire and other liberationists present in this regard a new version of the old and popular "just war" theory and the "right to rebellion" rationale: manifest or objective social injustice and economic and political oppression—i.e., structural and institutional violence—make necessary, and therefore justifiable, the participation of the Christian in armed confrontation in order to correct or transform the situation. For a practical discussion of just-war thinking suitable for religious education context, see John Howard Yoder, *When War Is Unjust* (Minneapolis: Augsburg, 1984).

111. This stance represents, of course, a mirror image of the right-wing Christianized justification of political and armed repression on the part of Latin American regimes, especially United States-supported dictatorships or so-called "authoritarian" governments and oligarchies in power. Also, it rings structurally analogous to the rationale for direct intervention and military and other forms of aggression against regimes opposed to the imperialist and neocolonialist policies of the United States.

112. One interesting illustration of appropriation of liberationist contributions, especially Freire, for revitalizing the theory and practice of religious education is the proposal of Kevin Nichols, "Education as Liberation," in *Religious Education and the Future*, ed. Dermot A. Lane (New York: Paulist, 1986), pp. 135-147. Nichols underscores five points for the groundwork of a restated distinctive Catholic theory of religious education: 1) an *evangelical option for the poor* and looking for ways in which the disadvantaged can become aware of themselves, aware of their environment and able to transform it; 2) the educational goal of *threefold conversion*, including conversion of the mind as well as moral and religious conversion; 3) a Christian idea of education that adopts the established forms of *knowledge for the task of humanization*; 4) a deep faith in *human creativity* linked to

the conviction of the work of the Holy Spirit in the transformation of the world; 5) a look at *action in the world* as the pivot of the approach of Christian religious education.

113. The liberationist critique of conscientization is practically nonexistent, and the appropriation of liberation theology (including Freire) in the field of religious education does not include adequate critique either. See note 4 in the Preface.

114. James Michael Lee has argued convincingly that the duality posited between content (what) and method (how) in religious education—or in any form of education for that matter—involves the fundamental error of ignoring that *method is (structural) content.* Because "method is a form of process and process is a full-fledged content in its own right" ("Process Content in Religious Education," in *Process and Relationship: Issues in Theory, Philosophy, and Religious Education,* ed. Iris V. Cully and Kendig Brubaker Cully [Birmingham, Ala.: Religious Education Press, 1978], p. 22.) Lee refers to two basic forms of molar content: a) *structural content* alludes to the way in which content is brought into activity and sustained in its activity, such as in the case of conscientization seen as a *pedagogical procedure* and *strategy;* b) *substantive content* refers to the form in which content appears (e.g., conscientization *product* content as tangible content entails deeper consciousness, new insights, changes in self-esteem, transformed attitudes and lifestyle, etc. In addition to product content, the seven other molar forms of substantive content are *process, cognitive, verbal, affective, nonverbal, unconscious, lifestyle*). In light of our present interest, it can also be indicated that conscientization illumines, among other things, the relationship of intimacy, complementarity, and tension, that links (substantive and structural) *process content* and (substantive) *product content,* e.g., the conscientization process of awaring, awakening, and the actual awareness raised, including the will for transformation. Conscientization also illustrates, then, that *process content* is a type of structural content and also a type or mode of substantive content. Structural content is the theme of Lee's *The Flow of Religious Instruction.* (Birmingham, Ala.: Religious Education Press, 1973), and substantive content is the topic of *The Content of Religious Instruction* (Birmingham, Ala.: Religious Education Press, 1985).

115. James Michael Lee identifies five kinds of structural content which he places in a taxonomy proceeding from the most general to the most specific: style, strategy, method, technique, and step. In, *The Flow of Religious Instruction,* pp. 34-35.

116. Freire, *Pedagogy of the Oppressed,* pp. 77-81.

117. Bruce O. Boston asserts that to take the reflexive aspects of liberation education seriously is to reflect upon, criticize, redirect, and transform the appearances of Christian faith until its rationale begins to appear: "Each doctrine, each ethical precept, each teaching of Christ and/or the church, each bit of the tradition will be perceived differently....They will become problems to be solved rather than data to be banked. Once the rationale begins to appear, we will begin to pronounce ourselves in our own world and not simply echo the utterances of others. . . . A reflective style of Christian education will mean the self-conscious recognition that our current educational practice is already a method of politicizing, socializing,

and culture-building" ("Conscientization and Christian Education," *Learning for Living* 13:3 [January 1974], pp. 100-105). The point is that, equipped with the tools of conscientization, we can uncover our real concerns, whether or not they are being met, or whether what we do in Christian education is a way of side-stepping those concerns in the name of the gospel.

118. Loder, "Transformation in Christian Education," *Religious Education*, 206 ff. We employ in this section Loder's foundational contribution, including his reference to the learning tasks, in critical dialogue with the liberationist perspective already reformulated in terms of creativity.

119. Review the discussion of conscientization as fostered creativity in the first section of this chapter.

120. Loder puts it well in "Transformation in Christian Education": "The ultimate and decisive conflict is not 'my suffering,' 'their suffering,' or 'our suffering.' Rather, what is God doing in this world . . . to create a people who are truly human according to the humanity of Christ? That is the conflict to face and embrace with perseverance because, in its many particular forms which always engage human suffering, that is the conflict that initiates transformation as Christ's living answer" (p. 218).

121. On the theme of suffering, liberation, struggle for justice and the spirituality of the oppressed, see Gustavo Gutiérrez, *We Drink from Our Own Wells: The Spiritual Journey of a People*, trans. Matthew J.O'Connell (Maryknoll, N.Y.: Orbis, 1984).

122. The most consistent appropriation of the reflection and action paradigm proposed by the liberationist pedagogy and theology corresponds to Thomas Groome's "shared praxis approach" for Christian religious education. The dynamics described in this section are explained in terms of present dialectical hermeneutics in the fourth and fifth movements which Groome proposes for his educational sequence: dialectical hermeneutic between the Christian Story and the participants' stories and dialectical hermeneutic between the Christian Vision and the participants' visions. The last moment includes the challenge for decision making and choosing a faith response, in Groome's paradigm. See *Christian Religious Education: Sharing Our Story and Vision*, part iv. We will return to discuss Groome's important contribution in chaps. 3 and 4. For now we must indicate that his treatment of Paulo Freire and liberation thought fails to take adequately into account their weaknesses and limitations on epistemological and theological grounds.

Chapter 2

Prophetic and Utopian Vision

"Seek first the kingdom and the justice of God."[1]

JESUS

"The backdrop for the idea of the kingdom of God is the eschatological and apocalyptic vision of reality . . . the world as we find it contradicts the design of God. The first and primary aspect of following Jesus is proclaiming the utopia of the kingdom as the real and complete meaning of the world that is offered to all by God. Second, the following of Jesus means translating that utopia into action. We must try to change the world on the personal, social, and cosmic level . . .

"Third, God's liberation translates into a process that will entail conflict and struggle."[2]

LEONARDO BOFF

"Christian education does not consist primarily in the transference of a set of ideas from one generation to another, but rather in the cultivation of intelligent will. There can be no successful Christian education that does not increase the amount of effective, not merely sentimental, brotherhood in the world . . . measured by concrete evidence such as health, food, laws, ballot-boxes, homes, streets, schools, happy children, and happy husbands and wives. . . . In and through his growing participation in the creation of an ideal society the pupil will realize his fellowship with the Father . . . by doing God's social will even to the point of suffering with him."[3]

GEORGE ALBERT COE

68

INTRODUCTION

Liberation theology has recaptured the centrality of the biblical symbol of the reign[4] of God and has suggested its fresh appropriation in the context of a keen interest in the person and the ministry of Jesus. In fact, one important clue for understanding the character and orientation of this theological movement is to perceive the way it views Jesus and the reign of God.

The gospel quotation from Matthew 6:33 is especially fitting because the content of that verse is essential to Jesus' teaching in the "sermon on the mount."[5] It is the key to what we might suitably call the *kingdom curriculum* in chapters 5 through 7 in the Gospel of Matthew. The focus on the reign and the righteousness (or justice) of God carries a twofold meaning: It points to divine majesty, power, and will, and it also points to the social order and lifestyle unfolding in response to that majesty and power and in tune with divine will. Not only does Jesus teach and demonstrate that the coming of God's reign creates a new way and a better quality of life—e.g., through healing, forgiveness and reconciliation, and empowerment to love—but he also speaks of *seeking* (and entering) the kingdom. Thus, Jesus suggests choice, commitment, and active involvement on the part of his disciples. Further, we must notice the startling contrast between Jesus' vision and teaching regarding the reign of God and the prevailing cultural consciousness and conventional wisdom. Subversively enough, Jesus criticizes traditional values, normal concerns and understandings of reality, and personal loyalties, and he announces a radically different way while inviting persons to join in his journey empowered with the new vision.

The prophetic and utopian vision, so central in the ministry of Jesus, is especially affirmed in the Christology of liberation, as indicated in the quotation from Leonardo Boff at the beginning of this chapter. For Boff, becoming an authentic disciple involves appropriating and proclaiming the gospel utopia, actual engagement in "kingdom praxis," and embracing Jesus' very way of the cross and resurrection. The vision is to inspire and orient the life and mission of the church and to illumine its educational task.

The prophetic and utopian vision seeks to elicit a creative and transforming learning process involving, in the words of George

Albert Coe, "growing participation in the creation of an ideal society" and "doing God's social will." Faced with the issue of the social and political significance and implications of the Christian faith, Coe posed the crucial question: Shall the primary purpose of Christian education be to hand on a religion or to create a new world?[6] It is clear that, in his view, religious education must be oriented toward social transformation because "continuous reconstruction is of the essence of the divine work in and through the human."[7]

In this chapter we will explore further the utopian and prophetic character of liberation theology which, Freire claims, "leads naturally to a cultural action for liberation, and hence to conscientization."[8] Such a utopian orientation is forcefully vindicated by Rubem Alves in a classic response to the criticism that liberation theology represents a form of "soft utopianism."[9] Alves lucidly articulates three background assumptions or "silent agreements" behind the utopian vision in a manner that is useful for our discussion of liberation theology in dialogue with religious education.[10]

First, *Christian utopianism is not a belief in the possibility of a perfect society but rather the conviction of the nonnecessity of this imperfect order.* While not claiming that it is possible to abolish sin, it nonetheless affirms that there is no reason for us to accept present sinful structures that control our society.

Second, *Christian utopianism understands "reality" as existing, not because of divine or demonic necessity, but as a human construction.* Hence, whenever we call "reality" a provisional social game built by humans we commit idolatry, i.e., we give divine or demonic ultimacy to something that is not destined to eternity.

Third, *the categories "utopian" and "impossibility" are not absolute but relative to the systems to be transcended.* When a system despises certain visions as being utopian or incapable of realization, it says little about the real possibility or impossibility of those visions, but it definitely confesses its own limitations. The Christian utopian and prophetic vision assumes that all social systems are under God's historical judgment and must not be taken as the ultimate criteria for what is possible or impossible. Therefore, history can never be seen as self-enclosed but open, in hope, to surprise and to transformation.

We will discuss first the key question of Jesus Christ liberator and the main features and emphases of liberation Christology. Then we will reflect on the centrality of the biblical metaphor of the reign of God by underscoring the political and eschatological dimensions of the gospel from the vantage point of religious education. That will in turn lead us to reformulate the guiding principle and the overall purpose of the educational ministry in light of the interplay of liberation theology and religious education.

JESUS CHRIST LIBERATOR

In his study of the images of Jesus in the history of Western culture, Jaroslav Pelikan observes that, alongside the conventional pictures of Jesus as the pillar of the status quo in church and state, there has been a continuing traditon of portraying him as the liberator.[11] In his own time and in every age that would follow, Jesus has been seen by many as the one who challenges every social order and calls it to account before the judgment of God. Pelikan finds that it has been above all in the nineteenth and twentieth centuries that "the first-century Prophet who had preached the justice of God as it was directed against all the oppressors of humanity became Jesus the Liberator: And Jesus the liberator became—and in our time has become and is—a political force that overthrows empires, even so-called Christian empires."[12] These words apply very fittingly to the Latin American situation where, beyond the inherent theological and political ambiguity of such a reading of the ministry and message of Jesus, it continues to inspire the movement for liberation and justice. As Pelikan puts it, Jesus the liberator is being pitted against all the "grand inquisitors" both sacred and secular. And his original statement about the bread and the word of God (Matt. 4:4) now reads that bread is as essential as the Word. Jesus the liberator not only blesses spiritual poverty that awaits supernatural bliss in the life to come but walks with the poor and oppressed of this world in the search for human well-being in this life and in this world, even in the framework of a Christology of revolutionary praxis.[13]

Liberation Christology affirms consistently that portrait of Jesus Christ the liberator. It does so by focusing on the key question, "Who is Jesus Christ in Latin America today?" The question is dealt with on the intersecting levels of description, analysis, and praxis, and from the complementary viewpoints of historicobiblical, theological, and pastoral perspectives.[14] The christological reflection thus formulated flows naturally from the central and founding metaphor of God as liberator. That key metaphor points to the paradigmatic Exodus event and story that unites creation and redemption in the promise and hope of historical fulfillment. Given the traditional confessions about Jesus of Nazareth as the Christ and the Son of God, God incarnate, and Jesus Christ as Lord, the liberation metaphor is also essential to perceive the person and the praxis of Jesus, beginning with a candid look at the gospels in light of the present situation. Jesus Christ effects and models liberation in his active compassion and solidarity with the poor, the oppressed, and the marginal; in his prophetic and utopian proclamation and teaching about the reign of God; in his confrontation of worldly and spiritual powers; and in his overall work for transformation and humanization in love and justice. Jesus Christ actually liberates, and his resurrection confirms the truth of the life of Jesus and the ultimate truth of his person.[15] The victory of the resurrection in turn sets free the power of Christian faith in the model of "Christ liberating culture" as a practical correlation between the quest for justice and the Christian praxis of solidarity with those who suffer.[16]

The discussion that follows deals with three interrelated considerations of liberation Christology. We start with the critical view of the alienating and oppressive Christologies associated in principle with the Spanish legacy of conquest and colonization. Next, we consider other main features of this Latin American contribution, including some weaknesses or shortcomings, and a special reference to resurrection as total liberation.

Beyond the Christology of Oppression

Jon Sobrino contends that ethical indignation, in addition to an epistemological suspicion, lies at the base of the Latin American Christology of liberation, thus underscoring its critical character. That is, christological reflection does not emerge here in response to doubts or challenges concerning the mystery of Christ. Rather, that reflection confronts first the manipulation of Christ on the part of the powerful with its corresponding distortion of his message and the justification of the oppression of the poor.[17]

Liberation theologians have addressed the question, "Who is Jesus Christ in Latin America today?" mainly in a descriptive and analytical mode, by focusing on how Jesus Christ is actually perceived and how we can comprehend the images of him. The careful observation of prevailing pictures of Christ remarkably confirms the Christology of oppression described masterfully by John A. Mackay almost half a century before any liberationist discussion of the matter.[18] The typology of these pictures unveils first of all the predominant portrait of the suffering, defeated, and basically passsive Christ as often depicted in art: hanging on the cross, as a corpse, and as a helpless child on the bosom of Mary. The other classic image of Christ in Latin America is that of the idealized and glorified heavenly king, presented in imperial garments as the almighty Ruler. Both are historically associated with Spain's imperialist and colonialist project in the Americas. To analyze these images critically is crucial for understanding the negative side of the Spanish Catholic heritage and its lingering ramifications; a critical analysis is also crucial as a prerequisite for a christological restatement that can inform a conscientizing religious education in the framework of prophetic biblical faith and Christian ecclesial community.

The Conqueror-Colonizer's Christ. Jesus Christ was literally brought to Latin America with Christopher (or, Cristóbal = "Christ bearer") Columbus (or, Colón = "one who peoples anew," almost "colonizer") in 1492.[19] Spain carried out its mystic motive of the conquest, colonization, and christianization with a sense of mission realized in the fashion of a religious and military crusade. The striking symbolism of the name Christopher Columbus suggests christianization-colonization and evokes the merger of faith and politics, Christ and state, cross and flag in the Spanish project of expansion and search for domination, grandeur, and wealth to be carried out by the *conquistadores* representing the throne. Thus, the dream of a unified religious and political structure—a Catholic kingdom that could never be realized in Europe—was transplanted to Latin America as a colonial theocracy.[20] It is in the perspective of this background that the Christ brought from Spain is found to be deceptive and alienating. In

Mackay's terms, that Christ has put people in agreement with life; he has told them to accept life as it is, and things as they are, and truth as it appears to be.[21] This is the Spanish Christ of the conquest, colonization, and christianization, classically represented in the twofold picture of abject lord and heavenly king.

Christ, Abject Lord. This is the portrait of Jesus overcome, dolorous, humiliated, and defeated who remains as the suffering Christ of popular veneration. His steps have been traced by Mackay and others from the time of Spain's own subjection under the Muslims to the conquest and colonization and beyond.[22] In that pilgrimage Christ has represented the tragic victim and the focus of a cult of death as an expiatory creature with neither personality nor power. He has shown how to die rather than how to live, not to mention the promise of "abundant or fulfilling life" (John 10:10). This is the Christ "known in life as an infant and in death as a corpse, over whose helpless childhood and tragic fate the Virgin Mother presides . . . (no wonder, then, that) fullblooded men with a passion for life and liberty found their religious inspiration in the figure of the Virgin who had never died."[23] Several features of a "traditionalist" religiosity (in Freire's typology) are associated with this Spanish and later the "Creole" Christ, such as lack of ethical thrust and intellectual content and the magical character assumed by the relationship with God and Christ.[24] Liberationists have reconfirmed and radicalized Mackay's assessment. They observe that when the faithful people venerate this image of Christ, when their spirit is seared through life by a pedagogy of passivity and submission, it is their own destiny that they encounter there, and accept and worship with masochistic resignation.[25] In other words, the impotence of the dolorous Christ is interiorized or appropriated by the oppressed, thus validating the function of the Christology of subjugation and domination and resignation and marginalization as well.

Christ, Heavenly King. The second portrait of Jesus Christ in Latin America is that of a glorified celestial monarch resembling Ferdinand of Aragón (while the Blessed Virgin Mary, equally overadorned in royal costumes, evokes an eternal Isabella of Castile). This image serves to proclaim a very earthly power which "for centuries, in Latin America and elsewhere, has planned and executed the death of aborigines, the subjugation of peoples, and the accelerating exploitation of the poor by the rich."[26] This power is thus transposed and established and receives legitimation and ulitimate anointing from "above." For Latin American liberation theologians this situation clearly illustrates that the powerful of this world will be interested in the people's love and veneration for their heavenly counterparts. In Latin America, the traditional function of Christology has been baptizing and sacralizing the *conquista* and colonial establishment and the resulting oppression, including the making a virtue out of suffering (i.e., the claim that suffering leads to glory and expresses communion with the crucified Christ).[27] In Freire's words, since the Conquest Latin America has been basically a subjugated region: "Its colonization consisted of transplantation by the invaders."[28] The role of religion and religious education in such a process could be further assessed, for instance, in terms of the "portraits" of the colonizer and the colonized.[29] Consistent with colonialism and related political projects, religious education has played a functional role in a domesticating and alienating fashion. What Mackay and others describe regarding the prevailing situation in the history of religious education in Latin America correlates with the traditionalist and missionary types of church and religion critiqued by Freire, as indicated in chapter 1.[30]

A twofold ideological distortion of Easter has thus been diabolically established: The Jesus of the cross is transfigured into a symbol of the defeat and resignation of the people; the risen Christ of glory is effectively demoted to the rank of a propaganda minister in the service of oppressive regimes and systems.[31] Hugo Assmann contends that those portraits of Christ are actually the two complementary dimensions of a Christology of oppression. In other words, the reference is to the same alienating Christs, with two sides or faces as counterparts to one another. On the one hand, there is the Christ of "established impotence," eliciting resignation that refuses to struggle because it has been dominated and alienated; on the other hand, there is the Christ of "established power," evoking a subjugation that has no need to struggle because it has overcome already.[32]

The aforementioned liberationist political interpretation indicates that the creation and popularization of such representations of Jesus Christ clearly favors the interests of the powerful. What

Mackay had perceived and stated in light of his own approach, the Latin American theologians later reformulated with a different perspective and the aid of Marxist analysis. A liberating Jesus Christ must be presented then as confronting and transforming the Christology of oppression. The sociology of knowledge is basic for understanding the contrasting global perceptions of reality which emerge from diverse social praxis and definite ideological options. That being the case, Assmann concludes, the conflict of Christologies cannot be analyzed or resolved outside the dialectic of sociopolitical conflicts, which has always been its real conditioning factor in the first place.[33] Other approaches to the problem are bound to be saturated with idealism. The conflict of Christologies, conditioned as it is by the historical contradictions of our societies, will not be solved in the near future because there is no prospect for an immediate solution for the grave social contradictions in our "Christian America."[34] The corollary is, then, that reactionary and revolutionary Christs will coexist while the former are presented as the more "authorized" versions or portraits of Jesus Christ which sanctify and cement the existing social order. Faith in the liberationing Christ is associated with solidarity with the poor and oppressed and with a partisan option for and with them. The main claim is, therefore, that the power of Christ the liberator must be found and rekindled in the midst of the struggle for liberation and justice. Further, the conscientizing potential of that praxis can free us from false consciousness and from the ideology of the bourgeoisie.

Over against a Christ that promotes adjustment and conformity, the authentic Christ of biblical faith—the One, perhaps, akin to "the other Spanish Christ"[35]—must be welcomed anew: this is the Christ who invites people to follow him in the light of the liberationing and re-creating vision and vocation of the reign of God.

Liberating Christology

The affirmation of Christ the liberator leads Latin American liberation theologians, not only to denounce and negate the Christology of oppression in the actual history and experience of their people, but rather to suggest an alternative to the "sublime abstraction"[36] of classic or traditional Christologies. This is why

Boff, in his early description of Christology in Latin America, refers to the primacy of the *critical* element over the dogmatic. He thus underscores continuing opening to the future and the need to refine and purify the core of Christian experience so that it can be made incarnate within the present historical situation we are living.[37] That is of course another reference to the liberationist motif of the prophetic-utopian vision which points to one specific Latin American contribution to theology in the North Atlantic.[38]

Essentially, the christological reformulation proposed by liberation theologians consists of an interested focus on the "historical Jesus" in light of present experience—especially oppression and suffering—for the sake of greater faithfulness on the part of the church and its mission. In other words, there is a practical interest and a pastoral concern at the service of the renewal of the Christian and ecclesial praxis. Further, major attention centers on the teachings and actual ministry of Jesus, particularly his consistent confrontation of injustice and his death resulting, precisely, from his liberating witness in words and deeds.[39] We must also notice that liberation theologians perceive a certain analogy between conditions of oppression and injustice in the historical situation of Jesus, on the one hand, and in the prevailing scene of massive suffering in Latin America, also referred to as a sinful situation, on the other hand.[40] It is in light of that assumed correlation that liberation Christology underscores the gospel of the reign of God and the Christian stance of solidarity with the poor and oppressed. From there three major emphases follow—the primacy of orthopraxis, the preeminence of the social dimension, and the centrality of the utopian/hope-filled future—which are especially significant from the perspective of religious education. To them we now turn our attention in order to indicate both strengths and limitations in this liberationist view.

Orthopraxis: A Matter of Lifestyle. Christological reflection provides further substantive content to the overall liberationist emphasis on "orthopraxis" (i.e., active engagement in concretely living out biblical faith or the gospel of the reign of God), already alluded to in the previous chapter. For liberationists, the main concern is whether that reflection orients and correlates with a distinctively Christian ethic and lifestyle. In short, truth is a matter of life rather than belief. Hence, as Boff puts it, correct acting in the light of Jesus the Christ has primacy over correct thinking or believing (i.e., "orthodoxy") about him. It also follows that doing theology must be at the service of creating new habits of acting and living in the world.[41] The emphasis on orthopraxis in this context is another way of affirming *discipleship*—the faithful following of Jesus—by loving God and neighbor in the midst of the concrete historical situation. The biblically supported claim is, of course, that orthopraxis is a more authentic test of Christianity than orthodoxy. Or, as Jesus said when addressing the question of false and true prophets, "by their *fruit* you will recognize them" (Matthew 7:20).

The ethical and epistemological dimensions intersect here because, in Sobrino's words, the only way to get to know Jesus is to follow after him in one's own real life. This involves trying to identify oneself with Jesus' historical concerns and trying to fashion the kingdom in our midst. Hence, "only through Christian praxis is it possible for us to draw close to Jesus. Following Jesus is the precondition for knowing Jesus."[42] Therefore, the Christology of liberation not only claims to illumine substantive content about Jesus Christ, to be apprehended in the form of beliefs and ethical guidelines, for instance, but also the very manner—process and context—of knowing Christ himself.

The Social Dimensions and Expressions of Christian Faith. Closely related to orthopraxis is the question of the primacy of the social dimension of the gospel of Jesus Christ, which we discuss in more detail in the section on the reign of God. Critically viewed, this stress on orthopraxis balances the almost exclusive focus on the individual and interiority which liberationists rightly perceive as distorting Christian faith and, therefore, alienating. The alternative understanding stresses both the Christian ecclesial community (and the Trinity-evoking metaphors of people of God, body of Christ, temple of the Spirit) and the role of the church in the larger social and cultural context. Therefore, communal spirituality has primacy over individual spirituality, and societal transformation becomes a major concern and objective. Also, the base Christian communities are seen as paradigms of the prophetic-utopian church and living models of the coming reign of God offered to society at large.

A Utopian, Hope-Filled Future. A third major tenet of liberation Christology is intimately associated with both orthopraxis and the social dimension of the gospel. This tenet has been referred to by Boff as the primacy of the utopian over the factual. Liberationists aim to transcend the lingering (and mainly European, colonialist) past and to move toward fashioning an alternative future in hope. They thus affirm the activating function of utopia with a permanent openness to transformation.[43] And authentic faith in Jesus Christ, as evoked by liberation Christology, embraces both the promise and partial fulfillments or demonstrations of the new creation to be fully realized in Christ.

Limitations and Weaknesses of Liberation Christology

Before indicating specific shortcomings, we must notice that, in many ways, this is a very orthodox theology as far as major doctrinal statements of the Christian faith are concerned.[44] Therefore, the first critical observation regarding liberation Christology has to do not with its being "unorthodox" but rather with the *risk of separating orthopraxis from orthodoxy.* The tendency to overemphasize orthopraxis does not do justice to the correspondence, complementarity, and mutual explanation in the praxis and message of Jesus. The inner unity of deeds and words must be maintained and they cannot be considered in isolation.[45] At stake is a fuller perception of the multidimensional character of the Christian faith which, among other things, is essential for the ministry of religious education. As Juan Alfaro states, the confessional, decisional, and praxis aspects of faith are all united with one another, and only their unity constitutes the fullness of faith; the same applies to the connection between orthodoxy and orthopraxis.[46] A corrective formulation, consistent with liberationist epistemology, is that orthodoxy and orthopraxis must also be seen in a mutually influencing, or dialectical relationship. Furthermore, "orthopraxis" must explicitly include the affective domain and really holistic lifestyle, as indicated in the next chapter.

A second critical observation is that the combined stress on praxis and the social expressions of the Christian faith potentially becomes a shortcoming whenever and wherever *the mission of the church is narrowly focused* in terms of social emancipation and the vindication of the socioeconomically and politically oppressed. This is in fact a perennial problem of radical Christianity which tends to define biblical faith almost exclusively in terms of the struggle for a new social order. In other words, overreaction to narrow individualism and interiority may result in another kind of unbalance in the understanding of Jesus and the gospel. By unilaterally underscoring the corporate and structural character of evil and sin we may thus fail to realize the very personal nature of human alienation and lostness. In connection with that risk, we must notice that there is often a facile identification, or confusion, between the political statement—"the situation of dependency calls for liberation" and the theological assertion—"subjection to sin calls for liberation."[47] Furthermore, the accent on the influence of circumstances on acts of violence and injustice often leads to *underestimating the pervasive and destructive quality of sin in all people.*

We also observe the serious anthropological issue implicit in the previous comments, together with the question of Christ's atonement: the meaning of the cross tends to be unduly restricted to the (correct but partial) political interpretation of the unjust death of Jesus the revolutionary prophet.[48] And this in turn raises the problem of *hermeneutic selectivity* in making Jesus normative, primarily and even exclusively, as the prophet who confronts and subverts the social order.[49] His specific call to the way of the cross and the uniqueness of his vision is then often overlooked or minimized, including of course his original rejection of violence.[50]

Finally, we must note that liberation theologians tend to present an open, unqualified eschatology which arises out of the present praxis or concrete historical struggle for liberation and justice. When a *prophetic future* is affirmed *rather than an apocalyptic future* (which irrupts from the future to the present) there is a *risk of collapsing eschatology.*[51] This is so because of the resulting obsession and enthusiasm with the meaning and the direction of history and the social concern generated by the desire to make history march in the right direction.[52] The actual attempt to control the course of history includes a number of assumptions which often go uncritically claimed or unchallenged, such as these: 1) all relationships of cause and effect are apparent, understandable, and manageable, so that as we make our choices according to our future hope(s) for society, society will indeed move in the right direction; 2) we are adequately equipped to set for ourselves and the rest of society the utopian goal toward which we seek to move; 3) effectiveness in approaching the goal(s) which we have envisioned is itself a moral yardstick. All these and related assumptions are based on the axiom that it is a high good to make history march in the "right" direction.[53] What is called for, then, is, first of all, a stance more consistent with the overall liberationist thrust of conscientization and critical reflection and, second, an integration of the prophetic and apocalyptic dimensions of the eschatological vision. To a certain extent, the treatment of the resurrection, briefly discussed below, illustrates the suggested direction.

Resurrection Is Total Liberation

A fuller appropriation of Easter—that is, fuller than the previous sketchy references to Easter in this volume would suggest—has led liberation theologians to deal more constructively with the issues of new creation and resurrection especially. In fact, it can be argued that *resurrection*, rather than liberation as such, is the definitive biblical model for salvation.[54] Resurrection, new creation, and new humanity are key New Testament motifs that illumine the questions of freedom not only as emancipation but as freedom to care and to create as well. The following comments highlight the crucial place of resurrection in liberation Christology.

Leonardo Boff discusses resurrection in terms of the "realization of a human utopia."[55] He views resurrection as an eschatologization of human reality, an initial entry of the whole human person into the reign of God, and a complete realization of the capacities that God placed within human existence. Hence, all the alienating elements that truncated and disfigured life, such as hatred, pain, void, sin, and death, have been annihilated. In Jesus' resurrection human hope was fulfilled and is being realized already in every person. To the question, what is to become of humankind? Boff adds: Christian faith joyfully responds to *resurrection* as the complete transformation of the corporal and spiritual human reality.[56] Further, the resurrection of Jesus must be perceived as intimately related to his life, his announcement of the reign of God, and his death on the cross. There is an essential connection between liberation, resurrection, and the gospel of the reign of God. "Reign of God" connotes total liberation; Jesus' life was a liberated and liberating life, and his death was his completely free offering up of that life; therefore, "his resurrection realizes and fulfills his program in eschatological form."[57] God's ultimate intention for creation is revealed in the resurrection. It is the victory of life and the making explicit of all its potentialities as a gracious divine gift. In other words, the resurrection points to the dream and goal of every genuine process of liberation: achievement of complete and definitive freedom. And because of his own resurrection, Jesus continues to minister among human beings, especially through his Spirit and through the church. Thus, all instances of human emergence such as the enhancement of justice and the freedom for creativity—that is, expansion of life and community building—represent ways in which the resurrection is realized here and now while its future fulfillment is prepared and expected.[58]

The import of the resurrection motif as related to human history and destiny is further illumined by Jon Sobrino. A new kind of life, based on love and hope, has been offered to humanity: "Because the resurrection also confirms the life of Jesus himself, we are not offered the possibility of living a particular way of life in the footsteps of Jesus. We can and should live as new, risen human beings here and now in history."[59] In other words, the resurrection of Jesus is essential for an effective and hopeful Christian alternative to the present reality. The Christian claim that the messianic age of peace, justice, and reconciliation has already broken into the old age is based on the belief that God raised Jesus from the dead. And because of the resurrection, the gospel of the reign of God is not a naive fantasy but the reliable utopia and promise of God.

Sobrino also discusses resurrection from a hermeneutical vantage point, and suggests four interrelated considerations. First, the expression "resurrection of the dead" indicates total transformation of people and history in light of the biblical model of hope *against* (rather than merely *beyond*) death and injustice.[60] Second, in order to grasp the meaning of resurrection it is necessary to have a historical consciousness that views history as both a promise and a mission to be accomplished. Third, something radically new has entered the world with Jesus' resurrection. The experience of the resurrected empowers the disciples to become engaged in the historical praxis of the following of Jesus. Like Jesus, his followers must serve the project of making things new and establishing a new order under the sponsorship of the liberating and creative Spirit of God. Fourth, knowing the resurrection of Jesus, like knowing God, is not a one-time event. The horizon of perception must be constantly fashioned anew. The praxis of love and Christian hope must be kept alive and operational at all times and under all circumstances. That is the way to grasp Jesus' resurrection as the resurrection of the "firstborn" and as the promise that history will encounter fulfillment and completion.[61]

The liberation Christology at this point converges with the confession of Paul and any other committed disciple-apostle: "I want to know Christ and the power of his resurrection" (Philippians 3:10). Dialectically speaking, this power lies in the fact that *resurrection radically negates the negation of life.*[62] It is the power claimed for transformation and for participation in the liberating and re-creating project of the reign of God in the midst of history.

THE GOSPEL OF THE REIGN OF GOD

We indicated in the Introduction of the present volume that liberation theology has recaptured the centrality of the biblical symbol of the reign of God and has suggested a fresh appropriation of it. In fact, liberation theology claims that affirming the pertinence of the kingdom gospel and the very expectation of the coming reign of God are crucial to grasp the whole biblical thrust and the meaning of Christian faith itself. Therefore, we must discuss now the implications of that claim and especially its political and *eschatological*[63] dimensions. We will focus mainly on the work of Boff and Sobrino in light of our appraisal of strengths and limitations from the explicit perspective of religious education.

The reign of God symbolizes divine liberation and re-creating action, will, and promise as depicted in the Bible and, mainly, in light of the ministry of Jesus. He promised and provided signs of the fulfillment of that utopia of total liberation as a reality introduced by God: the defeat of alienation and evil and the annihilation of the consequences of sin—suffering, violence, and death. The reign of God would be the manifestation of divine sovereignty over all. Boff asserts that it is a total, global, and structural transformation of human reality (i.e., transformation into Christlikeness). And the reign is also the cosmos completely restored and full of the reality of God. God's kingdom is actually the old world transformed into a new one. The reign that Jesus announces is not merely liberation from economic hardships, political oppression, from other specific evils or from sin alone. The reign cannot be narrowed down to any particular aspect or dimension. The whole of life and reality will be transformed by God. And it is in this light that the words "God's reign is among you" (Luke 17:21) mean that we already have access to the new order that God has introduced.[64]

In the following three sections, we will consider three kinds of implications of the assumed centrality of the gospel of the reign of God—formal, critical-material, and constructive-material implications. The discussion will establish biblicotheological foundations for Christian religious education which inform the questions of guiding principle and overall purpose in terms of the liberationist contribution.

Jesus, History, and Political Obedience

The formal implications of the central place of the kingdom gospel suggest at least three major considerations interrelated that we will discuss briefly now. They refer to the person of Jesus, history and community, and political obedience.

The Person of Jesus. The affirmation of the reign of God calls for taking seriously the one who reigns. An adequate hermeneutics must focus on the person of Jesus as having an eschatological perception that his mission was to assist in the coming stage of the inbreaking order of the rule of God. Jesus does not teach primarily about himself or about the church but about God's reign. This biblical symbol is the center and clue of his message, the longing of Israel. Jesus promises that it will no longer be a utopian dream but a reality ushered in by God. In fact, Jesus' total ministry must be seen in light of the coming reign of God. Thus miracles performed and the forgiveness of sin are signs that the kingdom is already breaking in and fermenting within the old world; oppression is overcome and transformation takes place. Those and other signs witness to God's liberating and re-creating will and action. The personal presence and work of Jesus negates the negation of life: impure demons are dislodged by God's Spirit (Matthew 12:28),[65] diseases are healed (Matthew 8:16-17), sins are forgiven (Mark 2:5), death is transfigured into sleep (Mark 5:39), and struggle is changed into victory and joy (Mark 5:41-43; Luke 7:11-17). The reign of God implies total liberation brought about by divine grace and power. It is *God's* reign and—as Boff notes—Jesus sees himself not only as a prophet of this gospel but as a key element of the new transformed situation: he is the new human person, God's reign already present although veiled in weakness. Hence, commitment to Jesus the Christ is an indispensable condition to participate in the new order that God introduces.[66]

Jesus teaches and proclaims God's reign, and he is also the new way to enter the kingdom. Sobrino deduces the nature of Jesus' distinctive consciousness from his praxis, and suggests that: 1) *He is aware that in and through his own person, God's reign is drawing near*, as reflected in connection with the "signs" mentioned above (Luke 11:20) and his teachings (Matthew 5:22, 28, 32, 34, 39, 44), especially the kingdom parables (Mark 4:30ff). 2) *Jesus is bold enough to assert that eschatological salvation depends on the stance adopted toward his own person* (Mark 8:30; Luke 12:8ff).[67] In Jesus' teaching, discipleship has a salvific function as service within God's reign and is linked to his own person (Matthew 8:19-22; Mark 8:34ff). Further, the gospels make clear that Jesus is not only aware of having a mission on behalf of God's reign but he is also conscious of a special communion with God as Father. An unconditional trust and obedience to the Father's will make explicit that kind of consciousness.

Finally, while proclaiming a message of radical liberation from all alienation and oppression, Jesus himself appears as the new human, the paradigm of new humanity. Boff underscores creative imagination as one of the fundamental qualities of Jesus because is a form of liberty born in confrontation with reality and established order; "it emerges from nonconformity in the face of completed and established situations. . . . Imagination postulates creativity, spontaneity, and liberty."[68]

History. The reign of God involves actual history. The ministry

of Jesus confirms God's purpose of being actively involved
among and through human beings. Thus, the kingdom is not
something outside of this world or purely transcendent or "spiritual." It is rather the whole of this social and physical world being
incorporated within the rule of God. It is the expression of liberation and new life for the whole creation (Romans 8:18ff). The
symbol of God's reign suggests that God gives ultimate meaning
to the world and that divine intervention will bring restoration
and "a new heaven and new earth" (Revelation). That which still
does not fully exist, the *utopia*, becomes *topia*, i.e., that which
exists somewhere. Yet, the kingdom cannot be regionalized in
any social system, or even the church, because no liberation
process within history can define the ultimate form of the reign of
God which is an eschatological gift.[69] At the same time, it must
be noted that there is but one history and one liberation process
that culminates in Jesus Christ. Hence, God's reign is essentially
a historical reality to be searched for, seen, valued, proclaimed,
shared, and celebrated, *eschatologically*.[70] This calls for affirming
the conflict and complementarity between present and future:
The core of the eschatological dimension of the gospel lies in the
tension of what is to come, the expectation of new action which
demands a fresh look at the present and participation here and
now.

God's reign involves history as *community* formation and
transformation. The Pauline references to "new creation" (2 Corinthians 5:17) and "new man" (Ephesians 2:15) point to new
humanity in the process of becoming the people and the family of
God. "Kingdom" symbolizes a new way of being in social relationships involving total renewal in human selves and societal
structures. The final goal is total *reconciliation* which confronts
and transforms present reality in the direction of *justice*. In Sobrino's words, to effect reconciliation is to do justice, because
"Jesus does not propose to leave people as they are and simply
console them in their plight; he proposes to re-create their present
situation and thus do 'justice' to them."[71]

Political Obedience. Faith and obedience, and theology and
ethics, must not be separated. The announcement of God's reign
(Matthew 4:23) is followed by the proposal of a new ethical
model (Matthew 5-7). Therefore, the gospel of the reign of God

requires *radical discipleship* and involves *kingdom politics.*

The biblical documents establish a correlation between ontology, epistemology, and ethics: "God is" and "God exists" mean and imply that "God reigns"; the essential reality of God is inseparably united with the operative reality of the reigning of God. And, as we will discuss in the next chapter, to have faith—to know God—means and implies obedience, or faithfulness, to God, or being in tune with divine will (or with the reign of God). Analogously, Sobrino asserts that our relationship with Jesus must embody the same relational character: Only through Christian praxis is it possible for us to identify with Jesus and draw close to him. Following Jesus is the precondition for knowing Jesus. Jesus' intrinsic relationship to the kingdom means that our communion with him will come primarily through following Jesus in the service of God's kingdom.[72] The reign of God presupposes radical transformation in patterns of life and human relationships. The Sermon on the Mount programatically presents the new lifestyle of authentic disciples. It involves limitless love and human beings truly liberated for greater and creative accomplishments.[73] The essence and the heart of Jesus' "kingdom curriculum" is the affirmation that love, service, and truth constitute the only kind of power capable of anticipating the reign of God, the command to love one's enemies expressing the complete radicalness of discipleship in the context of the kingdom.[74]

The gospel of the reign of God also points to *politics* due to its concern with the issues of structures, interests, power, and socioeconomic and political projects. Thus, the wrong assumption about Christian neutrality, which Freire and others castigate, involves, not just a reactionary stance that contradicts the broad social dimension of love for the neighbor, but the hermeneutical mistake of overlooking the political pertinence of Jesus.[75] The symbol of the reign of God is eminently political in the long and rich tradition of biblical faith.[76] However, Jesus corrects the messianic and apocalyptic expectations of the people by challenging nationalistic positions even though political messianism was perhaps a major temptation for him (Mark 1:12ff; 11:10; Luke 15:26; 24:21). The great drama of the life of Jesus Christ, says Boff, was to try to take the ideological content out of "kingdom of God" and make the people and his disciples understand that he meant something more profound, namely that he calls for personal conversion and for a radical transformation of the human world.[77] The political character of the reign of God involves a more comprehensive reality both in the negation or subversion of present establishments and in the vision of creative alternatives that enhance life and build the human community. The biblical notion of *shalom*, which connotes peace, wholeness, well-being, and salvation itself,[78] corresponds closely to the symbol of the kingdom. The rule of God is the reign of shalom which informs both the content and process of the politics of God.

The Kingdom, Power, and Service

Now we want to consider material implications of the assumed centrality of the reign of God. We will reflect critically on the absolute claims of the kingdom gospel, the radical uniqueness of God's reign, and the association of power and service that it dictates.

Only One Kingdom. We said before that there is but one history. We must add now that within this one history there may be several kingdoms. The reference to the reign of God implies a distinction regarding other, lesser kingdoms. The confession that Jesus Christ rules (i.e., is Lord)[79] implies that others do not rule in the same way. In other words, the radical obedience to Jesus necessitates that other commitments and loyalties become secondary, or are even canceled in case of contradiction. This is of course an affirmation of the exclusive, conflictive, and confrontative nature of the reign of God which may require civil disobedience (as Peter said, "We must obey God rather than men!" Acts 5:29). Indeed, authentic disciples of Jesus will always be, in some way and to some degree, aliens in the midst of smaller "kingdoms" whose cultural and politicoeconomic structures tend to present manifold negations of life according to the reign of God.[80] Ambivalence, discomfort, and conflict then become normal experiences for the disciple-kingdom citizen en route to a world that is more human and just, i.e., closer to the will and the dream of God.[81] God's rule confronts and calls into question partial and immediate interests whether they be social, economic, political, or religious. It thus retains its characteristic totality and universality.[82] The radical demand for discipleship must be seen in terms of the mutually exclusive alternatives that the reign of God presents to the established order. In Sobrino's words, the alternatives can be described in theological terms (God or wealth), christological terms ("they who are not with me are against me"), or anthropological terms ("they who would preserve their lives will lose them, but those who lose their lives for my sake and the gospel's will preserve them").[83]

God's Reign: Upside-Down Kingdom.[84] A second critical observation about the reign of God is a further note on the radical social and personal transformation that the expression connotes. As Boff asserts, Christ makes two fundamental demands: He requests personal conversion and postulates a comprehensive restructuring of the human world.[85] The subversion of this human world, the formation of "kingdom beachheads" with efficacious signs of God's will being done, affect the normal order and social conventions and confront the oppressive and alienating powers. Further, conversion is not only essential in the first phase of this process of transformation and human emergence. The disciples must remain open and attuned to the liberating and re-creating work of the Spirit of God and Christ, which may appear in seemingly impractical, illogical, ineffective, or even scandalous ways, such as in the summons to love the "unlovable," to expect the impossible, or not to seek retaliation in the face of violence. This is also a call for affirming an *abnormal* epistemology[86] that challenges conventional wisdom. The announcement of the coming reign as a divine gift requires indeed an alternative way of knowing and appropriating truth. Those who need to be receptive to divine revelation cannot simply dictate or predetermine the future contours of liberation and salvation. Otherwise, there are unpleasant surprises, disappointments, and frustration so dramatically experienced in regard to the fulfillment of the messianic expectation: Jesus changes radically the meaning and connotations of "kingship" because *service* defines the new context for the symbol of the reign of God. A fundamental inversion of values is involved: Jesus the Christ is a Servant Lord (Matthew 20:25-30; Luke 22:25-30; John 13:13ff). Royalty is defined in terms of service, and the gospel of God's reign is advanced by sharing in the way of the cross and in the power of resurrection.

Power and Service. Just as Jesus does not impose himself by force, a corollary of the rulership-as-servanthood motif is that the kingdom gospel is offered in love while affirming human freedom. At the same time, the proclamation of the reign of God requires us to acknowledge the central place of the question of *power*. The temptations of power—or, to become a typical or "normal" king/lord—seem to have been crucial, frequent, and definitely rejected by Jesus. Therefore, to the extent that Jesus is normative, a twofold stance is in order: suspicion concerning the claims of lesser, moral "lords," political leaders, or whoever practices the kind of authority rejected by Jesus; and the invitation to participate in the creation of viable alternatives in social transformation—or, the "untested feasibilities," as Freire would say—in the direction of life in the reign of God.

An important aspect in Jesus' teaching is the relationship between the essence of power and the essence of sin. He discusses in that light both the personal features of sin and its social and structural dimensions. Sobrino states that, for Jesus, sin consists of the rejection of the reign of God and that the anthropological base of sin is the self-affirmation of persons which leads them to assert their own power in negative ways (i.e., by securing themselves against God and by oppressing others). "Only one kind of power is proper if one seeks to anticipate the kingdom. It is the power of love, of sacrifice, of service, of truth."[87]

Creativity, Discernment, and the Messianic Community

In our final set of considerations regarding the centrality of the gospel of the reign of God, we focus on some key constructive material implications involving creative power for transformation, critical discernment, and the question of the church as messianic community.

Creative Power. The announcement of the kingdom gospel assumes creative power for transformation. Essentially, that proclamation in hope assumes a special sensitivity and concern for human suffering, together with the critique of the present order and the promise of the renewing power of forgiveness, love, and service. The reign of God concerns the totality of the human experience, that is, not only the structural or global dimensions; the whole arena of human life and relationships is involved, from the divers facets of daily life to the socioeconomic and political institutional orders. Furthermore, the very presence of a nonconformist, alternative ecclesial community, which we discuss below as a special bearer of that gospel, is already an agent of change that creates new social and interpersonal models of human existence.

Ultimately, salvation—or full liberation and resurrection—and the coming of God's reign is a gracious divine gift in Jesus Christ. Yet, consistent historical realizations assume active human involvement and participation. There is ample space for hope and expectations beyond faulty (i.e., unrealistically utopian) views of human beings. In this vein, Rubem Alves criticizes traditional Protestantism for having concluded, in his view, that there is no room for human creativity in history. Grace, instead of making humans free for creativity, makes creativity superfluous or impossible.[88] He states the need to affirm both grace and human creativity: "God's grace, instead of making human creativity superfluous and impossible, is therefore the politics that makes it possible and necessary."[89] The claim is not that God simply depends on humans for fashioning the coming divine utopia but, rather, that the gift of the reign of God includes the invitation, the equipment, and the empowerment for humans to be partners in God's project of liberation and recreation. The claim is also that any truly disalienating and humanizing program necessitates divine grace and power in the Spirit of the risen Christ. It is in light of these understandings that the challenge to become engaged in the building of the new order is viewed. The challenge amounts to fulfilling the human "ontological vocation," as Freire says, to be subjects in making history and fashioning the future.

Critical Discernment. The gospel of the reign of God includes the affirmation that its ethical thrust must be the standard for discerning what it means and implies to be consistent with the politics of God—in Paul Lehmann's happy expression, "the power to will what God wills . . . what it takes to make and to keep human life human."[90] That gospel points to a quality of life which is impossible if God's reign is not coming (Matthew 3:2ff; Luke 3:11-14; 4:18-21). The "already" of God's reign is discerned wherever and whenever there is sharing with the needy, forgiveness, overcoming evil with good, creating more just and humanizing alternatives. The critical discernment illumines those con

crete, historical situations insofar as they correspond to that perception of "making human life more human." What is claimed
here is that referring to the ethical import of the gospel of the
reign of God is less subjective and less ideological than other
criteria associated with either "order" (e.g., reactionary preconceptions) or "revolution" (e.g., dogmatic projections of the course
of history), or the mere "reading" of history in terms of the
relative success or failure of a given social movement.[91]

In light of the biblical documents, the quality of life which
corresponds to the reign of God—and, therefore, possesses eschatological meaning—can be envisioned in terms of *shalom* and
resurrection, as already indicated, and their specific manifestations in justice and peace and freedom to create and to build
community on the basis of love and work. The appraisal and
critique of the present order requires the use of criteria stemming
from the gospel of the reign of God[92] which points to the ultimate
fulfillment of all creation, the definitive form of liberation and
salvation. Thus the question is to what extent our present world
and praxis are attuned to the politics of God concerning the signs
of the kingdom. The reign of God provides criteria for discerning
both the negation and the affirmation of the new creation in
society at large and also within the church. It also evokes hopes,
dreams, and aims for future realizations. In other words, the
moral content of the reign of God, announced and expected, is
the main criterion for critical reflection and discernment. Hence
the Sermon on the Mount, for example, outlines the basics of the
ethical originality of the reign of God: a new quality of life which
corresponds to the coming kingdom. Further, God's reign is discerned—even when God is not mentioned—whenever events fit
that definition of what it means "to make human life more
human."[93]

The Messianic Community. The conviction about the reign of
God is affirmed together with the claim that the ecclesial community is called to become a paradigm of kingdom living and a
sacrament of history. The vocation of the church is that what was
manifest in Jesus ought to be manifest in the community of his
disciples. In Boff's words, the ecclesial community must be characterized by complete openness to God and others, an indiscriminate love without limits, and a critical spirit which culti-

vates the creative imagination and challenges cultural structures in the name of love and of the liberty of God's children.[94] In its life and mission the ecclesial community must announce the gospel of the reign of God in the midst of human history by the very nature of worship, by sharing the gospel of *shalom*, the experience of human communion (*koinonia*), a nonconformist lifestyle, and a liberating model of social service. It is to become a healing community of reconciliation where the following of Jesus is duly contextualized in terms of the actual historical situation. Gutiérrez asserts that as a "sacramental community"—or as revelatory sign—the church finds its meaning in its potential to signify the reality in function of which it exists; and the church is indeed oriented toward the fulfillment of the reality of the reign of God which has already begun in history.[95] The call for the ecclesial community is to become a *contrast-society*[96] in the sense of an alternative community with a countercultural consciousness, in the terms of Walter Brueggemann.[97] The coming of God's reign is necessarily a temporal, historical, and social reality whose prophetic announcement involves the creation of structures for freedom, justice, peace, and community. Those concrete social realities are expected to be manifested primarily within the faith community that confesses the rule of the risen Christ. That is the meaning of key metaphors that Jesus used, such as the salt of the earth, the light of the world, and the city on the hill (Matthew 5:13-16). In words and action, the church's announcement of the reign of God reveals to the rest of society the very aspiration for liberation and justice by pointing to new ways in human emergence. Although partial and imperfect realizations, those expressions of a new order in the making may in turn open up further the dream and hope of complete liberation and salvation.

RELIGIOUS EDUCATION FOR THE REIGN OF GOD

Liberation theology, and especially the theological reflection on the reign of God, amounts to a compelling commentary on the meaning and implications of the summons of Jesus—"seek first the kingdom and the justice of God." As indicated before, that reflection—and the overall work of liberation theology—is done explicitly for the sake of greater faithfulness on the part of the church and its mission. In this context, the practical interest and pastoral concern at the service of renewal in the Christian and ecclesial praxis directly affects the task of religious education. This is a theological reflection which purports to be both *background* and *clue* (in Randolph Crump Miller's terms[98]) for the educational ministry. In that capacity it can supply much of the substantive content or subject matter for the teaching-learning process and the curriculum, for instance. Thus, there is a gospel message to be rediscovered and shared; the story of the liberating and re-creating work of God is to be learned in actual Christian praxis together with the vision of the coming reign of God. And this (substantive) content is intimately related to issues of structural content and context. Hence the liberationist contribution can also play a certain guiding role[99] in the theological assessment of the enterprise, for example, with the theological critique of alienating Christs taught, or indoctrinating instructional techniques, and the theological endorsement of dialogue, critical discernment, and a utopian-hopeful orientation.

We must recognize that the prophetic and utopian vision, as a key liberationist thrust, has actually inspired and informed a number of correctives, emphases, and new directions in the field of religious education, among which we can mention the following. Thomas H. Groome presents the need for a "critical principle" and a vocational redefinition in terms of the task of prophecy.[100] Drawing from the theologians of hope and liberation, Mary Elizabeth Moore calls attention to the hope and future dimensions in Christian religious education, in order to supplement the common concerns with historical tradition and contemporary experience.[101] John L. Elias proposes that religious education make accessible hopeful visions for the future and foster the social and political imagination that enables us to view and understand society in a larger historical context.[102] Utilizing similar theological foundations, Michael Warren advocates politicization in the context of youth ministry and religious education for peace and justice.[103] And William Bean Kennedy presents radical critiques and explores alternative futures for religious education in a variety of settings.[104]

The liberationist foundations detectable in those and other contributions lead to a restatement of a guiding principle and the overall purpose of Christian religious education in terms of the focus on the gospel of the reign of God. In the next two sections we discuss the concrete significance and some practical ramifications of such a proposal.[105]

A Guiding Principle for Religious Education

The liberationist theological reflection deals with the interrelation of three foci which are the Word and the Spirit of God, the ecclesial community, and the sociohistorical situation. Actually liberation theologians explicitly assume a threefold commitment in terms of those distinct but intimately related realities so that three sets of interconnected agendas of theological reflection can be identified, as represented below:

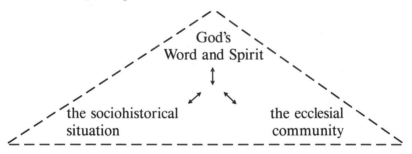

The articulation of the three vectors converge or intersect in the gospel of the reign of God, which points to the gift, the promise, and the demands of the inbreaking reality of the new creation under the rule of Christ.

The theological input may help clarify three major concerns of religious education in the ecclesial context, namely, the interpretation of the scriptures and God's Spirit's work, understanding the nature and mission of the church, and a Christian view of the historical situation. Thus the reign of God is not perceived as a transcendent, other-worldly reality, and it is not located somehow in the mind of God, yet it is affirmed as God's will and dream, gift and promise of the new creation in Christ. The Bible does not present a clear definition or complete picture of the kingdom, yet the scriptures provide indispensable clues and illustrations of divine and human liberating and re-creating work through the narratives, symbols, teachings, and confessions that point to the life of freedom, justice, and peace. The church must not be identified with the reign of God, yet it is called to become a sign and a foretaste, a beachhead of the kingdom emerging with its life and values. No social order can ever be equated with God's reign, yet that reign is to be realized and discerned in the midst of historical sociocultural and political-economic structures.

Furthermore, the integrity and interrelations of those vectors and the threefold commitment must be maintained as in the case of the "hermeneutical circulation" process which we discuss in chapter 4. For now we can indicate more specifically what is meant by the resulting "agendas" that can inform the religious education task. We can do that with the help of another diagram which builds on the previous one:[106]

The discernment of the work of God in promoting the reign of *shalom* in the light of the biblical documents corresponds to "God's revealed agenda" of Word and Spirit, in dialogue with the other two. The history, the tradition, and the living story of the people of God, including the actual life and ministry of a given ecclesial community, constitute the core of the "agenda of the church," also in connection with the other two. And the comprehensive natural and social context with its cultural, political, and economic dimensions comprise the "world's agenda," also in association with the other two. Obviously, all of these dimensions must be seen both as interrelating in divers ways and also in a certain tension with each other. What we have called the "agenda of human emergence" is deliberately placed at the center because it signifies the life, learning, growth, and transformatiaon of actual persons and groups of people who participate in the educational ministry or who are affected in some way by it.

The rediscovered centrality of the gospel of the reign of God inspires a *guiding principle* for the church's educational ministry consistent with the life and mission of the ecclesial community. The theory and the task of Christian religious education can be illumined, directed, and evaluated on the basis of that principle as conceptualized by D. Campbell Wyckoff.[107] The choice of the gospel of the reign of God meets Wyckoff's criteria for the guiding principle concerning theory, practice, and communication.[108] Not only is this gospel central in contemporary theology but, more importantly, it is at the heart of the teaching and ministry of Jesus whose utopian and eschatological vision we wish to underscore. Further, the very person of Jesus Christ is freshly affirmed by liberation Christology and its focus on the political and eschatological dimensions of the gospel in the face of today's world. That guiding principle evokes the tension between the "already" and the "not yet" of the reign of God as well as the experience of alienation and hope in the midst of the present social structures. It also suggests a corrective alternative to prevailing instructional practices which foster passivity, conformity, or the domestication of consciousness.

"Seek first the kingdom and the justice of God" means, in this light, that the gift, the promise, and the demands of the new creation become the main value and focus of concern as well as the driving force in the life of the ecclesial community within our historical situation. If that is, indeed, the case, then *the educational task of the church must be perceived, directed, and evaluated in the light of the gospel of the reign of God.* This is the guiding principle, that is, the essential core on the basis of which we can arrange both meaningfully and relevantly all facets of the religious education task.

The Overall Aim of Religious Education

The main categories and principles of religious education can be seen as ramifications of the guiding principle. That includes, in retrospect, our illustrative discussion of teaching and learning in the context of conscientization and creativity, as well as other practical considerations in the next chapters. In fact, their interconnections become more apparent when seen in that light.

The question of the overall aim or purpose is here the fundamental issue of *why* engage in the task of Christian religious education? or, what is the end toward which the educational ministry in the ecclesial context strives? That aim can be stated basically in terms of the persons, the process, and the scope involved in the task. It provides the direction for the whole enterprise; it functions as the main criterion for setting goals and planning instructional activities; and it serves as a means for evaluation.[109] Simply and broadly stated, in light of our guiding principle, *the overall aim of religious education is to enable people to appropriate (i.e., make their own) the gospel of the reign of God.* "Appropriation" in this context connotes both conversion and the nurture of Christian lifestyles, transformations as well as formation and empowerment in the sense of lived Christian faith in response to the gift, the promise, and the demands of the new creation. This is a comprehensive approach concerning persons because the whole ecclesial community must be engaged; it is comprehensive regarding the diverse and multidimensional processes involved on the part of groups and individuals; and it is comprehensive also in terms of scope, because the whole realm of human life is subject to be seen and acted upon in light of the coming reign of God.

Another general observation to reiterate is that the overall aim of Christian religious education here is explicitly consistent with the church's mission of being a sign of the good news of the kingdom. Hence, the task of religious education can also be defined as serving in the formation, transformation, and empowerment of the (alternative) ecclesial community in light of the gospel of the reign of God. From this perspective, the centrality of that task and ministry can be seen as enabling for *worship*, equipping for *community*, and empowering for *mission*.[110] And this central role of religious education in the ecclesial community must be correlated in turn with more specific references to the overall aim as stated above. For that we may refer again to the four interrelated "agendas" in order to spell out further the meaning and implications of the overall aim.

1) To appropriate the gospel of the reign of God implies *existentially responding to Jesus Christ and fulfilling the call to discipleship*. The Christian claim is that God's reign has been inaugurated in Jesus Christ. His person, teaching, ministry, cross, and resurrection are normative for human emergence as expression of the gift, the promise, and the demands of the new creation. Hence, from the vantage point of the ecclesial community, it is essential to grow into Christlikeness, which necessitates participation in the community's life and ministry.

2) To appropriate the gospel of the reign of God implies *promoting social transformation for the increase of freedom, justice, and peace*. This means to get involved in the liberating and re-creating work of God in society and history. In light of the "agenda of the world" the purpose of religious education is to sponsor critical awareness, Christian solidarity, and social engagement. Societal transformation for freedom, justice, and peace may be realized in divers ways: by denouncing oppression and alienation and their sustaining ideologies, values, and practices; by becoming involved in various projects of social service and action; by guiding and assisting vocational choices and engagements on the part of persons and groups; by discerning and promoting more humanizing alternatives, and by becoming a paradigm ("the city on the hill") or a sacrament of the reign of God.

3) To appropriate the gospel of the reign of God implies *to know and to love God* as creator, redeemer, and Holy Spirit. This is the God whose will is *shalom* and who makes accessible the freedom from bondage and alienation as well as the freedom to care and to create. (A double corrective is intended in the face of distorted views of God's character and defective notions about the process and context in which communion with God develops.) Communion with God—or, "to know and love God"— is seen in terms of fidelity, commitment, and obedience (i.e., "orthopraxis") which points back to the previous references to the overall aim in regard to discipleship and service.

4) To appropriate the gospel of the reign of God implies, in Freire's terms, *to become more human*, or *"to be more."* Conversion (*metanoia*) and nurture of the service-oriented Christian lifestyle supply the basic content for those expressions. On the personal level, the gift of salvation—essentially, another name for

the gift of the kingdom—involves self-affirmation and integration as well as empowerment to care and create as expressions of identity and vocation. "To become more human" means to be closer to Jesus Christ as a member of the prophetic-messianic community of faith that serves the world and to grow in knowing and loving God.

Those four manifestations of the overall aim of religious education must be seen as closely interrelated. Indeed, they should be considered together in order to affirm the comprehensive nature of that general purpose. Further, we must notice that the fourfold aim applies analogously to the persons involved in the educational ministry and to the ecclesial community as such and its corporate emergence into Christlikeness. The guiding principle ultimately reminds the church of its call to be that revolutionary community of Jesus Christ meant to be a foretaste and promise of the new humanity and new society. The educational ministry is supposed to communicate and sustain that vision, and to foster its appropriation and fulfillment. And the summary statement of purpose is that *the overall aim of Christian religious education is to enable people to appropriate the gospel of the reign of God by existentially responding to the call to conversion and discipleship in the midst of the ecclesial community which is to promote social transformation for the increase of freedom, justice, and peace, make accessible knowing and loving God, and foster human emergence, wholeness, and fulfillment.*

The claim is that the truly liberating thrust of that overall aim lies in the fact that human emergence is thereby sponsored in terms of the coming reign of God. The claim highlights again the political and eschatological dimension of the gospel which we have addressed in our discussion of the prophetic and utopian vision as a major liberation motif. From the vantage point of religious education, what we thus perceive is a strong summons to reaffirm the prophetic stance and commitment to transformation. Peace and justice become core metaphors[111] in the liberationist approach to the educational ministry. That approach calls in turn for a redefinition of faith as participation in the work of God and a restatement of epistemology in terms of praxis and obedience. That is the agenda for the next round of dialogue, in chapter 3, between liberation theology and religious education.

Notes

1. Matthew 6:33.
2. Leonardo Boff, *Jesus Christ Liberator: A Critical Christology for Our Time*, trans. Patrick Hughes (Maryknoll, N.Y.: Orbis, 1978), pp. 280, 291-292.
3. George Albert Coe, *A Social Theory of Christian Education* (New York: C. Scribner's Sons, 1917), p. 56.
4. We prefer to use the term *reign* of God because it is a more dynamic metaphor (i.e., closer to the original symbol in the teaching and preaching of Jesus) without the geographical, structured, and to some persons sexist connotations of "kingdom." The term kingdom will be used sparingly.
5. "Teaching on the mount" is probably a much more appropriate designation. The gospel account actually starts and ends with specific references to Jesus' moral and religious teaching (Matt. 5:1-2, 7:28-29). It begins with the beatitudes, and, at the end of the text, it asserts that people were amazed at his teaching, "because he taught as one who had authority, and not as their teachers of the law." Furthermore, Matthew (and Lk. 6:20, in the parallel "sermon on the plain") makes clear that Jesus' ethical instruction is addressed primarily to his disciples who are expected to realize the new social order of the people of God intended for the whole of Israel and, ultimately, for all humanity. On this point, see Gerhard Lohfink, *Jesus and Community: The Social Dimension of Christian Faith*, trans. John P. Galvin (Philadelphia/New York: Fortress/Paulist, 1984), pp. 26ff.
6. George Albert Coe, *What Is Christian Education?* (New York: C. Scribner's Sons, 1929), p. 29. Coe is undoubtedly one of the major religious educationists of the century whose contribution to the field reflects clearly certain theological and educational foundations. Influenced by the Social Gospel movement and liberal theology and by the progressive movement in American philosophy of education, Coe envisioned the contours of the new social order—which religious education would assist in creating—in terms of the "democracy" (rather than kingdom) of God.
7. Ibid., p. 35.
8. Paulo Freire, "A Letter to a Theology Student," *Catholic Mind* 70 (1972), p. 1265.
9. Thomas G. Sanders, "The Theology of Liberation: Christian Utopianism," *Christianity and Crisis* 33:15 (September 17, 1973), pp. 167-173. Following Reinhold Niebuhr, Sanders considers liberation theology as a moralistic ideology in utopian form. In working out his interpretation of Christian realism, Niebuhr objected to utopian moralism on the grounds that: a) utopianism contradicts the biblical view of human nature (i.e., although liberated from sin, Christians continue to be human and sinners) and history (i.e., history is not a progressive unfolding of moral aspirations but a permanent dialectic between human hopes and undermining contradictions); b) utopianism gives insufficient consideration to the moral ambiguity that characterizes all forms of social existence (i.e., every social system will always be imperfect, and relative achievements of freedom and justice flow from a precarious balance of power in any given social context.)
10. Rubem A. Alves, "Christian Realism: Ideology of the Establishment," *Christianity and Crisis*, pp. 173-176. Alves contends that Christian real-

ism accepted the axioms of positivism and that its rejection of utopias "is a sign that it participates in the revolt against transcendence that characterizes Western civilization." He also charges that realism (including pragmatism) is an American ideology which is functional to the system, contributes to its preservation, and gives it ideological and theological justification. Rubem Alves is not only a liberation theologian but a poet and philosopher as well. In his *A Theology of Human Hope* (St. Meinrad, Ind.: Abbey Press, 1969) Alves discusses the importance of language and presents a vision of theology as a language of freedom. His *Tomorrow's Child: Imagination, Creativity, and the Rebirth of Culture* (New York: Harper & Row, 1972) provides a trenchant critique of Western culture and its suppression of the imagination. See also, Rubem A. Alves, *La Teología como Juego* (Buenos Aires: La Aurora, 1984), *What Is Religion?* (Maryknoll, N.Y.: Orbis, 1984) and *I Believe in the Resurrection of the Body*, trans. L. M. McCoy (Philadelphia: Fortress, 1986).

11. Jaroslav Pelikan, *Jesus Through The Centuries: His Place in the History of Culture* (New Haven, Conn.: Yale University Press, 1985), pp. 206-219. Pelikan presents a gallery of cultural incarnations of Jesus Christ cherished by particular ages through the centuries. He suggests that each age has created Jesus in its own image and, therefore, a key to understanding a given age is to observe the way Jesus has been depicted then.

12. Ibid., p. 209.

13. Ibid., p. 218.

14. See José Míguez Bonino, "Who Is Jesus Christ in America Latina?" in *Faces of Jesus: Latin American Christologies*, ed. Jose Miguez Bonino, trans. Robert R. Barr (Maryknoll, N.Y.: Orbis 1984), pp. 1-6.

15. Jon Sobrino, *Jesus in Latin America*, trans. Robert R. Barr (Maryknoll, N.Y.: Orbis, 1987), pp. 14, 89ff.

16. On this question of "Christ-liberating-culture" see Rebecca S. Chopp, *The Praxis of Suffering: An Interpretation of Liberation and Political Theologies* (Maryknoll, N.Y.: Orbis, 1986), chap. 7, especially pp. 130-133. Chopp observes that the model of Christ liberating culture depends on two important and specific theological arguments for liberation theologians: 1) The reason Christians relate to culture in the liberating praxis of solidarity with those who suffer, is *because of God's option for the oppressed*; 2) the second argument for the Christ liberating culture model identifies *justice as a primary analogue for faith* (i.e., faith that sets free from sin and for God and world; faith working through love in bringing about human justice through structural and personal transformation).

17. Sobrino, *Jesus in Latin America*, p. 12.

18. John A. Mackay, *The Other Spanish Christ: A Study of the Spiritual History of Spain and South America* (New York: Macmillan, 1932). Mackay's study illumines the historical conditioning of the Latin American situation in terms of the transplanting and establishment of the Christian religion. His major observations—in spite of his different cultural and religious background—are consistent also with later historical and anthropological discussions as noted below. The *purpose* of Mackay's classic work was to propose a pioneer's comprehensive view of the religious situation in Latin America in the face of the apparent contradiction presented by massive, nominal Christianity in need for radical re-evangelicalization and

religious education. His major *hypothesis* was that, in order to appreciate the spiritual pilgrimage of the continent it is necessary to know "the psychic forces emanating from Spain and Portugal, which have molded all life and history of the countries which compose it, from the time of the Conquest until now (p. ix). At many points Mackay's approach comes close to representing a kind of "psycho-historical" perspective (see, for example, Erik H. Erikson "On the Nature of Psycho-Historical Evidence: in Search for Gandhi," in *Psychoanalysis and History*, ed. Bruce Mazlich, [New York: Universal Library, 1971], pp. 181-212). What is missing in Mackay's work, however, is an appraisal of the Protestant missionary movement to Latin America, which correlates with the neo-colonialist expansion of the United Kingdom and the United States (on this topic, see Jose Miguez Bonino, "The Recent Crisis in Missions," in *Mission Trends*, ed. G. H. Anderson and T. F. Stransky [New York: Paulist 1974], pp. 37-48). In attenuated and subtle ways, many Protestant mission projects in Latin America and elsewhere have reproduced a pattern somewhat analogous to that of the Catholic colonization and evangelization, from a "Christ-of-culture" in the metropolis to a "Christ-transformer-of-culture" in the so-called mission fields (roughly similar to H. Richard Niebuhr's typology in *Christ and Culture* [New York: Harper & Row, 1951], chaps. 3 and 6).

19. The year 1492 is, of course, doubly crucial for Spain: the struggle against the Arabs-Muslims is finally over (after eight centuries) and Ferdinand and Isabella determine that a unified and expanded Spain would be for Christ and for Christians; and Christopher Columbus, a rare combination of mystic and adventurer, "discovers" a new world for the crown of Spain and, hence, for the "kingdom of God." See Saúl Trinidad, "Christology, *Conquista*, Colonization," in *Faces of Jesus*, pp. 49ff.

20. Ibid., pp. 56-57. For an excellent study of the history of the church in this context, see Enrique Dussel, *A History of the Church in Latin America: Colonialism and Liberation (1492-1979)*, (Grand Rapids, Mich.: Eerdmans, 1981).

21. Mackay, *The Other Spanish Christ*, p. 124.

22. Ibid., first part.

23. Ibid., pp. 102, 63. Anthropologist Eric Wolf picked up Mackay's assessment concerning the Virgin Mary and confirmed it in the important case reported in his interesting study "The Virgin of Guadalupe: A Mexican National Symbol," *Journal of American Folklore* 71 (1958), pp. 34-39. Wolf concludes that there is, indeed, a symbolic identification of the Virgin with health, hope, and life, while Christ is symbolically identified with defeat, despair, and death. Wolf also indicates that in Hispanic artistic tradition in general, Christ is seldom depicted as an adult man but either as a helpless, harmless child or—more often—as a figure that is defeated, tortured, and killed. For further reference to the Virgin of Guadalupe, see Victor Turner, *Dramas, Fields, and Metaphors: Symbolic Action in Human Society* (Ithaca, N.Y.: Cornell University Press, 1974), the chapter, "Hidalgo: History as Social Drama."

24. Mackay, *The Other Spanish Christ*, pp. 98ff. Mackay includes the awakening of fear as another feature of this alienating religion which fosters what could be called a "necrophilous" (or death loving) Christ. (Curiously,

Erich Fromm—one of Freire's sources—reports that he adopted the use of the term necrophilous, also present in some of Freire's writings, from Miguel de Unamuno who had inspired Mackay before. Erich Fromm, *Anatomy of Human Destructiveness* [Greenwich, Conn.: Fawcett, 1973], p. 368.)

25. Georges Casalis, "Jesus—Neither Abject Lord Nor Heavenly Monarch," in *Faces of Jesus*, p. 73.

26. Ibid., p. 74.

27. Trinidad, "Christology, *Conquista*, Colonization," in *Faces of Jesus*, p. 59.

28. Paulo Freire, "Cultural Freedom in Latin America," in *Human Rights and the Liberation of Man in the Americas*, ed. Louis Colonnese (Notre Dame: University of Notre Dame Press, 1970), p. 169.

29. See Albert Memmi, *Portrait of the Colonizer and the Colonized* (New York: Orion, 1965).

30. Among Catholics worldwide religious education reflects the background of several approaches to the mission of the church in society. The most *traditionalist* one—still predominant in many places—may be associated with the old "Christendom" motif which identifies Christianity with culture and with national citizenship in particular, promotes a strong sacramental stance and aims at the formation of a "Christian" mentality in conjunction with the established civil (or military) power. This approach has been directed basically to the popular masses and has betrayed an indoctrinating and repressive character like that observable in the old catechetical models.

A "new Christendom" approach corresponds to the *modernizing* type of church and religion. This new approach shows the influence of Jacques Maritain, particularly since the 1930s. It aims at creating Christian institutions such as political parties, the revitalization of schools, and Christian labor unions. Less militantly "religious" than the traditionalist alternatives, it has attracted a considerable intellectual and political elite who are concerned with sociopolitical reform. Religious education here provides both support and foundation for those endeavors as an effective instrument for the formation of exemplary democratic citizens and institutions.

A major movement of renewal in religious education has taken place since the Catholic Bishop's Conference in Medellin, Colombia, in 1968. The main trends of this thrust have been characterized as follows: 1) an anthropological catechetics as the starting point, in the sense of "situational catechetics"; 2) a Christocentric emphasis in which Jesus Christ is proclaimed as liberator beyond the many forms of "pietistic" deformation; 3) a communitarian approach centered on grassroots congregations or base communities; 4) a more consistent focus on Bible study; and 5) a religious education oriented toward the promotion of social transformation in the face of poverty and injustice. (In Cecilio de Lora, "A Fuller Account of Catechetics in Latin America since Medellin," *Lumen Vitae* 30:3-4 [1975], pp. 357-374.) A stated priority of these efforts is the "re-evangelization" of adults among the majority of "nominal" Catholics. The general emphasis tends to reflect a "reconstructionist" approach to religious education among those actively involved in working toward transforming and adapting the church's educational task. The roles and aims of religious instruction are seen in terms of several categories, such as: forming human beings, serving the poor, proclaiming Christ the liberator, forming missionary communities, providing an ordered, progressive, and continuous faith education, and evangelizing the cultures. The training of catechists is to be defined by four salient traits: specialized, incarnated, communitarian, and permanent. (In Enrique Garcia Ahumada, "The Training of Catechists for Latin America," *Lumen Vitae* 38: 2 [1983], pp. 219-229). The "base ecclesial communities" offer a significant paradigm regarding this *prophetic* approach, as indicated in chapter 5 of this volume. It should also be noticed that, parallel to the contradiction of Christologies mentioned above, in many instances there exists a real polarization between views and practices representing "traditionalist" or "modernist," and "prophetic" approaches. This is also the case, of course, in other Christian denominations where the coexistence of differing or even conflicting models of religious education often creates severe tensions.

In the case of Protestants, the overall situation of religious education tends to present a poor reflection of the prevailing "banking" model in the public school system so sharply criticized by Freire. Another characteristic is the uncritical appropriation of curricula, methods, and organization designed mainly by North American missionary agencies and publishing houses. Much of Protestant Christianity consistently reveals the influence of the missionary enterprise in planting and supporting the churches. Thus congregational religious education has reflected a *traditional theological approach* (see Harold W. Burgess, *An Invitation to Religious Education* [Birmingham, Ala.: Religious Education Press, 1975], chap. 2) basically concerned with the transmission of an authoritative divine message of salvation, according to the theological bias of the missionary "mother churches" and their boards of missions. Gerson A. Meyer identifies consistent patterns of religious education inherited from Europe and the United States which have been transplanted in an uncritical and indiscriminating manner. The importation of cultural elements thus imposed on the people while disregarding their social and cultural heritage has been a major problem, together with several specific traits pertaining to the transplanted patterns such as the following: a conservative approach to the Bible and to Christian doctrine; a ghetto mentality; disassociation from social reality; narrowness of objectives; and fragmentation of the religious education programs. ("Patterns of Church Education in the Third World," in *Foundations for Christian Education in an Era of Change*, ed. Marvin J. Taylor [Nashville: Abingdon, 1976], pp. 231-233.)

31. Casalis, "Jesus—Neither Abject Lord Nor Heavenly Monarch," in *Faces of Jesus*, p. 74.
32. Hugo Assmann, "The Actuation of the Power of Christ in History: Notes on the Discernment of Christological Contradictions," in *Faces of Jesus*, p. 74.
33. Ibid., p. 127.
34. Ibid.
35. That is precisely Mackay's main assumption regarding a "subterranean tradition" in the spiritual history of Spain. For him, to this tradition belong the great mystics of the sixteenth century and other Christian "rebels" and prophets down to the present. The pro-life ("biophilic") Christ is there presented with traits associated with personal spirituality as

well as a social ethical lifestyle. A strong prophetic and utopian stance, a conflict affirming religious experience and perspective, new power to live, and Jesus Christ as actual mediator of death and life, are other features in the portrait of "the other Spanish Christ" that needs to be rediscovered. See *The Other Spanish Christ*, chap. 8.

36. This eloquent expression comes from Jon Sobrino, *Christology at the Crossroads: A Latin American Approach*, trans. John Drury (Maryknoll, N.Y.: Orbis, 1978), p. xv. Sobrino's work presents two essential guidelines for a Latin American Christology of liberation: 1) the centrality of the historical Jesus; 2) discipleship as the basic means for knowing Christ. He goes on to state that Latin American Christology is not a complete Christology in the traditional sense because Latin America does not treat all the themes dealt with in classic Christologies. Sobrino adds that liberation Christology generally proceeds from a point of departure in the historical Jesus and only then moves to the various New Testament, conciliar, and traditional Christologies. Further, Sobrino and others indicate that liberation Christology—like any other Christology—must be enriched by the formulations of the New Testament as well as the ecclesiastical magisterium concerning Christ. (*Jesus in Latin America*, pp. 8, 168.)

Other Latin American contributions include the following types: For a christological reflection in terms of spirituality, see Segundo Galilea, *Following Jesus*, trans. Helen Phillips (Maryknoll, N.Y.: Orbis, 1981); for a scholarly presentation of the historical Jesus that Segundo himself calls somewhat paradoxically an "antichristology," see Juan Luis Segundo, *The Historical Jesus of the Synoptics*, trans. John Drury (Maryknoll, N.Y.: Orbis, 1985) vol. II of a five-volume series, *Jesus of Nazareth Yesterday and Today*. Here Segundo aims to determine what contribution Jesus of Nazareth—and the tradition stemming from him—makes to the process of humanization. He attempts to discuss Jesus "in such a way that it may open people up to seeing him as a witness to a more humane and liberated human life" (p. 16). And his suggested *antichristology* seeks "to open a road between Jesus of Nazareth and our present reality, amid the various christologies. It seeks to connect him with the problems of our anthropological faith" (p. 21).

37. Boff, *Jesus Christ Liberator*, p. 45.

38. This point is confirmed by Claus Busmann, *Who Do You Say?: Jesus Christ in Latin American Theology*, trans. Robert R. Barr (Maryknoll, N.Y.: Orbis, 1985). Busmann presents a comprehensive survey of liberation Christology until 1980. In the concluding remarks, he asserts that never again will it be possible to do Christology in the absence of a raised consciousness of the social reality in which this Christology must be formulated—the reality of First World-Third World relationships—or in the absence of reflection on the political meaning and implications of the life and mission of Jesus and the church (p. 144). For a helpful survey of a contemporary Christology, see Thomas N. Hart, *To Know and Follow Jesus* (New York: Paulist, 1984).

39. It is obvious that this view of the suffering Christ is very different from that of the "Christologies of oppression" already discussed. Liberationists affirm the Suffering Servant who is actively obedient to God, even unto death, in solidarity with the human predicament; he suffers because he

confronts evil and struggles for liberation and salvation (i.e., he is not a passive, defeated victim who epitomizes suffering as a virtue in itself).
40. Sobrino, *Christology at the Crossroads*, pp. 12-13.
41. Boff, *Jesus Christ Liberator*, pp. 46-47.
42. Sobrino, *Christology at the Crossroads*, p. xiii. See also Sobrino's *Jesus in Latin America*, pp. 16, 95ff and, especially, chap. 5, "Following Jesus as Discernment," pp. 131ff. For Sobrino, typical of liberation Christology is its proposition of the following of Christ—discipleship—as indispensable for knowing Christ. The idea is not novel, however, and it was forcefully presented, for instance, in the sixteenth-century Radical Reformation movement, as in the case of Hans Denck: "No man may truly know Christ, except he follow him in life" (*mit dem Leben*). Cited in Cornelius J. Dyck, "Hermeneutics and Discipleship," ed. Willard Swartley, *Essays on Biblical Interpretation: Anabaptist-Mennonite Perspectives* (Elkhart, Ind.: Institute of Mennonite Studies, 1984), p. 30.
43. Boff, *Jesus Christ Liberator*, pp. 44-45.
44. Thus, for example, in his *Jesus in Latin America* Sobrino explicitly reaffirms crucial traditional theological tenets, such as the divinity of Christ; the normative and binding character of the christological dogmas of the church; the metahistorical fullness of Christian eschatology; and the integral, all-encompassing nature of salvation as total and final liberation.
45. This point is rightly made by Juan Alfaro in his Foreword to Sobrino's *Jesus in Latin America*, p. xi.
46. Ibid., p. xii.
47. This is one of the very few critical observations included in Claus Busmann, *Who Do You Say?*, p. 143.
48. Cf. Andrew Kirk, *The Good News of the Kingdom Coming: The Marriage of Evangelism and Social Responsibility* (Downers Grove, Ill.: InterVarsity, 1985), pp. 20ff. Balanced critiques of liberation theology and theologies of revolution appear also in J. Andrew Kirk, *Liberation Theology: An Evangelical View from the Third World* (Atlanta: John Knox, 1979) and *Theology Encounters Revolution* (Downers Grove, Ill.: InterVaristy, 1980).
49. The problem is already apparent in the case of Gustavo Gutiérrez. When he discusses Jesus and the political order, at the center of his discussion of eschatology and politics in *A Theology of Liberation*, Gutiérrez concentrates on three major issues: Jesus' attitude toward the Jewish leaders, his relationship with the Zealots, and his death in the hands of the political authorities. Gutiérrez stresses prophetic confrontation without substantial reference to the constructive alternatives proposed by Jesus in light of the proclamation and actual coming of the reign of God as he (Jesus) saw it.
50. John Howard Yoder, *The Politics of Jesus* (Grand Rapids, Mich.: Eerdmans, 1972), p. 100. The whole question of transformation and violence is, of course, a complex one, and Latin American liberation theologians tend to follow the mainline traditional Christian approach to the so-called lesser evil of the "just war" (or "just revolution"). With few exceptions (e.g., Dom Helder Camara and Adolfo Pérez Esquivel, who hold that physical violence is always inappropriate for a disciple of Jesus Christ) liberationists have failed to address creatively the problem of violence and alternative practical means for societal transformation. Ironically, yet understandably enough, proliferation just-revolution ethical thinking has the

same logic, and the same pitfalls, as the proestablishment (and often antiliberation) just-war reasoning. A related concern that liberationists normally neglect to address is the perennial temptations of "Constantinianism" on the part of the church, i.e., the question of getting hold of the power structures in order to establish a "Christian" social order for all, that is, regardless of discipleship commitments. On these issues see John Howard Yoder, *Christian Attitudes to War, Peace, and Revolution: A Companion to Bainton* (Elkhart, Ind.: Goshen Biblical Seminary,1983), especially, pp. 511ff. See also Yoder's *The Priestly Kingdom* (Notre Dame, Ind.: University of Notre Dame Press, 1984), chap. 7, "The Constantinian Sources of Western Social Thinking."

51. This point on prophetic and apocalyptic eschatology in liberation theology was originally argued by Orlando Costas in *The Church and Its Mission: A Shattering Critique from the Third World* (Wheaton, Ill.: Tyndale, 1974). Costas asserts that in liberation theology hope is not grounded so much in a God who is ahead, coming to us, and pulling us toward Self, but on a God who has come along with us and is leading us to the future which is in the making. Costas concludes that both the prophetic and the apocalyptic vision seem to be supported in the New Testament and that those two eschatological visions are integrated in the ministry of the Spirit. "On the one hand, he is the continuation of the incarnation, the one who makes Christ present in the historical situations of life. On the other, he is the spirit of promise" (p. 261).

52. Yoder, *The Politics of Jesus*, pp. 223ff.

53. Ibid.

54. From the perspective of the Christian Orthodox tradition, this point is treated by Paul Verghese, in *The Joy of Freedom* (Richmond, Va.: John Knox, 1967) and *The Freedom of Man: An Inquiry into Some Roots of Tension between Freedom and Authority in Our Society* (Philadelphia: Westminster, 1972).

55. Boff, *Jesus Christ Liberator*, chap.7. The treatment of resurrection by liberation theologians would appear to assume a "pre-Bultmann" position on the matter. However, liberationists would argue that their position is in fact *post-Bultmannian*. Liberation theologians actually criticize Bultmann as "the most tragic heir of the theology and . . . the solitary spirituality of the pietistic traditions coming down from Luther to Kierkegaard." (George Casalis, *Correct Ideas Don't Fall from the Skies: Elements of an Inductive Theology*, trans. Jeanne Marie Lyons and Michael John [Maryknoll, N.Y.: Orbis, 1984], pp. 65-66, 74.) Casalis and others take Bultmann severely to task for ignoring history and thus failing to integrate it in hermeneutic research. Liberationists consider that his effort at "demythologization" fails to understand the scriptures and the narrative of power. They conclude that a real understanding of the Bible—including the great myths found unacceptable by existential and historical interpretation— must be found in history, politics, and praxis.

56. Casalis, *Correst Ideas Don't Fall from the Skies*, p. 135.

57. Ibid., pp. 290-291.

58. Ibid.

59. Sobrino, *Christology at the Crossroads*, p. 377.

60. Ibid., p. 380.

61. Ibid., p. 381.

62. For this notion I am indebted to James E. Loder who refers to resurrection as *transformational negation* (i.e., the negation of the negation such that a new integration emerges, establishing a gain over the original condition or state). Loder discusses the crucified and resurrected Christ as the paradigm of the mediator of transformation at the level of existential negation. The Christ event creates an ontological gain for those whose existential nature is defined by his nature: "Christ becomes the adequate 'grammar' for existential transformation because in his crucifixion he takes the ultimate annihilation into himself and in his resurrection existential negation is negated." ("Negation and Transformation: A Study in Theology and Human Development," in *Towards Moral and Religious Maturity,* ed. James Fowler and Antoine Vergote [Morristown, N.J.: Silver Burdett, 1980], p. 169. See also, James E. Loder, *The Transforming Moment: Understanding Convictional Experiences* [New York: Harper & Row, 1981] chap. 6, "From Negation to Love.")

63. Sobrino discusses aptly the *eschatological* nature of the kingdom in terms of a fourfold description as follows: First, eschatology *means crisis* because God passes judgment on present reality in order to re-create it. This is consistent with Jesus' basic demand for conversion (*metanoia*). Second, Jesus' eschatology has a historicotemporal character: The present order is not the ultimate possibility for us. The future is not just an extrapolation based on the present; it is an as yet unrealized utopia. Third, we can pose the matter of the relationship between God and human beings in terms of a tension between fashioning the kingdom on the one hand and affirming that God is growing near in grace on the other. Fourth, eschatology presents the question of God in a new light: it points to God's relationship to the future as a mode of God's own being. *(Christology at the Crossroads,* pp. 61ff., 354ff.)

64. Boff, *Jesus Christ Liberator,* pp. 53, 55.

65. Here and elsewhere, the New Testament references are only suggestive and illustrative.

66. Boff, *Jesus Christ Liberator,* p. 64.

67. Sobrino, *Christology at the Crossroads,* p. 68ff.

68. Boff, *Jesus Christ Liberator,* pp. 90ff. Jon Sobrino also affirms forcefully that Jesus is the norm of liberation, especially in response to the critique of reductionism in liberation theology. For him, one of the "antireductionist" elements of liberation Christology is that Christ is presented, not only as the one who moves humanity toward liberation, but also as the *norm* of liberative praxis and the *prototype* of the new human being for whom liberation strives." Jesus is *norma normans* of liberation, not its *norma normata*." *(Jesus in Latin America,* pp. 11-12.)

69. Ibid., p. 281.

70. The rediscovery of the eschatological dimension of biblical faith has had far-reaching consequences for theology which was thus led to reconsider the crucial role of historical praxis. Gustavo Gutiérrez puts it clearly: "The Bible presents eschatology as the driving force of salvific history radically oriented toward the future. Eschatology is thus not just one more element of Christianity but the very key to understanding the Christian faith." (*A Theology of Liberation,* trans. Caridad Inda and John Eagleson [Maryknoll, N.Y.: Orbis, 1973], p. 162.)

71. Sobrino, *Christology at the Crossroads,* pp. 119-120.

72. Ibid., pp. xiii, 50.
73. Boff, *Jesus Christ Liberator*, p.69.
74. Sobrino, *Christology at the Crossroads*, p. 56.
75. For a thorough exposition of this theme see Yoder, *The Politics of Jesus.*
76. Historically, the theme of the kingdom of God is central in postexilic literature and in the inter-Testament times. For the Jews, it obviously possessed a political import since politics and religion were so much interrelated. For them, the effective *symbol* kingdom of God denoted liberation from oppression and life at its fullest potential. God's rule over all had also to be demonstrated politically: the Messiah would inaugurate the reign of God. Norman Perrin states that the symbol was indeed effective because it evoked the story (myth, in his terms), by means of which the Jews had come to understand themselves as people of God, the beneficiaries of divine rule in the world. The symbol is dependent upon the myth, and it is effective because of its power to evoke the myth. The myth in turn derives its power from its ability to make sense of the life of the Jewish people in the world. (*Jesus and the Language of the Kingdom: Symbol and Metaphor in New Testament Interpretation* [Philadelphia: Fortress, 1976], p. 23.) For further discussion on Perrin's contribution see Bernard B. Scott, *Jesus, Symbol-Maker for the Kingdom* (Philadelphia: Fortress, 1981). Other helpful discussions of kingdom of God are included in the following: G. R. Beasley-Murray, *Jesus and the Kingdom of God* (Grand Rapids, Mich.: Eerdmans, 1986); Bruce Chilton, ed., *The Kingdom of God in the Teaching of Jesus* (Philadelphia/London: Fortress/SPCK, 1984); John Gray, *The Biblical Doctrine of the Reign of God* (Edinburgh: T & T Clark, 1979); George E. Ladd, *Jesus and the Kingdom* (New York: Harper & Row, 1964); Wolfhart Pannenberg, *Theology and the Kingdom of God* (Philadelphia: Westminster, 1969); George V. Pixley, *God's Kingdom—A Guide for Biblical Study* (Maryknoll, N.Y.: Orbis, 1981).
77. Boff, *Jesus Christ Liberator*, p. 60.
78. *Shalom* is a broad, complex concept which connotes a condition of well-being resulting from sound relationships among people and between people and God. It covers human welfare, health, and well-being in both material and spiritual dimensions. Peace, justice, and salvation are essentially synonymous terms for the condition of wellness generated by right (i.e., according to God's will or intention) social relationships. See Walter Brueggeman, *Living Toward a Vision: Biblical Reflections on Shalom* (Philadelphia: United Church Press, 1982), and Perry B. Yoder, *Shalom: The Bible Word for Salvation, Peace and Justice* (Newton, Kans.: Faith and Life, 1987).
79. In the case of Paul's writings, the use of the kingdom motif is rather limited (although Luke ends the book of Acts with a reference to the apostle's "preaching the reign of God and teaching about the Lord Jesus Christ." [Acts 28:31], in the very heart of the Roman empire). Paul appears to make a distinction between Christ's kingdom and God's kingdom (e.g., 1 Cor. 15:24). However, in light of our present discussion, it can be argued that the lordship or rule is essentially another symbol for the same confession.
80. For instance, an incisively prophetic analysis of society and culture from

the perspective of fidelity to God's reign in the midst of the capitalist system, can be found in John Francis Kavanaugh, *Following Christ in a Consumer Society: The Spirituality of Cultural Resistance* (Maryknoll, N.Y.: Orbis, 1981). See also, John Kavanaugh, "Capitalist Culture as a Religious and Educational Formation System," *Religious Education* 78:1 (Winter 1983), pp. 50-60.

81. Boff, *Jesus Christ Liberator*, p. 69.
82. Ibid., p. 281.
83. Sobrino, *Christology at the Crossroads*, p. 127.
84. The meaning of "upside-down kingdom" is explored and developed at length in a challenging study of the reign of God in the snyoptic gospels by Donald B. Kraybill, *The Upside-Down Kingdom* (Scottdale, Pa.: Herald Press, 1978).
85. Boff, *Jesus Christ Liberator*, p. 64.
86. This point is discussed by John Howard Yoder, "La Expectativa Mesiánica del Reino y su Carácter Central para una Adecuada Hermenéutica Contemporánea," in *El Reino de Dios en America Latina*, ed. C. René Padilla (El Paso, Tex.: Casa Bautista de Publicaciones, 1975), pp. 110ff.
87. Sobrino, *Christology at the Crossroads*, p. 55.
88. Alves, *A Theology of Human Hope*, p. 142.
89. Ibid., p. 136.
90. Paul Lehman, *Ethics in a Christian Context* (New York: Harper & Row, 1963), p. 101. In the same paragraph Lehman claims that the Christian *koinonia* is the foretaste and sign in the world that God has always been and is contemporaneously doing what it takes to make and to keep human life human (on this point see below our discussion of the messianic community).
91. Yoder, "La Expectativ Mesiánica del Reino y su Carácter Central para una Adecuada Hermenéutica Contemporánea," in *El Reino de Dios y América Latina*, pp. 114-115.
92. This point is also made by Thomas H. Groome in his discussion of the kingdom of God, *Christian Religious Education: Sharing Our Story and Vision* (San Francisco: Harper & Row, 1980), pp. 35-55.
93. Yoder, "La Expectativa Mesiánica del Reino y su Carácter Central Para una Adecuada Hermenéutica Contemporánea," in *El Reino de Dios y America Latina*, p. 115.
94. Boff, *Jesus Christ Liberator*, p. 97.
95. Gutiérrez, *A Theology of Liberation*, p. 261.
96. Gerhard Lohfink uses the concept of "contrast-society" in his discussion of the church as the community of the disciples of Jesus. Lohfink asserts that this is the church *for* the world and not an elitist community, and that it is precisely by not becoming of the world (or just dissolved in it) that the church can serve and transform the world. He argues that in the Bible the people of God is always understood as a contrast-society whose conduct must correspond to the liberating and re-creating action and justice of God by becoming a holy people (Israel, the church) with a distinct social ethic. The call to be an alternative type of society implies a good measure of resistance and refusal, although not for the sake of contradiction itself. It also implies the efficacious perspective of a new society, one which stands in sharp contrast to social orders or systems marked by the will to over-

power and control. The last point in turn underscores the centrality of Jesus' call for nonviolence and the renunciation of domination. Finally, Lohfink asserts that the creative "contrast" that the church lives and represents does not stem from efficacy and moralism but from the miracle of the inbreaking reign of God. (*Jesus and Community*, pp. 66ff; 122ff; 157ff.)

For a compelling articulation of this ecclesiological and eschatological vision from the perspective of a distinctively Christian ethics—with its far-reaching implications in religious education—see the outstanding contribution of Stanley Hauerwas, including *Vision and Virtue: Essays in Christian Ethical Reflection* (Notre Dame, Ind.: Fides/Claretian, 1974); *Character and the Christian Life: A Study in Theological Ethics* (San Antonio: Trinity University Press, 1975); *Truthfulness and Tragedy: Further Investigations in Christian Ethics* (Notre Dame, Ind.: University of Notre Dame Press, 1977); *A Community of Character: Toward a Constructive Christian Social Ethic* (Notre Dame, Ind.: University of Notre Dame Press, 1981); *The Peaceable Kingdom: A Primer in Christian Ethics* (Notre Dame, Ind.: University of Notre Dame Press, 1983); *Against the Nations: War and Survival in a Liberal Society* (Minneapolis: Winston, 1985); *Suffering Presence: Theological Reflections on Medicine, the Mentally Handicapped, and the Church* (Notre Dame, Ind.: University of Notre Dame Press, 1986). For Hauerwas' view of the church as Christian education, see his "The Gesture of a Truthful Story: The Church and Christian Education" *Theology Today* 42:2 (July 1985). For an illuminating debate on Hauerwas' contribution and, especially, the questions of sociological and epistemological sectarianism, see "Symposium," *Theology Today* 44:1 (April 1987), pp. 69-94.

97. The expression *alternative community with a countercultural consciousness* is inspired by Walter Brueggemann and his *The Prophetic Imagination* (Philadelphia: Fortress, 1978). In light of our discussion of conscientization and creativity in chapter one, and current considerations on the prophetic and utopian vision, Brueggemann's view of the *task of prophetic ministry* (including, of course, prophetic religious education) is very appropriate. For him, that task is to nurture, nourish, and evoke a consciousness and perception alternative to the consciousness and perception of the dominant culture around us. Further, the alternative consciousness to be nurtured serves to *criticize* in dismantling the dominant consciousness and to *energize* persons and communities by its promise of another time and situation toward which the faith community may move (p. 13). Other helpful contributions on biblical perspectives by Brueggemann include, *The Creative Word: Canon as a Model for Biblical Education* (Philadelphia: Fortress, 1982); *Hopeful Imagination: Prophetic Voices in Exile* (Philadelphia: Fortress, 1986); and *Hope Within History* (Atlanta: John Knox, 1987). See also his article "Passion and Perspective: Two Dimensions of Education in the Bible," *Theology Today* 42:2 (July 1985), pp. 172-180.

98. See Randolph Crump Miller, "Theology in the Background," in *Religious Education and Theology*, ed. Norma H. Thompson (Birmingham, Ala.: Religious Education Press, 1982), pp. 17-41. Miller's position is that some kind of theology stands in the background of any religious education

theory and that theology is in fact the "clue" for understanding and carrying out the religious education enterprise. The conclusion is that all religious educationists must be well aware of their own theological assumptions. See also Randolph Crump Miller, *The Theory of Christian Education Practice: How Theology Affects Christian Education* (Birmingham, Ala.: Religious Education Press, 1980), especially chaps. 3 and 9, and "How I Became a Religious Educator—Or Did I?" in *Modern Masters of Religious Education*, ed. Marlene Mayr (Birmingham, Ala.: Religious Education Press, 1983), pp. 65-86. For a critique of what he calls "theological imperialism" (and particularism) see James Michael Lee, "The Authentic Source of Religious Instruction," in *Religious Education and Theology*, pp. 146ff. Lee asserts, however, that theology has a valuable necessary internal and external role in religious education: "Theology's internal role is properly enacted when it becomes a dimension of religious instruction's substantive content (religion) not on theology's terms but on the terms of religious instruction's own substantive content. Theology's external role is properly enacted when it reflects on the theological meaning of religious instruction—not on the religious instruction meaning, but on the theological meaning" (pp. 155-156). In the same volume edited by Norma Thompson, which consists of an excellent collection of essays, Gabriel Moran states that theology can supply just a small part of the content of religious education, as a "modest contributor"; however, in the ecclesial context he sees Christian theology as being "almost by definition the guiding hand of catechetical instruction." ("From Obstacle to Modest Contributor," p. 57.)

99. Sara Little presents five alternatives concerning the relation between theology and religious education: theology as content to be taught; theology as norm; theology as irrelevant; "doing theology" as educating; and religious education in dialogue with theology. "Theology and Religious Education," in *Foundations for Christian Education in an Era of Change*, ed. Marvin J. Taylor, (Nashville: Abingdon, 1976), pp. 30-40. It can be argued that liberation theology may relate to religious education in terms of Little's categories of content, norm, theologizing, and dialogue. Another helpful discussion of theology and religious education appears in Norma H. Thompson, "Current Issues in Religious Education," *Religious Education* 73:6 (November-December 1978), pp. 611-627.

100. Thomas H. Groome, "The Critical Principle and the Task of Prophecy," *Religious Education* 2:3 (May-June 1977), pp. 262-272.

101. Mary Elizabeth Moore, *Education for Continuity and Change: A New Model for Christian Religious Education* (Nashville: Abingdon, 1983), pp. 14ff.

102. John L. Elias, *Studies in Theology and Education* (Malabar, Fla.: Krieger, 1986), chap. 13, "Social Imagination and Religious Education."

103. Michael Warren, *Youth and the Future of the Church: Ministry with Youth and Young Adults* (Minneapolis: Seabury, 1982); "Youth Politicization: A Proposal for Education Within Ministry," *Religious Education* 77:2 (March-April 1982), pp. 179-196; *Youth, Gospel, Liberation* (Harper & Row, 1987).

104. William B. Kennedy, "Toward Reappraising Some Inherited Assumptions about Religious Education in the United States," *Religious Education*

76:5 (September-October 1981), pp. 467-481; "Pursuing Justice and Peace: Challenge to Religious Educators," *Religious Education* 78:4 (Fall 1983), pp. 467-476; "Ideology and Education: A Fresh Approach for Religious Education," *Religious Education* 80:3 (Summer 1985), pp. 331-334; "The Ideological Captivity of the Non-Poor," in *Pedagogies for the Non-Poor*, ed. Alice Frazer Evans, Robert A. Evans, and William Bean Kennedy (Maryknoll, N.Y.: Orbis, 1987), pp. 232-256.

105. This discussion follows closely my treatment of this topic in Daniel S. Schipani, *Conscientization and Creativity: Paulo Freire and Religious Education* (Lanham, Md.: University Press of America, 1984), pp. 100ff.

106. This conceptualization involves the contribution of liberation theology with a constructive reformulation.

107. The concept of the guiding principle in Christian religious education is proposed by D. Campbell Wyckoff in his *The Gospel and Christian Education* (Philadelphia: Westminster, 1959), pp. 86ff. This principle is seen as the nucleus or heart of the matter to be communicated to the participants in the diverse facets of the enterprise. It is an essential principle which informs those different aspects of religious education such as setting goals, selecting curriculum, orienting methodology and administration. For an assessment of the concept, see Donald B. Rogers, "The Empowering Gospel: Wyckoff's Concept of the Guiding Principle," *Princeton Seminary Bulletin* 5:1 (New Series 1984), pp. 21-27. And James E. Loder proposes a guiding principle focused on transformation, in "Transformation in Christian Education," *Religious Education* 76:2 (March-April 1981), pp. 204-221. For Loder, that guiding principle formulates, in a way that is both theologically and behaviorally sound, the nature of the essential reality with respect to which all the various subdivisions and aspects of Christian education must be defined, directed, and evaluated; the guiding principle tells one in the field how to perceive oneself in relation to the fundamental reality that is at stake (p. 216).

108. Wyckoff, *The Gospel and Christian Education*, pp. 87ff.

109. See James R. Shaefer, *Program Planning for Adult Christian Education* (New York: Newman, 1972), p. 83.

110. Our choice of *worship, community,* and *mission* is deliberate because we assume that together they correspond to the three main facets of the life of the church and its very reason for being. Notice also that worship, community, and mission can be seen as expressing the trinitarian nature of the church and, somehow connected, respectively, with the biblical metaphors of Covenant People of God, Body of Christ, and Temple/Community of the Spirit.

111. See Jack L. Seymour, "Approaches to Christian Education," in *Contemporary Approaches to Christian Education*, ed. Jack L. Seymour and Donald E. Miller (Nashville: Abingdon, 1982), pp. 25ff.

Chapter 3

Praxis Way of Knowing

"Do the will of God, and you shall know . . ."[1]

JESUS

"To know the Lord is to pattern one's life after God's own creation. . . .

"Obedience is not a *consequence* of our knowledge of God, just as it is not a precondition for it: obedience is included in our knowledge of God . . . obedience *is* our knowledge of God. This is what is meant by emphasizing the intrinsic demand for Christian truth to become historical, to be 'truth in the facts.'

"The God of the covenant has himself designed a pattern of action which such words as justice, righteousness, the protection of the poor, active love, help us to discern."[2]

JOSÉ MIGUEZ BONINO

"The nature, purpose, and context of Christian religious education calls for a way of knowing that can hold past, present, and future in a fruitful tension, that fosters free and freeing lived Christian faith, that promotes a creative relationship with a Christian community and of that community to the world. . . .

"Since a praxis way of knowing always has the purpose of promoting further praxis, the knowing which arises from a reflective/experiential encounter with the Christian Story and Vision seems capable, by God's grace, of sponsoring people toward intentionally lived Christian faith."[3]

THOMAS H. GROOME

INTRODUCTION

According to the gospels, the teaching of Jesus generated admiration and inspiration among the people. But it also elicited perplexity and indignation on the part of those individuals who were confronted or indicted in the light of that teaching. John 7:14-18[4] illumines both Jesus' liberating and offensive teaching as well as his own view of the fundamental source of his educational ministry.

Jesus' teaching in the context of that worshipful celebration—the Feast of Tabernacles—is amazing as well as disruptive. The question is soon raised (John 7:15): "How did this man get such learning without having studied?" (or, more literally, "How can this uneducated man read the scriptures?"). The Jews wonder how Jesus can teach if he did not himself study under a teacher. In light of our discussion on Paulo Freire in the first chapter of the present volume, it is interesting to note also that this is in principle a question concerning literacy or "knowing letters." According to his contemporaries, Jesus is supposed to be illiterate. His authority as a teacher is being questioned given his apparent lack of formal training. The familiar assumption is that, in order to "know," a man has to go to rabbinical school and learn from the respected masters of the past under the authority of some duly authorized teacher.

In other words, Jesus is confronted with a question about his own schooling and curriculum (and *curriculum vitae* in particular). His answer is astonishing and brilliant: Rather than addressing schooling and curriculum, he chooses to focus on epistemology, i.e., the question of the authentic source of knowledge and truth. He asserts simply, "If anyone chooses to *do* God's will, such a person will know. . ." which is to say that the practice of divine will authenticates the teaching of Jesus. That teaching needs to be existentially owned—it is a matter of choice and commitment—and needs to be tested and validated in actual practice.[5] Further, we must notice that the question raised by the Jews was linked to the past—where is Jesus coming from? His response is future-oriented and obedience-focused. Jesus thus challenges the educational and political establishment, not only in terms of what he teaches, but also by changing radically the whole notion of what authentic teaching, learning, and knowing are about.[6] Only in faithful action can we find our way into the truth of his teaching. Put in other terms we might also say "whoever lives by the truth comes into the light" (John 3:21a).

The gospel references from John are especially fitting in terms of the agenda of the present chapter, an agenda which is plainly announced in the two opening quotations from José Míguez Bonino and Thomas Groome. That is the case because of the unique and interchangeable views of knowing, truth, love, believing, and obedience, present in the Johannine gospel and epistles. Essentially, what we see there is the clearest biblical expression of the unity and integration of faith and fidelity, which we can restate with the equation, *knowledge of God=faithful covenant practice* (i.e., the practice of love and justice consistent with God's will and word). According to John, this is for Jesus a matter of life and death or, rather, a question of passing from death to *eternal life* (i.e., the Johannine equivalent for the symbol of the reign of God).[7] Interestingly enough, it is in that sense that *believing/knowing* God (John 5:24; 17:3) and loving (John 3:14) are both equally associated with eternal life. And that special quality of life is made possible by the historical facts of the very life, ministry, cross, and resurrection of Jesus, the *word* made flesh (John 1:1, 14), the *light* of the world (John 1:9; 8:12), and the *truth*-ful *way* to God (John 14:6). Further, the new life described in what John often calls the "words," "teachings," and "commandments" of Jesus is unequivocally defined in terms of loving (e.g., John 13:1-20; 15-17; 1 John 2:3-5). In turn, love is plainly seen as a concrete, historical course of action having to do with our relationship with actual human beings (1 John 3:17-18) including an identification of love with righteousness and justice (1 John 2:29; 3:10; 4:7). In other words, John states very clearly and explicitly what is otherwise also apparent in authentic biblical faith and in the whole of the biblical records, namely, that there is no such thing as a theoretical, abstract, or merely contemplative "knowledge of God." Rather, knowing and loving God—an essential purpose of religious education, as indicated in the previous chapter—is a matter of personal choice, conviction, and commitment; trust and fidelity; and consistent, active engagement in the politics of the reign of God in light of the covenant.[8]

This third chapter is pivotal in our discussion of the encounter between liberation theology and religious education. It has been placed deliberately at the center of the book because it deals more explicitly with the key issues of knowing, truth, and Christian faith, issues which actually permeate the overall treatment of our subject in the rest of the chapters. We will begin with a general reference to the liberationist praxis epistemology which attempts to restate and contextualize the preferential "biblical way of knowing." The twofold emphasis there is on obedience to the will of God and on discipleship—i.e., concrete and daily faithful following of Jesus Christ—as the means for the epistemological and ethical discernment of the divine will in the midst of the current historical situation. Then we will focus on the corresponding performative (i.e., praxis-oriented) view of the Christian faith, again with a twofold emphasis on doing justice and participating in the re-creative and liberating project on the reign of God in and for the world. Finally, after a brief critical assessment of the liberationist praxis epistemology, we will indicate some principles of religious education theory and practice stemming from the dialogical interface with liberation theology.

A PRAXIS EPISTEMOLOGY

Our discussion of Paulo Freire's philosophy of education in the first chapter highlights the strong epistemological base of his work and thought. In fact, Freire perceives education both as a certain way of knowing and as a theory of knowledge put in practice. Furthermore, he presents a view of learning and education with an explicit epistemological perspective.[9] The notion of praxis as the dialectic relationship of action and critical reflection is central in such a perspective. In Marxian fashion, Freire contends that authentic liberation can only be achieved through a process of social transformation whereby human beings actually make their own destiny. Praxis is, in this light, the human activity essential to transforming the world in the face of injustice, oppression, and suffering. Thus, by articulating his own praxis-focused liberationist stance from a Christian standpoint, Freire assisted in laying the base for the methodological approach of

Latin American liberation theology. Indeed, consistent with Freire's conscientization approach, liberation theologians define the theological task in terms of *critical reflection on Christian praxis in the light of the Word.*[10]

In the second chapter, we discussed the prophetic and utopian vision. There our reflection on the political and eschatological dimensions of the gospel of the reign of God yielded further substantive content to the overall liberationist emphasis on *orthopraxis* (i.e., commitment and active engagement in concretely living out the Christian faith; or, the faithful following of Jesus Christ in the midst of the historical and existential situation). That liberationist christological reflection is foundational for our present focus on praxis epistemology in light of the two essential guidelines of this kind of epistemology, namely (a) a radical and biblical interest in the historical Jesus vis à vis the present experience, especially oppression and suffering, and (b) discipleship considered as the basic means for actually knowing Christ and the will of God. That christological approach assumes in turn a practical and pastoral concern at the service of the renewal of the Christian and ecclesial praxis. In liberation theology, commitment to praxis fundamentally connotes a sharing in the life and struggles of the poor and oppressed in search for liberation, justice, and peace. That sociopolitical option in turn calls for further affirmation of an epistemological stance that assumes the paradoxical privilege of the poor and oppressed and the corresponding need for conversion and solidarity as requisites for transformational knowing and learning and creative theologizing.[11]

At this point we need to probe further the liberationist praxis epistemology in light of its own critical and constructive agenda. Hence, we must first consider the liberationist rejection of the idealistic (and also rationalistic) conception of knowledge and truth in traditional and academic theology together with the emphasis on recapturing the biblical epistemological focus on obedience. Second, we must look at the germane question of truthful discernment of divine will as a patterned process of discipleship.

Knowing as Obedience

Liberation theologians have confronted a classical conception of truth deemed to have come to a crisis in the tasks of theology and education. They critique the classical view for failing to correlate with key biblical understandings on knowing and faith; further they redefine theology itself in terms of commitment to praxis. The main liberationist concern in this regard is the question of the relation of truth to actual historical practice, or knowing and obedience.

Beyond Idealism and Dualism. Liberationists attack the conception of an absolute, timeless Christian truth (or "principle") somehow enshrined in the scriptures and in the formal set of teachings of the church. Such a conception typically assumes that there are, besides, more or less imperfect applications of that truth. In this view truth belongs to a certain world of truth which is a universe complete in itself and subsequently reproduced or copied in "true" or "correct" propositions, or in a theory which corresponds to that universal truth. These abstract universal principles are, when the situation arises, applied to give the correct answers to any particular exigency. This so-called classical view is therefore faulted for assuming that truth is preexistent to and independent of its historical effectiveness.[12] The classic view of theology relegates the realm of history and action to a second level of inferences and consequences of "truth" seen as the correspondence between certain conceptual formulations and universal ideas or principles.

José Míguez Bonino lists three serious problems which he sees as deeply embedded in the epistemology of the classical theological tradition: 1) It facilitates a discussion between theories and ideas regardless of the historical courses of action to which such intellectual conceptions are related; 2) it posits ideas as floating in a heaven of abstraction, as if they were conceived out of nothing, unrelated to the existential conditions of the peoples and groups who generated them; and 3) it creates the classical ethical dilemmas by assuming that there are "ideal courses of action" stemming from the conceptual firmament of truth and asking afterwards for the degree of compromise acceptable to accommodate the actual conditions in which action must be undertaken.[13] That idealistic perspective has been consistently rejected by liberation theologians. They have done so by affirming, essentially, that there is no such thing as truth outside or beyond the concrete historical situation involving human beings as agents, and that, therefore, there is no knowledge except in action itself, in the process of transforming the world through participation in history.[14] The earlier liberationist essays are especially forceful in this regard, as in the case of Gustavo Gutiérrez' emphasis on a praxis-oriented "epistemological split,"[15] Hugo Assmann's rejection of "any *logos* which is not the logos of a *praxis,*"[16] and José P. Miranda's correlating and integrating Marxist and biblical epistemological views.[17] A major epistemological claim on the part of all liberation theologians, without exception, is that a *biblical* view of knowing and truth must be recovered and reappropriated in theology and education alike.

The Biblical View. From the liberationist perspective, there is no question that the classical (idealistic and rationalistic) perspective which has dominated much of the theological, ethical, and educational scenes does not correspond to the biblical understanding of knowledge and truth. The dualistic distinction between a theoretical knowledge of truth and practical applications of it simply cannot claim a biblical base because the scriptural records point to correct or right knowing as being contingent on faithful doing. In other words, the knowledge that counts and matters—the knowledge of God—is disclosed in righteous action. Wrongdoing is ignorance and disbelief; further, there is no such thing as neutral knowledge (or lack of it).

The basic liberationist claim that true knowledge of God is equivalent to conforming to divine will is found supported throughout the Bible and specifically confirmed in two blocks of scriptural material, namely the prophetic writings in the Old Testament and the Johannine literature in the New Testament already referred to in the Introduction of the present chapter. In both cases, as Míguez Bonino indicates, knowing God is not abstract theoretical knowledge but active obedience to divine will—obedience *is* our knowledge of God. There is not a separate *noetic* moment in our relationship with God. There is an imperfect faith, a faltering faith, but there cannot be a *believing* disobedience—unless it is the "dead faith" of which James speaks and which "profits nothing" (James 2:14-26).[18]

By the same token, the biblical view of the Word of God is not a matter of conceptual communication but the reality of creative and liberating event, history-making and redeeming "prouncements," with the supreme and definitive expression in Jesus, the

Word-made-flesh. The inherent truth of that Word of God does not consist in some correspondence to an idea but in its power to carry out God's promise and to fulfill divine judgment. Consequently, what is expected from the people of God is not an ethical inference but an obedient participation—in suffering as well as in service—in God's creative and liberating work in the world.[19]

Liberationists particularly highlight the prophetic identification between knowing God and practicing justice in the face of the biblical affirmation of God's (or Yahweh's) own character (e.g., Jeremiah 9:23-24). Hence, to know God is to pattern one's life after God's own way of being and acting. Authentic biblical knowledge, then, is intrinsically ethical in nature, and the juxtaposition of knowing and doing justice (e.g., Jeremiah 22:14-16; Hosea 4:1-6; 6:6; 10:12; 12:6) is grounded in God's nature and action in history (Hosea 14:3). Further, in the Bible the practice of justice encompasses much more than interpersonal relationships and social virtue; it is the very nature of the covenant with Yahweh who consistently practices mercy and justice.[20] Therefore the epistemological distortions of theological thinking characteristic of Western academic theology involve also the perversion of the biblical doctrine of God with two momentous consequences, in Míguez Bonino's words: 1) God is robbed of the particular divine identity (i.e., God becomes objectified in our thought apart from divine action; thus we make an image apart from the words and commandments in which God has defined the covenant terms); and 2) the fact that God's identity is revealed to us precisely by announcing actions specifically involving the neighbor and the world (e.g., inviting, commanding, forbidding), is actually ignored or contradicted in the classical view of knowledge and truth.[21]

In short, those are the fundamental considerations pointing to a biblically grounded major epistemological revision which must serve both the theological task and the educational ministry.[22]

A Praxis Theology. The liberationist rejection of the idealistic and rationalistic theological approach includes the broader critique of European (and North American) theologies as having been, by and large, an idle non-reality-oriented academic exercise. In that light, North Atlantic or First World theologizing has falsely assumed the possibility of constructing a "pure" theology derived from scripture and church tradition, a theology which was first systematized and then applied to real life ethical, pastoral, and practical concerns. This is, once again, a manifestation of the assumption that it is possible to acquire and develop a knowledge of truth separated from truthful action or the practice of truth. Inevitably, revelation is then reduced to communicating "divine truths" and faith becomes intellectualized. Liberation theology proposes that the theological task consists in proclaiming the truth that is called gospel for the purpose of the obedience of faith. An epistemological restatement, therefore, becomes imperative.

Jon Sobrino lucidly compares "European" and "Latin American" theologies, broadly speaking, by defining two ways of conceiving the theological task which have evolved within the boundaries set by the epistemological challenge of the Enlightenment. His reflection explains the purported "liberating" character of contemporary theological understanding, including the relation between theory and practice.[23] Sobrino refers to the two distinct phases of the Enlightenment represented by Immanuel Kant and Karl Marx. The liberation of reason from all authority and the courage to use the human intelligence corresponds to Kant and the first phase or movement of the Enlightenment. The second phase looks to liberation from the wretched condition of the real world rather than seeing liberation as the autonomy of reason from which the total liberation of the human person would automatically come. Such a Marx-inspired liberationist view requires not merely an autonomous way of thinking but a new way of acting as well. In other words, the liberation of the mind would be put forward in dialectical relationship with the liberation from the abject misery of the concrete historical situation. Sobrino contends that, broadly speaking, modern European theology has been oriented to the first *(Kantian)* movement of the Enlightenment, mainly by underscoring the liberating role of theological understanding vis à vis dogmatic arbitrariness and all authoritarianism. Further, that theology has remained interested in the traditional task of explaining the truth of faith and in clarifying its meaning whenever it is obscured.[24]

For its part, Latin American liberation theology attempts to respond to the challenge presented by the second *(Marxian)* phase of the Enlightenment. The focus of its theological interest is the will for liberation. Hence, "critical reflection on Christian praxis in the light of the Word" is to serve the project of human liberation in the midst of the sociohistorical situation. Sobrino notes in this case the evident influence of Marx on the view of the liberating character of theological understanding, which paraphrases Marx's famous *Thesis XI on Feuerbach* (i.e., the paradigm for the liberative dimension and the import of theological understanding consists in the will for reality transformation in the direction of the politics of the reign of God). Transformation goes far beyond explanation and intellectual reordering of reality; it connotes working for the creation of another reality while the present order is theologically confronted in the most realistic and unideological way possible. Theological understanding is thus inseparable from the ethical and the practical realms and cannot be reduced to the production of explanation.[25] In fact, theological immersion in the reality of injustice, oppression, suffering, and conflict which calls for radical transformation comes first; that is, theological commitment is prior to reflecting on the theological implications of the task. In other words, this "praxis theology" calls for a major reformulation of the theological method.[26] And such a reformulation involves an additional claim included in the rejection of any idealistic and rationalistic epistemology, namely, that true appreciation and comprehension of liberation theology itself necessitates a prior understanding of the concrete historical process of the liberation of the oppressed and active participation in that process.[27]

Discipleship as Discernment

The question of knowing and obedience must be further explored by focusing on certain christological clues proposed by liberation theology. From the perspective of religious education, several significant propositions can then be highlighted concerning the "epistemological break" in Christian spirituality and in theological method and the structure and process of discernment viewed as an epistemology of obedience.

Epistemological Break. As already indicated in the previous chapter of the present volume, a major biblical affirmation of liberation Christology is that the only way to get to know Jesus (and, therefore, to know and love God) is to follow after him in one's real life. In fact, for Jon Sobrino, the following of Jesus—which is *the* precondition for knowing him—is the epistemological source for theological and christological understanding, which is by and large neglected in contemporary systematic theology and which liberationists reaffirm.[28] Further, the *way* of Jesus (and Jesus is the "truth" insofar as he is the "way"[29]) illumines and correlates both theological method and the authentic religious experience of Christian spirituality. Thus, liberation Christology claims to propose not only substantive content about Jesus Christ to be accepted believingly and known (for example in the form of instruction for moral conduct), but also the manner of knowing Christ which actually defines Christian *faith* itself. In other words, while embracing whatever can be known about Jesus—from correct pieces of information to orthodox formulations—states Sobrino, it is discipleship, or the concrete following of Jesus, that must be seen as indispensable for actually knowing Christ.[30]

The "epistemological break" consists in the existential and historical following that yields a praxis knowing which is *distinct* from "natural understanding" as well as *contrary* to it.[31] This is, of course, another way of referring to the "abnormal epistemology" of the upside down kingdom briefly discussed in chapter 2 of this book; there we indicate the radical challenge to conventional wisdom and the requirement of an alternative way of knowing and appropriating truth. Such an epistemological break is symbolized dramatically in Jesus' call to conversion *(metanoia)*. For his part, Paul interprets the break also in terms of scandal and foolishness in his reference to Christ as the wisdom and the power of God.[32] When it comes to integrating the epistemological break into theological understanding, liberationists argue that the difference between European and Latin American contributions lies in the fact that, for the latter, the break is more a matter of experience and praxis than of reflective thought.[33] And this is the case, even as discipleship—the actual following of Jesus—is viewed in terms of discernment, as presented below.

Discernment: Process and Structure. Discipleship as discernment is the concrete existential and historical realization of Jesus' claim that he is indeed the truthful way of life (John 14:6).

Christian discernment may be defined, then, as "the particular quest for the will of God, not only to understand it but also to carry it out. . . . [It is] a process in which the will of God carried out verifies the will of God thought."[34] Further, if being Christian means becoming children of God in the Son, then Christian discernment must have a structure analogous to the discernment of Jesus which can only be realized by faithfully following him. Thus, for Sobrino and others, Jesus' own experience and praxis of discernment provides the *prototype* of every Christian discernment because he is the believer by autonomasia, "the pioneer and perfecter of our faith" (Hebrews 12:2). However, we must realize that, on the basis of Jesus' own choices and historical commitments, we learn not so much specific solutions to our discernments as, more basically, how to learn to discern. Thus, along with Jesus' first appreciation of a God who is partialized love for the poor and oppressed, we see his appraisal of divine love as unconditionally placed between a "no" (i.e., the effective negation of dehumanizing sin in all forms) and a "yes" (i.e., effective affirmation of God's utopian project of liberation and reconciliation). Jesus' discernment was directed primarily to corresponding to the objectivity *in* history of God's "no" and "yes" *to* history. Hence, difficult as it may be to discern what needs to be done in particular situations, for Jesus there was at least a clear criterion of discernment. Insofar as it applies to the neighbor and concerns love, the will of God is not really a mystery. The first step toward Christian discernment is thus hearing the clear "no" given by God to the world of sin that dehumanizes human beings (which has nothing mysterious about it) and, above all, *carrying on* this negation throughout history without stifling or softening that voice in any way. The second step is hearing the divine "yes" to a world that has to be reconciled and, above all, *carrying on* this utopian "yes" as a task never to be abandoned even when history radically questions it. Therefore, discernment must be exercised by remaining fully open to the praxis of love and to the overcoming of sin objectivized in history (i.e., it is not so much a question of purifying our intentions with regard to love, nor of reconciling the sinners in their innerness).[35]

The paradigmatic record of Jesus provides us with four additional criteria for faithful discernment in the praxis of Christian love. The first criterion is *partialized incarnation;* for Jesus, becoming incarnate meant choosing that particular locus in history—the existential place of the poor and oppressed—which was capable of leading him to the totality of God. He affirmed that the poor and oppressed constituted the proper setting from which to discern the praxis of love. The second criterion is *effective signs* or *mediations* in the praxis of love; Jesus sought to do God's will by seeking particular and effective solutions. His public life, teaching, miracles, forgiveness, controversies, and renaming evil, point to his search to convert the good news into a good reality. Third, the *praxis of sociopolitical love,* or love that becomes justice, i.e., the efficacy of love must apply to the configuration of the whole of society because the gospel is the good news of the reign of God seeking total liberation and re-creation of the whole human being and all human beings and creation. Justice is the form of love corresponding to that type of social totality. The fourth criterion derives from the other three (partial, effective, sociopolitical love) and is *conflictive love.* Christian love is *for* all persons; however, its privileged embodiment is first and foremost *with* the oppressed *against* the oppressors for the humanization of all, for all to become members of God's family.

Finally, we must notice several *formal* features in the discernment practiced by Jesus in his quest for the divine will. Some of the formal characteristics of this discernment, and hence of true discipleship, are as follows: 1) It involves a learning process of historical development (stages of awareness, choices and commitments, for instance); 2) it calls for radicalness (e.g., presentation of alternatives—one cannot serve two masters; one cannot win life and keep it; and the exercise of critical will); and 3) it requires openness to verification (i.e., the question of "fruits;" the signs of service and sacrifice, persecution; modeling according to the Sermon on the Mount ideal, etc.). As Christians we exercise our discernment within the concrete existential and historical channel of discipleship, by following Jesus with identifiable values, criteria, and verification. Within this channel, we listen to the requirements of the Spirit given to us to enable us to go on making history and advancing God's reign in particular situations.[36]

In light of the previous considerations, liberationist praxis knowing may be reformulated as an *epistemology of obedience* strikingly reminiscent of a Radical Reformation view of discipleship and knowing. In this view, which is recaptured and contextualized by liberation theology, knowing and doing become a reciprocal experience of understanding and obeying. Thus lack of obedience is not only a lack of love but a lack of knowledge as well.[37] This perspective thus affirms the biblical notion that faith is not a *gnosis* but a *way* (i.e., lifestyle, including interpersonal and sociopolitical dimensions), a walking in concrete obedience to the will of God. Therefore Christian faith is seen as practically equivalent to discipleship, the dynamic, dialogical, and discerning following of Jesus Christ.

REDEFINING CHRISTIAN FAITH

Our comments on the liberationist conception of faith advance the discussion of praxis epistemology. Indeed liberation theology presents a performative (i.e., praxis-oriented) approach to Christian faith consistent with a prophetic and utopian vision of the reign of God and the political-eschatological dimension of the gospel. Consequently, liberation theology criticizes the inadequacies of prevailing theologies of faith which neglect or underestimate the biblically based emphasis on existential and historical commitment and faithful or obedient action. The critique also addresses popular notions such as the assumption that faith directly relates the individual "believer" to God (especially when objective beliefs are seen as mediating the link person-God, or even as a synonym for faith). Further, liberationists critically confront classical notions of faith in Christian tradition and European theology, with their intellectualist and fiducial emphases on assent and trust, respectively typical of Catholic and Protestant perspectives.[38] The intellectualist and fiducial understandings of Christian faith, as well as other views such as the mystical or illuminationist, are then replaced—or, at least, supplemented—with a notion that highlights the historical praxis of liberation. Two major related emphases can then be indicated in the liberationist constructive restatement of a theology of faith— justice as the primary analogue for biblical faith; and faith as the Christian's present mode of participation in the reign of God.

Faith as the Practice of Justice

Latin American liberationists have consistently focused theological reflection on the pressing reality of massive human suffering. Correspondingly they have also consistently proposed that the practice of justice must integrate Christian faith and love in effective responsibility for freedom at the level of social structures. Indeed, liberation theology contends that the practice of justice defines the distinctive shape of faith in our present historical situation. Several principles stemming from that major claim underscore converging concerns on Christian love for social transformation and discipleship for the reign of God.

Christian Love for Social Transformation. In the light of the biblical records, especially the ethical teaching and the ministry of Jesus, faith becomes practically identified with love of neighbor.[39] In this perspective the actual historical life of Jesus provides the historical grounding for the structure of Christian faith. The historical, moral, and loving nature of faith suggests that responsibility and voluntary action are intrinsic to the full and historically mediated reality of Christian faith. Further, the pervasive challenge of human suffering calls for the concern for social justice as a necessary intrinsic form of authentic Christian faith. This is so because such a concern is the determining form that structures faith's love for the neighbor.[40]

Simply stated, justice is that concrete form of love which "seeks to effectively humanize, to give life in abundance to the poor and oppressed majorities of the human race. . . . It is the form of love that is indispensable if the reign of God is to become a historical reality or if there is to be within history a reflection of the transhistorical utopian reality of that reign."[41] Sobrino goes on to highlight several historical features that distinguish justice from love in general and which, in his view, can generate a number of values essential to the gospel and to revelation generally. Those characteristics include the following: 1) Justice takes seriously the existence of the oppressed majorities (as well as the minorities), hence it also takes seriously the primordial fact of the *created world* in its present form. 2) Injustice and oppression reveal the destruction of the created order and the death of human beings which constitute the most radical negation of God's will and person. Justice thus concretely leads to the rediscovery of *sin*.

3) Justice attempts to recreate human beings and to make *life* possible for them. 4) Operating within history, justice requires the adoption of a *partisan* (for the weak, poor, oppressed) *and subjective perspective* (from below, from the underside of history) in the practice of love. 5) By fostering objective solidarity with the oppressed, justice promotes an *objective kenosis,* that is to say self-emptying or self-humbling. 6) The practice of love as justice often leads to a personal, radical *conversion* (i.e., the poor and oppressed often render a service to those who are trying to secure justice for them, thus realizing their privileged "evangelizing" potential, as we will indicate in chapter 5 of the present volume). 7) Justice highlights *service* as a major characteristic of love in which personal gratification does not often emerge as an immediate affective dimension (i.e., this service aspect of justice underscores the fact that love gives rather than receives). 8) In justice we move out, unconditionally and with a sense of urgency, to the poor and oppressed in order to make them our neighbors; hence, justice recovers the biblical notion of the *neighbor* as being not merely someone in close proximity to us but someone we *make* our neighbor. 9) More clearly than in other forms of love, justice tends to result in the *persecution* of those who practice it (i.e., sin thus shows its might and power in its historical reality against those who practice justice and are willing to "take up their cross," or the cost of discipleship). These historical features point to faith as the practice of justice as a basic demand of the gospel, essential to the following of Jesus today.[42]

Liberationists forcefully argue that justice is a necessary and historically privileged embodiment of Christian love. Several reasons are adduced to validate this argument: First, since the reign of God embraces the totality of human relationships, conforming to the God of all history requires that we see Christian love in terms of the totality of things which is implied in the ideal of justice. Second, the concretization of love in the form of justice has historically meant doing justice to the poor, the majority of the human race; justice is a necessary and effective way of enfleshing the biblical truth that God is partial to the poor and oppressed. Third, to give love the concrete expression of justice is to recall the unitive and mediating role of material things (i.e., persons are not pure spirits who relate to each other without material media). Fourth, injustice reveals the full extent of the evil that is sin, and justice concerns itself with the kind of oppressive relationships that arise among human beings which is sin par excellence (i.e., the usurpation of that which is the prerogative of God alone, namely dominion or lordship). Fifth, justice and injustice cut across the totality of human relations and their impact affects the forms these relations take in other types of grouping in the personal, familial, and associational arenas. Sixth, in the practice of justice the Christian paradox of the powerlessness of love becomes manifest with special or unique intensity (e.g., the risks and the potentially painful consequences of acting justly). Seventh, love as justice is a historical necessity in the face of both the current situation of the human race and the partially unmet responsibility of the church to embody this form of love (i.e., justice is a key for the Christian conscience of our day and the movement toward justice helps in the return of the church to its biblical roots).[43] In sum, faith and justice must be considered together as distinct but reciprocally related dimensions of the whole Christian response to the creative and liberating activity of God for the sake of the world. To be sure, the practice of justice does not exclude other expressions of authentic love from shaping the role of faith in Christian existence. Yet the practice of justice is necessary for faith to be in keeping both with its own content—the mystery of God—and with the demands of the present situation—massive human suffering.[44] The conception of Christian faith as a form of praxis is thus once again affirmed, a foundational affirmation, of course, in light of the definition of theology as critical reflection on Christian praxis (i.e., "Christian praxis seeking understanding," as it were).[45] By the same token, no understanding of faith which neglects justice as an intrinsic quality or form of faith is an adequate representation of Christian faith. Furthermore, all faith that lacks concern for social justice and social transformation is incomplete and suspect.[46]

Discipleship for the Reign of God. In liberationist perspective, any discussion of Christian faith must reiterate the centrality of its Christic structure together with its concern for the reign of God that Jesus taught and for which he lived and died. Faith is thus a practical way of life conceived in terms of commitment, following, doing and action, that is, discipleship oriented toward the coming kingdom. As indicated above in the discussion of discernment, discipleship consists in allowing the pattern or logic of Jesus' life and teaching to reveal or disclose a relationship with God through taking on or participating in that mode of redemptive—i.e., liberated and liberating—life. In other words, the first and primary way of knowing and loving God through Jesus Christ is by entering into the disclosive pattern of his life, a life characterized by love for the sake of the coming reign of God.[47] For Sobrino and others, the focus on discipleship for the reign of God provides the clue to resolve the question of relating faith and justice. A few additional comments on this matter might prove helpful.

The first and fundamental unity of the Christian faith is that God's reign—a reality in which people actually become brothers and sisters and children of God—should come into existence. Further, in the reality of the kingdom, which encompasses all areas of human life, history and transcendence become integrated and the vertical and horizontal dimensions of Christian existence are also unified together with two aspects of the human person— seeker of meaning and maker of meaning. Human beings appropriate meaning by allowing God to communicate with them; as meaning makers, they create meaning by cooperating in the building of God's reign. Therefore, faith and justice are brought into unity in the course of history, that is, in the interaction of building the kingdom and building it in obedience—i.e., in accordance with divine will: "Justice is the way in which the kingdom is built and becomes a reality. Faith is the way in which the kingdom exists in accordance with God, as well as the way in which meaning is found in the process of building, because the meaning comes from God."[48] Sobrino further suggests that the connection between the gratuitousness of faith and the requirements of ethical practice emerges in the new love commandment as stated in the Johannine writings, with an original approach to the link between faith and justice: God has taken the initiative by loving us first; we humans respond to divine love by conforming to its movement and loving "the brethren" (John 13:34; 15:12-17; 1 John 4:10, 19, 21; the synoptic gospels follow a comparable pattern by referring to the unity of the twofold commandment to love —Matthew 22:36-40; Mark 12:28-34; Luke 10:27). Faith is, then, not simply a human response to the love initially given by God, but it is also a concrete, historical and existential conformity to that love. And love, more than a requirement or a consequence of God's prior love for us, is also a constitutive factor in making possible the faith response. There is no opposition, then, between gratuitousness and human activity, because the most complete expression of gratuitousness is the "new hands" for doing, for fashioning a history at hand for the reign of God.[49] Finally, the continuity between the fullness of God's reign and history is to be found not in thought but in actual discipleship, in the faithful following of Jesus. Discipleship provides the living and the fashioning of a reality, of a kingdom "at hand," from which, at least in hope, an ultimate reality acquires meaning.[50]

Faith as Participation in God's Reign

The praxis way of knowing embraced by liberation theology includes a particular view of Christian faith with a strong emphasis on the practice of justice, as discussed previously. In this view, faith is understood in the face of the processive nature and dynamics of the unfolding, coming reign of God with its objective and subjective dimensions. Objectively, the faith that does justice corresponds to the mission of building God's reign which is evangelization in the fullest sense of the term (i.e., to evangelize is to make present the Good News that is becoming a Good Reality).[51] Subjectively—in the sense of the Christian active subjects who respond to and participate in God's work—the point is that one becomes a Christian disciple in the very process of concrete participation in constructing a "Christian" (i.e., God pleasing) reality. The becoming and the construction must be seen as a process.[52] Therefore, a liberationist redefinition of Christian faith suggests that *faith is the Christian's present mode of participation in the ongoing creative and liberating work of God in the world.* Having faith or, rather, being faithful, connotes that the reign of God effectively takes hold of persons and operates in them. Being faithful means becoming instruments in the transformational healing and reconciliation of the broken world; it means becoming agents of peace and justice and bearers of the power of God's reign. Therefore, more than intellectual assent and hope in what God will do without us, faith is also a present participation in what God is doing, namely the task of bringing *shalom*.[53] This conception of faith is especially significant in terms of the dialogical encounter between religious education and liberation theology.

Liberationists forcefully propose a normative and radical theological meaning of faith. Their proposal is consistent with a biblically grounded praxis epistemology including, as we have indicated, ethical and eschatological dimensions in a christological key. Liberationists also present a number of criteria or guidelines for interpreting and assessing faith—that is, what constitutes, indeed, faithful or obedient and appropriate participation in God's work in light of the mission of the church in the midst of the historical situation. Therefore, the potential significance of the liberationist contribution to Christian religious education becomes apparent, given the central concern of the church's educational ministry with the awakening, nurture, growth, and transformation of faith. This is, indeed, the case because, from the standpoint of the Christian ecclesial community, the view of the faith must emerge from within the faith community itself. In other words, the church and its educational ministry need a biblicotheological understanding of faith which involves, primarily, a theological task.

The liberationist theological view and its performative approach to faith may be then juxtaposed with other notions embraced or espoused by religious educationists. Of special interest in this connection is the understanding of faith proposed by Craig Dykstra who sees Christian faith as appropriate and intentional participation in the ongoing redemptive activity of God in the world.[54] While recognizing that faith is a reality of multiple dimensions which cannot be exhausted by just one meaning, Dykstra asserts that faith means to know and respond to God's redeeming activity by participating in it, and that we have been built into this in the church.[55] Broadly speaking, Dykstra proposes a certain performative approach to faith compatible with a liberationist theology of faith. The notion of "appropriate and intentional *participation*" certainly involves much more than praxis and doing justice as viewed in liberation theology.[56] However, a great deal of complementarity can be found in terms of what we have called discipleship for the reign of God. Thus,

Dykstra highlights the correlation of the gift of faith with God's character and action for the sake of the world, together with the view of faith as a willful, appropriate response, that is, faith as an activity which involves knowing and living on the part of the self as an active, intentional subject. Further, he asserts that participation in God's redemptive activity is transformational in nature. Such participation—which includes trust, loyalty, belief, commitment, and, especially, action—consists in finding a new life and following a new way that God has given to us and made possible.[57] Several implications relevant for faith development and religious education follow: 1) Growth or change in faith involves change in knowing and living; this growth or change is not necessarily progressive. 2) Growth in faith requires various particular kinds of practices in the arenas of worship, community, and mission, including certain intentional efforts such as Bible study and cultivating spiritual disciplines. 3) Those practices are in part expressions of growing faith as well as experiences through which growth in faith takes place. 4) Since participation in God's redemptive activity is an inexhaustible activity, there is no end to growing in faith. 5) Intentionality is an essential feature of Christian faith, hence the total dominant orientation of the self must be considered in the formation, transformation, and empowerment in Christ. 6) A number of capacities are needed to carry out the activity of faith; and what capacities are needed have to be determined by a theological description of faith together with the established criteria for discerning appropriate participation.[58]

It is obvious that such an understanding of faith coming from the field of religious education can complement the liberationist view. For its part, liberation theology can provide a supplement to that understanding in the light of its concern with suffering and oppression, its interest in freedom and social justice, and its commitment to the politics of the reign of God.

PRAXIS KNOWING AND RELIGIOUS EDUCATION

In the course of our discussion thus far, the value and the specific strengths of the liberationist epistemological perspective have become apparent together with its implicit limitations. Indeed, from the standpoint of religious education, both the assets and weaknesses must be examined in close relationship with each other. We will start this final section with a critical assessment of the contribution of liberation theology, indicating the main short-comings and ways to correct or to supplement the liberationist approach. Then we will suggest further ramifications of the inter-play between the two fields.

A Critical Appraisal

The liberationist view of knowing and Christian faith presents some limitations of special concern for religious education. We have chosen to highlight three of them which have to do with the danger of pragmatism and the questions of multidimensional faith and comprehensive orthopraxis. These three critical consid-erations must be seen, of course, as closely interconnected.

Danger of a Situational Pragmatism. The liberationist empha-sis on the historical and existential dimensions of truth with focus on praxis as obedience for understanding is certainly welcomed. A major question emerges, however, with regard to the possibility of evaluating Christian praxis on the basis of a norm somehow outside of historical praxis itself.[59] Assuming as we do that the end does not justify the means (in fact dichotomizing "ends" and "means" would be fallacious anyway) the challenge here is how to avoid the pitfall of a situational pragmatism, in the sense of the justification of functional praxis—i.e., praxis that "works"—for instance in the manner of political relevance or effectiveness. True, the Christian faith is not a gnosis but a way of life. Howev-er, Christian faith is specifically the way of Jesus Christ as special-ly informed by God's Word. Thus, there is still a message which is a logos to be appropriated; further we must affirm the substan-tive content of the epistemology of obedience in terms of the faithful confession of the lordship of Christ. Hence, praxis must be evaluated in light of criteria derived from revelation, and from biblical revelation especially[60] lest *doing* the truth becomes equiv-alent to *making* the truth through historical praxis, rather than *practicing* the truth which ultimately is being revealed to us.[61] In other words, praxis as the obedience of faith must occur in a historical contextual dialogue with scripture and the broader sto-ry of the Christian people and the vision of God's reign, including the church's teaching and discernment.[62] Appropriation of revelation and reflection on it must interface with the critical reflection on praxis. Therefore, for a fruitful conversation with a theological partner, religious education needs to confront not only the pitfalls of rationalistic and idealistic theologies concerned with "orthodoxy" narrowly defined but with the shortcomings of pragmatic theologies concerned with "orthopraxis" narrowly defined as well. Rather than emphasizing the unity of theory and practice, it is then preferable to highlight consistently the integration of *knowing* (theoretical or otherwise) and *obeying* with a twofold and simultaneous concern with both faithfulness to God's word and relevance to the historical situation. Praxis may then be seen as both reflective and contemplative as well as biblically anchored. Further, rather than primarily changing the world via social activism and politics and programs, the challenge for the educational ministry is learning and growth in obedience in all areas and levels of life including, to be sure, the socioeconomic and political realms.

Multidimensional Faith. The liberationist praxis way of knowing and view of Christian faith undoubtedly contributes needed correctives to traditional and popular epistemological views. Especially significant in this connection is the liberationist emphasis on active engagement in concretely living out biblical faith or the gospel of the reign of God (i.e., the faithful following of Jesus in the midst of the historical and existential situation). However, as already indicated in the previous chapter, there is a risk of overemphasizing "orthopraxis" thereby failing to restate the fullness and the multidimensional nature of the Christian faith, which is a central affirmation in the educational ministry. Two related shortcomings must be overcome. First, we should not simply subsume "orthodoxy" under "orthopraxis"; both must be seen in a mutually influencing or dialectical relationship. Further, while emphasizing the dialectical unity of orthodoxy and orthopraxis in the reality of the life of faith, we must also recognize that this dialectical unity is a unity in distinctness (i.e., *both* "word" *and* "deed" are involved).[63] Second, we must avoid reinforcing the oppositional dualism stated in terms of "orthopraxis" *versus* "orthodoxy"; after all, biblically speaking (especially in John) to believe truly is practically equivalent to living faithfully. These two principles are helpful to reaffirm the multidimensionality of

Christian faith from the standpoint of religious education, that is, beyond the performative liberationist approach.[64] In other words, faith dimensions such as conviction and belief, on the one hand, and personal trust and confidence, on the other hand, must not be undervalued;[65] further, interiority in the life of faith must be duly appreciated in a broader understanding of spirituality, which liberationists themselves in fact wish to embrace.[66] Third, the affirmation of the multidimensionality of biblical faith in turn invites us to highlight the *personal* as well as the *communal* nature of truth as convincingly presented in Parker Palmer's epistemology and spirituality of education.[67]

Comprehensive Orthopraxis. An additional question can be raised regarding the liberationist view of orthopraxis. This important question deals with the actual role of cognition in a well-rounded, holistic faith response and lifestyle. Given the pervasive emphasis on critical reflection in liberation theology,[68] it might be assumed that somehow cognitive knowing can directly elicit faithful action. That assumption, however, is no longer acceptable from the religious education viewpoint, as William Kennedy and others have argued.[69] Ironically enough, the assumption amounts to restating the psychology and epistemology that cognitive knowing is a sufficient prerequisite for action, which liberationists otherwise reject.[70] In any case, from the perspective of religious education the notion of a cognitively based lifestyle must be corrected. We need a more comprehensive view which includes various registers of behavior (e.g., the rich and complex affective domain), highlights the role of creative imagination,[71] and represents indeed a more holistic understanding, as the very concept of discipleship connotes.

Religious Education for Justice and Peace

Our treatment of a praxis epistemological foundation directly relates to the dialogical encounter between religious education and liberation theology which is presented in the first two chapters of this book. In fact, our present agenda develops and expands the main themes there introduced. In chapter 1 we focused on principles of liberating teaching and learning process in the context of the overall discussion of conscientization, liberation, and creativity. In chapter 2 we concentrated on the paradoxical symbol of the reign of God leading to a fundamental restatement of the guiding principle and the principal aim of Christian religious education; we concluded by highlighting a strong summons to reaffirm a prophetic stance and commitment to transformation. Justice and peace indeed become key foci in the liberationist approach to the educational ministry. In the light of the liberationist praxis epistemology, the guiding principle and the overall aim of religious education further point to the commitment to doing justice and making peace. Such a commitment requires a refocusing of concerns, the development of an adequate methodological approach, and a redefinition of Christian disciples as compassionate and responsible change agents.

Refocusing Concerns. One essential dimension of the overall aim of Christian religious education is *appropriation of the gospel of the reign of God by promoting social transformation for the increase of freedom, justice, and peace,* as explained in the previous chapter. This specific purpose of the educational ministry, seen in the context of a prophetic and servant view of the church, calls for religious education to be explicitly concerned with and involved in society's political and socioeconomic realms.[72] The corresponding political theory must face and deal adequately with a number of issues such as the question of uses and abuses of power, manifold expressions of oppression and of the search for justice and peace, the role of ideology and interest, the dynamics of social conflict, and the educational and political strategies. Such is the agenda articulated by Brian Wren and some other religious educationists.[73] Of particular interest in this area is the work of Suzanne Toton with regard to the evil of world hunger and the broader challenge of the public and political responsibility for Christian religious education. Toton proposes that those religious educators who are committed to the struggle for justice should move beyond education for consciousness raising (in the narrow sense of the term) and for value change. She contends that if justice is to be central to religious education, it must play a key role in effecting structural, systemic, and institutional transformation. In other words, a major concern and purpose of religious education becomes actual participation in creating a better world.[74] The task requires an adaptation of social analysis,[75] discernment of specific possibilities for change and the contours of responsibility toward a given situation, and concrete action for justice and peace as constitutive of the educational process.

Reorienting the Approach. Religious education for justice and peace necessitates the action-reflection paradigm as overarching dialectical process of learning, teaching, and transformation. More than a pedagogical strategy, the action-reflection paradigm encompasses a wide variety of activities in tune with the very mission of the church in the world. "Believing" and "doing" must be brought together in a mutually influencing dynamic relationship. Thus Sara Little indicates that the focus is on doing the gospel truth with reflective, critical thinking which informs and evaluates action; the "deed" of obedience is to inform and confirm the "word" of belief. "Praxis," as the dialectical interaction of action and critical reflection may thus become a means of enabling relationships among the cognitive, volitional, and conative dimensions of the self.[76] A number of processes are included, such as immersion into a given situation and "coversion" (i.e., making values explicit, or turning to values), observation, and description; analysis and use of both scripture and tradition as well as contemporary disciplines; problematizing and problem-solving; actual testing and revising assumptions; and further action and reflection.

Closely related to the substantive process questions of the action-reflection approach in religious education for justice and peace, we must include consistent teaching principles (structural process content) per se and the status and role of the educator, as indicated in the first chapter of the present volume. In short, in the words of Thomas Groome, because the ultimate purpose of Christian religious education is to lead people out toward the reign of God, it must *educate justly* and *for justice.*[77]

Christian Disciples as Active Subjects. Critically speaking, religious education for justice and peace amounts to confronting the values and habits of acquiescence, comfort, and respectability present in much of the religious education scene in North America. Indeed, the formation, transformation, and empowerment of young and adult disciples involves, on the one hand, confronting domestication (i.e., strategies for mere adjustment and compliance), indifference or silence, conformity and complicity with structures of injustice and oppression. On the other hand, there is a summons for active participation in God's reign as *compassionate and responsible change agents.* Thus Michael Warren proposes to reimagine the lives and the role of young people in church and society along the lines of Jesus' imagination. He contends that helping youth to rename reality, questioning the metaphors that interpret reality and finding forms of political action, become consistent objectives for religious education for youth, especially in the context of a "politicization" program aimed at critical consciousness and active commitment to justice and peace.[78]

It is apparent that compassionate and responsible involvement in social justice and change present a formidable challenge for religious education. The reason for that is probably threefold— the area of societal transformation is the weakest, the most difficult to educate for, and the most urgent to be approached. From a liberationist standpoint, North American and other First World religious education for justice and peace must deal with at least two interrelated issues—first, socioeconomic and political structures which internally maintain and justify alienation and oppression for both poor and non-poor;[79] and second, structures of domination in terms of imperialist and neocolonialist (e.g., related to world market system) policies, especially with regard to Latin America. Models of "transformative" education presented as pedagogies for the non-poor offer helpful guidelines for sponsoring Christian disciples as change agents on a variety of settings.[80]

Finally, by focusing on the formation, enablement, and empowerment of Christian disciples as compassionate and responsible agents of change, religious education aims at fostering not only societal transformation but the very maturing of faith itself.[81] The case can be made that the work for social justice is a necessary component of faith growth, as Ronald Marstin contends in terms of James Fowler's theory of faith development.[82] In fact, it can also be argued, beyond Fowler's cognitive-structuralist developmental perspective, a holistic commitment to social justice and peace is also necessary for the growth of faith understood as participation in the creative and liberating activity of God for the sake of the world.

Defining the Emerging Model. This chapter thus far suggests a number of principles for practice and theory in light of the encounter between religious education and liberation theology and the resulting mutual enlightenment for both fields in interplay. Further material for a more complete picture of religious education in a liberation key is presented in the next two chapters; meanwhile we can already characterize the emerging model of religious education as *radical sociopolitical;* as corresponding to a *revisionist* tradition; and as a *contemporary theological approach* with an *immanentist* theoretical perspective.

First, we perceive a reaffirmation of a Freire-inspired (i.e., "conscientizing") religious education for liberation, creativity, and peace and justice, which explicitly underscores, in Kenneth Barker's terms, the *political* approach to an education for freedom. This position is taken by those critical of a privatized arena of human freedom who emphasized the sociopolitical dimensions of freedom as both emancipation—freedom "from"—and enablement and empowerment—freedom "for" participating in the work of God's coming reign of justice and peace.[83] Further, as religious education for power and liberation, it represents a reconstructionist (i.e., oriented to societal transformation)[84] radical sociopolitical perspective, in John L. Elias' words, especially in the case of the religious education of youth and adults.[85]

Second, this emerging liberationist model may also be seen as a contribution within a *revisionist* standpoint of *Christian* religious education. This tradition is characterized by Kieran Scott as moving beyond ecclesiastical socialization by promoting both internal critical inquiry of tradition(s) and external reflectiveness on the public world. Indeed, the revisionist perspective fosters a critical dialectical, and intentional response to the historical and conditioning forces in the church community and its socio-cultural environment.[86]

Third, defined primarily as an *ecclesial* educational ministry the practice and theory of *Christian* religious education in a liberation key requires a strong infusion of theology as already indicated in chapter 2, thus fitting the description of a *contemporary theological approach* in Harold Burgess' typology.[87] Such an approach in fact focuses upon an organic relationship between religious education and the Christian ecclesial community in which theological input and reflection play a normative role. In our case, it is clear that the liberationist view emphasizes history and the immanence of the supernatural (e.g., God's indwelling power for freedom and creativity). Conversely, the liberationist perspective minimizes the distinctions between the sacred and the secular, and the workings of divine grace and human effort, among other common dualisms. In Ian Knox's terms, the theological metaperspective of liberationism can be seen as *immanentist*.[88] In the work for liberation, justice, and peace, Christian disciples participate with Christ in this world in bringing about the realization of the reign of God within history.

In sum, the encounter between religious education and liberation theology highlights a model of education which is dialogical and conscientizing, prophetic and eschatological in vision, and praxis oriented. We can also anticipate that the model calls for a critico-hermeneutical perspective and a communal ecclesial context at the service of God's mission in the world. On these two latter characteristics we must respectively concentrate our attention in the next chapters.

Notes

1. John 7:17.
2. José Míguez Bonino, *Christians and Marxists: The Mutual Challenge to Revolution* (Grand Rapids, Mich.: Eerdmans, 1976), pp. 40-41.
3. Thomas H. Groome, *Christian Religious Education: Sharing Our Story and Vision* (San Francisco: Harper & Row, 1980), p. 149.
4. Notice that this gospel passage is closely related to the one chosen for the first chapter of the present volume—John 8:31-32. The setting is the Feast of Tabernacles (or Booths, or Shelters) which was a week-long, joyous, thanksgiving festival celebrated by the Israelites in autumn after the completion of the harvest. It was a liberation festival—i.e., the Exodus was the key to the journey toward the promised land—commemorating God's protection of Israel during the wilderness wanderings (Leviticus 23:39-43; Nehemias 8:13-18). Starting with 7:1, John makes clear that Jesus is confronting an aggressive opposition and open hostility on the part of "the Jews." Jesus is not sure whether he should go to Jerusalem or not. Finally he does go in secret (7:6-10) and soon afterwards he is found teaching in the midst of that hostile setting. For an illuminating discussion of Jesus' praxis and teaching that addresses in detail the questions of freedom, liberating truth, and radical discipleship, see C. Hugo Zorrilla, "The Obedient Disciple: Agent of Liberation (John 8:31-32)," in *Freedom and Discipleship: Liberation Theology in Anabaptist Perspective,* ed. Daniel S. Schipani (Maryknoll, N.Y.: Orbis, forthcoming).
5. Frederick Herzog puts it well: Jesus does not promote himself, neither does he "authorize" himself. Rather, his teaching, unverifiable by sophisti-

cated intellectual argument, must be checked out by life. People must act their way into a new way of thinking rather than think their way into a new acting. This is a central concern of the Fourth Gospel. *(Liberation Theology: Liberation in the Light of the Fourth Gospel* [New York: Seabury, 1972] p. 111.)

6. We may underscore here that Jesus exposes an often oppressive cultural and political structure, namely the association of formal schooling and authority with a power issue including prestige, intellectual credibility, and social respectability. Indeed, even today, prominent teachers often become "masters" whose students are honored, in turn, for the privilege of studying *under* them (in fact, often serving them slavishly, as in the case of many a doctoral program.) Obviously, the situation invites these disciples to hope not so subtly that, one day, they too will become masters possessing knowledge to be handed down to others while enjoying power and public recognition.

7. Míguez Bonino, *Christians and Marxists,* pp. 35-36.

8. Ibid., pp. 37-38. On this matter, see also Groome's discussion in *Christian Religious Education,* pp. 143-144.

9. Freire asserts: "I see 'education as the practice of freedom' above all as a truly gnosiological situation. . . . In the education process for liberation, educator-educatee and educatee-educator are both cognitive subjects before knowable objects which mediate them." (Paulo Freire, *Education for Critical Consciousness* [New York: Seabury 1973], p. 149.) Freire's contribution to philosophy of education is due in part to the fact that the relationship between philosophy and education is especially apparent with regard to the theory of knowing and the theory of learning. Indeed, epistemology—the philosophical discipline which deals with the source and nature of knowing and with the validity and reliability of knowledge—has always been a fruitful source for a variety of fecund educational ideas. The reason for this foundational and relevant role on the part of epistemology in educational philosophy is at least threefold: 1) epistemology studies how human beings take hold of their world: 2) epistemology is a necessary check on the credibility of knowledge as well as a body of fundamental theory underlying the nature of the human mind and how it functions; 3) theories of knowledge and truth are, in a certain way, direct pointers to theories of learning (and, obviously, learning theory is central in any educational task). See Van Cleve Morris and Young Pai, *Philosophy and the American School: An Introduction to the Philosophy of Education* (Boston: Houghton Mifflin, 1976), pp. 169-170.

10. This topic is considered in depth in the next chapter. In that chapter we will deal at length with the references to commitment to praxis, epistemological break, and the "practical mediation" as methodological movement, as well as the principle of the primacy of orthopraxis in biblical interpretation.

11. Those and related themes are treated in the final chapter, in connection with the wider issue of the ecclesial context of the Christian base communities.

12. José Míguez Bonino, *Doing Theology in a Revolutionary Situation* (Philadelphia: Fortress, 1975), p. 88.

13. Míguez Bonino, *Christians and Marxists,* p. 30.

14. Míguez Bonino, *Doing Theology in a Revolutionary Situation*, p. 88.

15. Gustavo Gutiérrez, "Liberation Praxis and Christian Faith," in *Frontiers of Theology in Latin America*, ed. Rosino Gibellini (Maryknoll, N.Y.: Orbis, 1979), pp. 1-33.

16. Hugo Assmann, *Theology for a Nomad Church*, trans. Paul Burns (Maryknoll, N.Y.: Orbis, 1976), pp. 74-86.

17. José P. Miranda, *Marx and the Bible: A Critique of the Philosophy of Oppression*, trans. John Eagleson (Maryknoll, N.Y.: Orbis, 1974).

18. Míguez Bonino, *Christians and Marxists*, p. 40.

19. Míguez Bonino, *Doing Theology in a Revolutionary Situation*, p. 89.

20. Míguez Bonino, *Christians and Marxists*, p. 35.

21. Ibid., p. 40.

22. It is obvious that Christian religious education must give primary consideration to adopting a way of knowing consistent with the very reason for being and the purposes of the educational ministry. Thomas Groome spells out clearly his own view of the biblical way of knowing which nicely harmonizes with the liberationist epistemological understandings discussed in this chapter. Groome underscores the following: biblical faith and knowing is deeply experiential and relational in nature; God takes the initiative in the knowing-loving relationship with the people; knowing God demands active acknowledgement of the divine as Ruler and in turn calls for obedience to God's will (i.e., God is truly known in experience and obedient response); biblically speaking, ignorance is synonymous with guilt. In sum, Groome affirms that, in the biblical view, people come to know God in the midst of historical experience by reflecting on the activity of God there, by entering a relationship with God and God's people, and by their lived response to that relationship. Groome adds that their knowing is informed by and interpreted through the Story that has arisen from the previous "knowing" of God's people and is shaped by the hopes they have in the divine promise for their future. Then, from a biblical standpoint, "Christian religious education should be grounded in a relational/experiential/reflective way of knowing that is informed by the Story of faith from Christians before us, and by the Vision toward which that Story points." *Christian Religious Education*, pp. 141-145.

23. Jon Sobrino, *The True Church and the Poor*, trans. Matthew J. O'Connell (Maryknoll, N.Y.: Orbis, 1984), pp. 10-38.

24. Ibid., pp. 11, 20. Sobrino asserts that in "European theology" the starting point is the familiar and classical presupposition that there is a deposit of truth that must be transmitted, explained, interpreted, and made meaningful. Further, he states that it is in response to the challenge of the first phase of the Enlightenment, that this theology has produced the movement of depositivization, the historical-critical work in exegesis, the interpretation of dogma, and the development of various hermeneutics; all of these in its efforts to liberate faith and theology from historical error, authoritarianism, and myth, and from the obscuring of the meaning of Christian faith. Theological understanding is here supposed to be liberating by explaining the truth of faith and—when that meaning is under attack—by somewhat restoring the faith meaning. That is to say that the crises in the real world are viewed, theologically, as crises of meaning. (For Latin American liberation theology, however, the main interest is the

liberation of the real world from its wretched state, since the objective situations of oppression and suffering obscure the meaning of faith. In other words, rather than restoring the meaning of a threatened faith, the challenge taken up by liberation theology is the restoration of meaning to reality itself by assisting in the transformation of its sinful condition).

25. Ibid., p. 15.
26. The question of method in liberation theology is treated in detail in the next chapter of the present volume as a continuation of the discussion of praxis epistemology. See also the first two parts of chapter 5 concerning solidarity and the praxis of suffering and related topics, as further ramifications of the paradigmatic methodological stance of Latin American liberation theology. For the most comprehensive treatise to date on the epistemological grounding of liberation theology, see Clodovis Boff, *Theology and Praxis: Epistemological Foundations,* trans. Robert R. Barr (Maryknoll, N.Y.: Orbis, 1987). For a broader discussion of praxis and theological method, see Matthew L. Lamb, ed., *Creativity and Method: Essays in Honor of Bernard Lonergan* (Milwaukee: Marquette University Press, 1981), especially the essays by David Tracy—"Theologies of Praxis," pp. 35-51, and Matthew L. Lamb—"Praxis and Generalized Empirical Method," pp. 53-77. See also Matthew L. Lamb, *Solidarity with Victims: Toward a Theology of Social Transformation* (New York: Crossroads, 1982).
27. Leonardo Boff y Clodovis Boff, *Cómo Hacer Teología de la Liberación* (Madrid: Paulinas, 1986), p. 18.
28. Sobrino, *The True Church and the Poor,* p. 23.
29. Ibid., p. 24.
30. Jon Sobrino, *Jesus in Latin America,* trans. Robert R. Barr (Maryknoll, N.Y.: Orbis, 1987), p. 16.
31. Sobrino, *The True Church and the Poor,* p. 25.
32. See 1 Corinthians 1:18-31. Interestingly, Paul juxtaposes two different but, to a certain extent, complementary "normal" epistemologies—the Jews' who demand miraculous signs and the Greeks' who look for wisdom—as equally contrary to the power and wisdom of God in Christ, and to the cross particularly. "Stumbling block" and "madness" apply to "Jews" and "Gentiles" respectively when it comes to the presentation of the cross of Christ, unless conversion take place and the way of the cross is followed (with the fruits of holiness, righteousness, and redemption, 1 Corinthians 1:30).
33. Sobrino, *The True Church and the Poor,* p. 27.
34. Sobrino, *Jesus in Latin America,* p. 131. In this section on the process and structure of Christian discernment, we present, essentially, a summary of Sobrino's key considerations in his chapter 5, "Following Jesus as Discernment," pp. 131-139.
35. Ibid., p. 135.
36. Ibid., p. 139.
37. The reference to an "epistemology of obedience" comes from Cornelius J. Dyck in his work on sixteenth-century Anabaptism. Dyck has observed a correlation Anabaptists believed to exist between obedience to the known will of God and right biblical understanding and thinking, between obedience and the experience of further revelation. In other words, radical

obedience is there viewed as a major presupposition for biblical understanding. Furthermore, apprehension of new faith truths—knowing,
"orthodoxy"—is directly related to actual faithfulness in discipleship, the
following of Jesus—doing, "orthopraxis." Hence, discipleship *(Nachfolge
Christi)* has epistemological importance in connection with right thinking
(vera theologia) and is therefore much more than a question of piety and
ethics in the narrow sense of the terms. Further, discipleship, i.e., the way
to know Christ through conversion and following the "way of the cross,"
becomes participation in the very nature of God through the enabling
grace of the Holy Spirit. This epistemology thus poses a positive correlation between "practical" obedience and "spiritual" knowledge. (C. J.
Dyck, "Hermeneutics and Discipleship," in *Essays on Biblical Interpretation: Anabaptist-Mennonite Perspectives,* ed. Willard M. Swartley [Elk-
hart, Ind.: Institute of Mennonite Studies, 1984], pp. 29-44.) In the same
volume, see also, Ben C. Ollenburger, "The Hermeneutics of Obedience,"
pp. 45-61. For a comprehensive critical and dialogical overview of liberationist understanding in light of the Radical Reformation-Believers
Church tradition, Schipani, ed. *Freedom and Discipleship.*

38. On this and related topics, see the illuminating discussion of liberationist
views of faith in Avery Dulles, "The Meaning of Faith Considered in
Relationship to Justice," in *The Faith That Does Justice,* ed. John C.
Haughey (New York: Paulist, 1977), pp. 10-46. Dulles concludes that
liberation theology sees faith as a transforming acceptance of the Word,
which comes as a free gift of God, breaking into human existence through
the poor and oppressed, with whom Christ is seen to identify himself.
Dulles affirms the liberationist perspective for proposing the dialectical
interweaving of praxis and contemplation as a dynamic view of faith with
a solid biblical base. He also asserts that the corrective liberation theory of
faith is able to cope with the challenges raised by the sociotechnical civilization. Further, Dulles perceives that the liberationist view harmonizes
well with the growing sense of the power of human initiative to shape life
on this earth at the service of God's reign and that it is fully in tune with
the increased sense of human responsibility for the future of the world.
(Dulles' reservations regarding the liberationist view of faith are mentioned below, in note 65).

39. See Gustavo Gutiérrez, *A Theology of Liberation,* trans. Caridad Inda and
John Eagleson (Maryknoll, N.Y.: Orbis, 1973), pp. 198-203.

40. In this discussion I am partially indebted to Roger Haight for his treatment
of the liberationist conception of faith, in *An Alternative Vision: An Interpretation of Liberation Theology* (New York: Paulist, 1985), chapter 4,
"The Theology of Faith and the Ultimate Concern for Justice," pp. 64-82.
Haight discusses the main themes that govern the liberationist theology of
faith such as the assumption of an existential and historical approach, the
identification of faith and love, the question of faith as Christian praxis,
discipleship, and the reign of God. He also generalizes upon these themes
and articulates a certain theology of faith that includes the liberationist
contribution and seeks to be relevant to all Christians at the present age.

41. Sobrino, *The True Church and the Poor,* pp. 47, 53.

42. Ibid., pp. 50-53.

43. Ibid., pp. 76-79.

44. Ibid., p. 55.

45. Gutiérrez, "Liberation Praxis and Christian Faith."

46. Haight, *An Alternative Vision,* pp. 78, 80. Haight agrees with liberationists that concern for justice for whole groups of people who are alienated, marginated, and oppressed into social bondage and suffering as an intrinsic form of faith is a new teaching corresponding to a new historical consciousness and social awareness characteristic of our time. He adds that such a teaching depends on a realization of social structures and situations as changeable human structures, of social interdependence, and of the ways in which all people participate in those situations. Haight goes on to state that the insight regarding the social justice concern is in fact continuous with (and does not go beyond) Jesus' teaching on the reign of God and his manifestation of the informing power of this symbol in Jesus' own life. Further, the urgency and centrality of such a concern is augmented when we recall the primacy of the moral dimension of faith as the indicator of faith's reality and authenticity: "Active concern for other human beings on a social level, although never to the exclusion of concern for other levels of personal and transcendent freedom, constitutes real union with God by an implied faith" (p. 80).

47. Ibid., pp. 76, 81. It may be helpful for the reader to review the discussion of Jesus Christ liberator and the gospel of the reign of God in the second chapter of the present volume.

48. Sobrino, *The True Church and the Poor,* pp. 73-74.

49. Ibid.

50. Sobrino, *Jesus in Latin America,* p. 95. For Sobrino, the following of Jesus is the primordial locus of all Christian theological epistemology and, hence, of the understanding of eschatology as well. He asserts that the *thought* tension between gift of God and human task dissolves in Jesus' discipleship, where grace is *experienced,* not just in new ears for hearing the good news, but also—and furthermore as fullness of grace—in new hands for participating in the work of history making for the sake of God's coming reign: "The *thought* tension between the present and future of the kingdom is *experienced* as undying hope. In the *praxis* of love and justice one knows that the kingdom is at hand, is becoming present, and in conflictive *praxis* in the midst of the world's sin one maintains hope in God's future." (Ibid.)

51. Sobrino, *The True Church and the Poor,* p. 75

52. Ibid.

53. This performative, liberationist understanding of Christian faith is also highlighted by Avery Dulles in "The Meaning of Faith Considered in Relationship to Justice," pp. 43-44.

54. That faith is *participation in the redemptive activity of God,* is the first of five theses presented by Dykstra in a nicely crafted statement (his inaugural address as Thomas W. Synnott Professor of Christian Education at Princeton Theological Seminary) of a vision for the church's educational ministry, "No Longer Strangers: The Church and Its Educational Ministry," *The Princeton Seminary Bulletin* 6:3 (November, 1985), pp. 188-200. In that address, Dykstra establishes the fundamental connection between the church and faith. He states that "in Christ by the Spirit in the church we are being called into, led into, built into participation in the ongoing

redemptive activity of God in the world. We do not take over that activity for God. We do not exhaust that activity. But being built into it does mean that we come to know of it and are called to respond to it, living our lives and carrying out our own activity in the world in a way that is so governed by God's activity that we in fact participate in it with God" (p. 192).

55. Ibid. For Dykstra, then, the faith community is the privileged context of participation (thesis 2); and growing in faith involves the deepening and widening of participation in the church's life and mission (thesis 3). Further, given the peculiar nature of the church's practices, appropriate and intentional participation necessitates learning and teaching (thesis 4); finally, Christian education is the dialogical process of teaching and learning through which the faith community comes to know and participate ever more fully in the redemptive transformation of personal and societal life that God is carrying out (thesis 5).

56. See Dykstra's essay "What is Faith?: An Experiment in the Hypothetical Mode," in *Faith Development and Fowler,* ed. Craig Dykstra and Sharon Parks (Birmingham, Ala.: Religious Education Press, 1986), pp. 45-64. Dykstra here proposes his understanding of Christian faith as an alternative to the view of faith present in James W. Fowler's structural developmental theory of faith development. In the same book, Fowler finds Dykstra's approach illuminating as an alternative which is complementary to faith development theory, and he joins Dykstra in the affirmation that "faith is a 'doing,' a spiritual praxis that involves skills, intentionality, and faithful action." "Dialogue Toward a Future in Faith Development Studies," p. 285.

57. Ibid., pp. 55-57.

58. Ibid., pp. 59-62.

59. For these observations on the danger of pragmatism in the liberationist epistemology I am partially indebted to C. René Padilla, "Liberation Theology: A Critical Appraisal," in *Freedom and Discipleship.*

60. This challenge is addressed by liberation theologians in terms of their redefinition of theology as a hermeneutical task consisting in critical reflection on Christian praxis *in the light of the Word.* The topic is dealt with in detail in the next chapter of the present volume.

61. Padilla, "Liberation Theology."

62. In connection with this reference to praxis evaluation, Groome has proposed some guidelines for discerning the meaning of God's activity in history and appropriate faith responses. Those guidelines refer to *continuity* (past orientation), *consequences* (future orientation), and *community/ church* (present orientation). Groome contends that if we 1) maintain continuity with and faithfulness to the Story of the Christian people, 2) choose a response that is appropriate to the Vision of the reign of God, and 3) are informed by the teaching and learning of the whole church as well as by our own group discernment, then, with the help of the Holy Spirit (i.e., the Spirit of truth who will guide us into all truth, according to Jesus' teaching, John 16:13) we are most likely to discern God's will for us and what our response should be. *(Christian Religious Education,* pp. 197-201.)

63. At this point it is fair to say that a restatement of the liberationist emphasis on the unity of theory and practice (or, rather, knowing and obedience, as

suggested above) is itself also, at least partially, an expression of the Western theoretical tradition often castigated by liberationists. Further, in the light of this intellectual tradition religious faith often becomes an ideology for bringing about structural social change, among other things. More will be said about ideology and ideological captivity in the next chapter; for now it suffices to indicate that a symptom of the tendency for Christian faith to operate ideologically in liberation theology (as well as in other theological perspectives, to be sure) is the absence of significant self-critique.

64. Thomas Groome, who has adopted a praxis epistemology akin to the liberationist view, does present a multidimensional notion of Christian faith which includes three essential and constitutive dimensions: 1) a belief conviction (cognitive dimension); 2) a trusting relationship (affective dimension); and 3) a lived life of agape (behavioral dimension). For Groome, lived Christian faith—as believing, trusting, and doing—is the immediate purpose of Christian religious education (education for the reign of God being the ultimate purpose.) (Groome, *Christian Religious Education,* pp. 56-66, 73-81.)

65. Using a slightly different language, Avery Dulles states that faith includes three aspects: "a firm conviction regarding what is supremely important, dedication or commitment to what one believes in, and trustful reliance on the power and goodness of that to which one stands committed. The three components of faith are thus conviction, commitment, and trust." (Dulles, "The Meaning of Faith Considered in Relationship to Justice," p. 31. For a discussion of those three dimensions, see also Dulles' *The Survival of Dogma* [Garden City, N.J.: Doubleday, 1973], pp. 15-30.) For Dulles, the theories of faith, including that of liberation theology, can be mutually complementary and mutually corrective. His reservations regarding the liberationist performative approach arise at the point where he sees liberation theology adopting the specific theses of Marxian social analysis. Thus he indicates the following concerns: 1) The liberationist emphasis on external activity and societal involvement and transformation runs the risk of minimizing the dimension of interiority in the reality of faith. 2) Faith must not be viewed as a reaction to the historical situation rather than as a response to a personal call from God (i.e., without denying the historical mediation of faith, we may continue to insist that God succeeds in making Self immediately present to the human spirit, as shown by the transcendental theologians). 3) The assumed correspondence between gospel and Marxian analysis is sometimes too neat to allay the suspicion that the Bible is read through the eyes of those who are already convinced Marxists (e.g., the potential idealization of the poor and oppressed and the insistence of some liberationists that Jesus Christ is to be found necessarily in the poor and oppressed). 4) The liberationist rhetoric could engender confusion at the points of appearing to suggest that sociopolitical revolution is an essential means of bringing the poor and oppressed the salvation promised by the gospel. (Ibid. pp. 39-42.)

66. For expression of Latin American liberationist spirituality, see Leonardo Boff, *The Lord's Prayer: The Prayer of Integral Liberation,* trans. Theodore Morrow (Maryknoll, N.Y.: Orbis, 1984); Segundo Galilea, *Following Jesus,* trans. Helen Phillips (Maryknoll, N.Y.: Orbis, 1981), and *The Beati-*

tudes: To Evangelize as Jesus Did, trans. Robert R. Barr (Maryknoll, N.Y.: Orbis, 1984); Gustavo Gutiérrez, *We Drink from Our Own Wells, The Spiritual Journey of a People,* trans. Matthew J. O'Connell (Maryknoll, N.Y.: Orbis, 1984). (It could be suggested that liberation theology needs to enter into a serious dialogue with psychology and other social-scientific disciplines in order to supplement its fruitful interaction with other fields such as sociology and economics. The understanding of the human predicament and particularly the complex reality of faith itself could thus be enhanced). See also John L. Elias, *Studies in Theology and Education* (Malabar, Fla.: Krieger, 1986), chapter 14, "Liberation Spirituality: Theology and Models."

67. Parker J. Palmer, *To Know As We Are Known: A Spirituality of Education* (San Francisco: Harper & Row, 1983) especially chapters 1 and 4. Palmer emphasizes that the Christian tradition understands truth to be embodied in personal terms and that an education shaped by Christian spirituality draws us toward incarnate and personal truth, that is, a personal knowledge for healing and wholeness. He also asserts that we must look at the whole person whose authentic nature is to know in dialogical relationships, in a mutual process of transformation in which all parties subject themselves to the bonds of communal "troth." The intimate link between loving and knowing (and ethics and epistemology) implicit throughout the Bible—and explicitly stated in John—is consistently discussed by Palmer (pp. 1-18, 47-68).

68. Further critical comments regarding the liberationist focus on critical reflection appear in chapters 1 and 4 of the present volume.

69. William Bean Kennedy, "Toward Reappraising Some Inherited Assumptions About Religious Education in the United States," *Religious Education* 76:5 (September-October 1981), pp. 467-474. Kennedy asserts that, while logically we tend to affirm a dynamic interrelationship and balance between knowledge and action, or "content" and "experience," on the practical level it is easy to operate on a sequential assumption. He contends that religious education needs continually to radically reappraise the rationalistic assumption that learning occurs first in the head then in the heart and hands and feet. Further, he remarks that efforts to balance cognitive and affective (and physical); to explore right- and left-lobe types of experience; to rediscover and articulate the wholeness of learning continue to be important. In another essay, Kennedy analyzes two major questions related to the tension between cognitive knowing and right action, namely, how strategies of religious education have affected the knowledge-action issue and how the emerging ethical issues which demand religious action have influenced the "curriculum" in the educational work of religious educators. ("Pursuing Peace and Justice. A Challenge to Religious Educators," *Religious Education* 78:4 [Fall, 1983]: 467-476. See also the responses to Kennedy's paper in the same issue, pp. 477-524.)

70. By the same token, an analogous concern of serious import can be raised in the case of Groome's shared praxis approach to religious education. In the conceptualization of the approach, shared *reflection* (that is, reflection in terms of the plurality of individual "praxis") is not necessarily accompanied and followed in the selfsame lesson by an actual experience of social *action* as something intrinsic to the process. This point has also been

picked up by other authors such as Dermot Lane who critically notes that in Groome's approach the follow-through of conversion, decisions, and choices arising out of the Christian story and vision is not sufficiently embraced as constitutive of the process of religious education. ("The Challenge Facing Religious Education Today," in *Religious Education and the Future,* ed. Dermot A. Lane [New York: Paulist, 1986], pp. 155-156.) In other words, at least the impression is given that critical reflection and dialectical hermeneutics will somehow lead directly to action or to effectively carrying out the "faith responses" generated in the fifth movement of the "shared praxis approach." For a trenchant critique of Groome's contribution, see James Michael Lee, *The Content of Religious Instruction* (Birmingham, Ala.: Religious Education Press, 1985), pp. 72-73, 76-77, 702-703, 740-742. Lee repeatedly points out that "shared praxis" is not truly an action-reflection approach but, essentially, a cognitive pedagogical method and endeavor. Further, he asserts that there is no empirical evidence to support Groome's claim that "shared praxis" is indeed an effective teaching procedure. See also, for example, James Michael Lee, "The Blessings of Religious Pluralism," in *Religious Pluralism and Religious Education,* ed. Norma H. Thompson (Birmingham, Ala.: Religious Education Press, 1988), p. 117.

71. Having stated our concern with Groome's pedagogical approach (see note 70) it is fair to add that in later writings Groome has suggested that religious education must promote a way of knowing in which the creative imagination plays a major role. For instance, in his response to Kennedy—"Old Task: Urgent Challenge" (see note no. 69)—Groome alludes to the contributions of Amos Wilder, Kathleen Fischer, James Loder, and, especially, Sharon Parks. He affirms that the imagination can indeed hold our knowing and doing in dialectical unity and transcend the false dichotomy between the two. Imagination can thus bridge faith and action, religion and life, knowledge and power, and "outside" action and "inside" reflection. The challenge is, then, to gain a deeper understanding of the workings of imagination and how to intentionally engage that faculty in the religious education context. See also in chapter 1 of the present volume the reference to imagination and creativity in restating the Freirean, liberationist contribution, and chapter 2 in Daniel S. Schipani, *Conscientization and Creativity: Paulo Freire and Christian Education* (Lanham, Md.: University Press of America, 1984). Further correction and supplementation of the liberationist view of praxis knowing and faith that underscore the central role of spirit and imagination can be found in the following two fine essays: Maria Harris, "Completion and Faith Development," and Sharon Parks, "Imagination and Spirit in Faith Development: A Way Past the Structure-Content Dichotomy," in *Faith Development and Fowler,* pp. 115-156.

72. John Elias discusses the correlations between the "public of society" (together with the "publics" of the academy and the church) and concern for the political, socioeconomic, and cultural dimensions of social reality, on the one hand, and the ecclesial model of the church as servant to the world, on the other hand. Among other things, he underscores that education for peace and justice is a difficult venture, not only because of external opposition, but also due to the potential for resistance and divisiveness

within ecclesial communities themselves. *(Studies in Theology and Education,* pp. 23-25; 89-91.)

73. Brian Wren, *Education for Justice: Pedagogical Principles* (Maryknoll, N.Y.: Orbis, 1977). Review also *Religious Education* 79:4 (Fall 1983), "Education for Social Responsibility"; and 79:4 (Fall, 1984), "Pursuing Justice and Peace."

74. Suzanne C. Toton, *World Hunger: The Responsibility of Christian Education* (Maryknoll, N.Y.: Orbis, 1982). Toton correlates social analysis both with church teachings and with theological insights stemming from political and liberation theologies. Out of this matrix, she develops principles for practice and theory. She contrasts the individualism and the privatization of life in North American society and the spiritualizing of the radical gospel demands with the public and political nature of Christian faith and summons of the gospel.

75. See Joe Holland and Peter Henriot, *Social Analysis: Linking Faith and Justice* (Washington, D.C.: Center of Concern, 1983). Interestingly, Holland and Henriot propose a "circle of praxis" consisting of four phases— insertion, social analysis, theological reflection, and pastoral planning— which emphasizes the experience-reflection-action dynamics and resembles the liberationist theological methodology discussed in the next chapter of the present volume.

76. Sara Little, *To Set One's Heart: Belief and Teaching in the Church* (Atlanta: John Knox, 1983), pp. 40-41, 76-85. Little analyzes and compares five approaches to teaching with focus on formation and re-formation of belief and belief system—information processing, group interaction, indirect communication, personal development, and action/reflection. For her, the contribution of the action-reflection approach to belief formation consists in that faithfulness is related to believing when actual existential and historical experience, critically reflected on, is formulated as belief; hence, we *act* our way into *believing.*

77. Thomas H. Groome, "Religious Education for Justice by Educating Justly," in *Education for Peace and Justice,* ed. Padraic O'Hare (San Francisco: Harper & Row, 1983), pp. 69-82. In the same volume, see related essays by David Hollenbach, Mary C. Boys, Padraic O'Hare, and Russell Butkus.

78. Michael Warren, *Youth, Gospel, Liberation* (San Francisco: Harper & Row, 1987). Warren presents an insightful and hopeful contribution. His converging views of youth, culture, liberation thought, the gospel, the church, and the Christian faith, provide guidelines for youth ministry— and religious education especially—in the face of alienation, oppression, injustice, and violence.

79. We are not implying, however, that poor and non-poor are both oppressed in the same manner or with the same intensity. In the case of middle-class North Americans, it can be argued that, on the one hand, in global terms they form part of the "oppressors" class by virtue of their levels of consumption and their privileged (even if unwitting) participation in global structures of oppression. On the other hand, it can also be argued that middle-class North Americans are themselves subject to the dehumanizing forces of consumerist structures, including the strife to maintain the elusive material security offered by their relative wealth and the alienating drive to preserve the status—both at home and abroad—based on that

wealth and power. C. Arnold Snyder, "Liberation and the Fleshpots of Egypt: Towards a Pedagogy for the Oppressor," International Conference on Liberation Theology, Vancouver, Canada (February 8, 1986). For a wider treatment of a *"pedagogy for oppressors"* in the context of a First World liberation theology, see Letty M. Russell, *Growth in Partnership* (Philadelphia: Westminster, 1981), especially pp. 57-81, 110-134, 151-161.

80. See Alice Frazier Evans, Robert A. Evans, and William Bean Kennedy, *Pedagogies for the Non-Poor* (Maryknoll, N.Y.: Orbis, 1987). The authors and other contributors present a number of models of "empowering," "liberative," or "transformative" education designed for learning about injustice and for becoming actually engaged in effecting appropriate societal change in the direction of justice and peace. The book includes pertinent discussion and reflection significant for religious education of youth and adults as compassionate and responsible change agents.

81. As indicated in chapter 2 of the present volume, the four dimensions of the overall aim of Christian religious education must be seen together and as mutually influencing one another. Interestingly, a somewhat similar reference to religious education aims is made by Dermot Lane when he suggests the threefold goal of awakening an experience and knowledge of God, fostering maturity of faith, and promoting an explicit discipleship of Christ for the sake of the reign of God. (Dermot A. Lane, "The Challenge Facing Religious Education Today," pp. 160-163.)

82. Ronald Marstin, *Beyond Our Tribal Gods: The Maturing of Faith* (Maryknoll, N.Y.: Orbis, 1979). See also the references to faith development theory in chapters 1 and 4 of the present volume.

83. Kenneth Barker, *Religious Education, Catechesis, and Freedom* (Birmingham, Ala.: Religious Education Press, 1981), pp. 8-15, 128-159.

84. See note 11 in chapter 1 of the present volume.

85. John L. Elias, *The Foundations and Practice of Adult Religious Education* (Malabar, Fla.: Krieger, 1982), pp. 171-175; and *Studies in Theology and Education*, pp. 161-173.

86. Kieran Scott, "Three Traditions of Religious Education," *Religious Education* 79:3 (Summer, 1984), pp. 323-324, 328-333. Scott proposes a three-pronged typology of traditions as a scheme for ordering the field of religious education and a device for systematic reflection on it. Together with the "revisionist" tradition (corresponding to the Christian religious education theories of Thomas Groome and Mary Elizabeth Moore) he explores the "ecclesial enculturation" (represented by catechesis, Christian nuture, and socialization theories—e.g. C. Ellis Nelson, John Westerhoff, and Berard Marthaler), and the "reconceptualist" (i.e., the attempt to retrieve and reconstruct the root meaning of "religious education"—e.g. Gabriel Moran and Maria Harris) traditions.

87. Harold William Burgess, *An Invitation to Religious Education* (Birmingham, Ala.: Religious Education Press, 1975). Burgess explores four theoretical approaches ("traditional theological," "contemporary theological," "social science," and "sociocultural") in terms of six interpretive categories common to theorizing about religious education—aim, content, teacher, student, environment, and evaluation.

88. Ian P. Knox, *Above or Within: The Supernatural in Religious Education* (Birmingham, Ala.: Religious Education Press, 1976). Knox examines the

theological theme of the relationship of the natural and the supernatural as embodied in connection with religious education theory. The issue that he discusses is whether adopting a certain theological metaperspective bears an affinity with a certain religious education theory and practice; or, whether a correlation can be established between one's theological overview and the approach or theoretical position one adopts with regard to religious education. Knox studies the "transcendist," the "immanentist," and the "integralist" metaperspectives. For other references on the relationship between theology and religious education see notes no. 88 and 89 in chapter 2 of the present volume.

Chapter 4

Faith Seeking Understanding

"You have been given the secret of the kingdom of God."[1]

JESUS

"The fundamental difference between the traditional academic theologian and the liberation theologian is that the latter feels compelled at every step to combine the disciplines that open up the past with the disciplines that help to explain the present. And he feels this necessity precisely in the task of working and elaborating theology, that is to say, in the task of interpreting the word of God as it is addressed to us here and now.

". . . Liberation deals not so much with content as with the method used to theologize in the face of our real-life situation."[2]

JUAN LUIS SEGUNDO

"The interpreting community seeks to understand. It does this by proclaiming and reflecting on the meaning of the community's witness of faith (past, present, and future) in light of the richest possible understanding of its own experience and that of the world. . . .

"The traditioning community seeks also to act in the church and in the world. It seeks to act in the direction of the Kingdom of God, transforming and being transformed. . . .

"The primary goals of Christian religious education are knowledge with understanding and the transformation of persons' actions, beliefs, and values. . . . Neither goal can be met without the other."[3]

MARY ELIZABETH MOORE

INTRODUCTION

The discussion of praxis epistemology in the previous chapter leads us to consider another major liberationist motif, namely that of critical reflection and understanding for transformation. The dialogical interface between religious education and liberation theology may thus yield further foundation material as well as suggestive reformulations for both of the two fields in interplay.

The questions of process content and product content now come to the fore in a special way. In this sense, the gospel quotation of Mark 4:11, seen in its larger biblical context as well as in connection with our present agenda,[4] suggests at least three fundamental touchstones for both Christian religious education and liberation theology: 1) the prominence of the teaching ministry of Jesus and the unity and harmony of context, process, and product detectable in that ministry; 2) the fact that Jesus' teaching demands and elicits an active, personal involvement with subject-matter on the part of the learners in light of their present social environment; and 3) the realization that the gift of "the secret of the kingdom of God" assumes the most comprehensive educational outcome; indeed, much more than mere "understanding," it is a matter of Christian praxis, lifestyle, discipleship in community.

The question of critical interpretation and understanding for transformation, explicitly included in the representative quotations from Juan Luis Segundo and Mary Elizabeth Moore, will be addressed in the following overview of method in liberation theology in the next section. Then, we will focus on the liberationist perspective as more specifically related to religious education, first in the expanded discussion of "doing theology" and, second, in the reference to the purported liberation of the Bible. Finally, further analysis and critique will identify other strengths and weaknesses in the liberationist theological approach from the standpoint of religious education.

A New Way: Liberating Theology

One of the most common references to liberation theology is that it presents a "new way of doing theology" and that the whole of liberation theology is grounded in its methodology. In the already quoted words of Juan Luis Segundo "liberation deals not so much with content as with the method used to theologize in the face of our real-life situation." The question of method is indeed crucial for understanding this movement and especially so from the vantage point of religious education.

As explained in the first chapter, Paulo Freire's work and thought provided the original and key methodological principle for liberation theology in terms of the approach and philosophy of *conscientization.* Freire's pedagogical practice together with his reflection and writing provided a timely twofold impetus in Brazil and elsewhere. The first impetus spurred on the church's involvement with the poor and oppressed. The second impetus furthered the stimulation of new insights on Christian "praxis" which became decisive in shaping the method of liberation theology. In articulating his own liberationist view, which affirms the primacy of commitment and praxis, Freire helped to lay the foundation for the theological method adopted by liberation theologians. No wonder, then, that several key issues of concern for Freire appear later in the liberationist theological agenda. Examples of these key issues include the question of ideologies to be exposed, the problem of political-economic domination, and the challenge to work for the humanization of all in the midst of history.

It is apparent that this "new way of doing theology" involves far more than a matter of alternative theologizing as an intellectual or academic endeavor. In fact, traditional academic theology is radically criticized by liberationists[5] who have moved even beyond the progressive contributions of European (mainly German) political theology.[6] As Dennis P. McCann asserts, the question of method, once it is posed critically in theology, tends to be subversive of tradition. There is no need of methodological justification for an unchallenged tradition, but the attempt to criticize tradition does call for such a justification.[7] That being the case, a useful way to overview the method of liberation theology consists of examining briefly Gustavo Gutiérrez's definition "a critical reflection on Christian praxis in the light of the Word."[8] The three dimensions included in that definition are inseparable in practice as far as methodology is concerned. We will characterize them succinctly in the following paragraphs as an initial reference to the meaning of the purported "liberation of theology" on the part of Latin American liberationists. This discussion will be expanded in the next section.

"A critical reflection . . ." In liberation theology, this is not so much the beginning of the theological task as a special kind of focusing activity which presupposes a prior commitment to praxis. Put in simple terms, critical reflection consists of an analytical look at the situation in which Christian praxis occurs. Its twin purpose is 1) to discover and comprehend the character and causes of oppression, and 2) to understand as fully and clearly as possible the nature and dynamics of prevailing conditions which generate, sustain, foster, and justify oppression. In the case of Latin America, the question of unjust socioeconomic structures, repressive political systems associated with imperialistic policies, and supporting ideologies justifying militarism and the national security state have been the main subjects of concern. The realization of the widening gap between rich and poor countries and the increasing misery of the vast majority of the people have led liberation theologians to expose and denounce the failed policies of neo-colonialism, developmentalism, and capitalism, together with corresponding forms of domination, dependence, marginalization, and oppression. Naturally, these analyses have also pointed to the need for radical systemic transformation.[9] To the question of why critical reflection as a main theological task would address such temporal or mundane matters, liberation theologians unanimously respond that the divine gift of salvation from sin consists first and foremost of integral, holistic liberation. Salvation is the complete, total fulfillment of humanity; conversely, injustice, poverty, and oppression are social manifestations of sin, which is the fundamental alienation from God and humanity.[10] Obviously, this theological insight correlates with the "in light of the Word" component of the definition we are now explicating and to which we will refer below. Moreover, the insight on salvation and history is also connected with the question of the church and its action and thought (or lack of them) in terms of religious education, pastoral ministry, social teaching, and theology. In other words, the political and ideological critiques employed in liberationist theological reflection also include criticism of the church's views, of attitudes and practices concerning society and

culture, and of the political realm—for instance in terms of a "hermeneutic of suspicion"[11]—in light of the challenges being confronted (e.g., religious legitimation of prevailing structures and systems).

"On Christian praxis . . ." Commitment to praxis is the key because liberation theology underscores doing the truth—orthopraxis—rather than understanding revealed truth as the first and foremost theological task. The tilt is to orthopraxis rather than to orthodoxy. The critical reflection discussed in the previous paragraph derives from and illumines an active engagement by living out the gospel, and especially by sharing in the suffering and hope of the oppressed and the struggle for liberation and justice. This praxis is thoughtful, discerned action, reflectively and critically chosen, directed, and evaluated. It is practical engagement (e.g., in the planning for social change and implementation of alternatives) but not as a definitive criterion of truth in itself, for praxis needs to be subject to communal assessment.

As noted in the previous chapter, liberationists contend that modern academic European theologians have responded to the "first movement of the Enlightenment" (i.e., Kant—the liberation of reason from authoritarianism and establishment of its autonomy) whereas liberation theologians are seen as responding to the Enlightenment's "second movement" (i.e., Marx—the challenge of the radical transformation of reality). Thus, for Jon Sobrino, the interest moving the academic theologians to do theology is *rationality* (e.g., liberating faith from elements of myth or historical error). The motivation of liberation theologians to perform the same theological task is *transformation.* Liberationists see the need to confront the reality of the present sinful situation with the explicit purpose of confronting human misery and eliminating oppression.[12] Therefore, a praxis epistemology is entwined with the claim that liberation theology does indeed contribute a new methodology. That claim of newness is sustainable for at least two reasons. For one thing, liberationists are concerned first of all with Christian praxis in the present situation rather than starting with the Holy Scripture or with the teachings of the church as traditional academic theology has normally done. Second, liberation theology has recaptured the insight that theological truth cannot be grasped and appropriated through study alone but through commitment and active, communal engagement in tune with the project of the reign of God. Much more than a variation of theological methodology, what we have here is a basic *paradigm shift* in the context, the experience, the content, and the interpretation of Christian faith.[13] It must be reiterated in this light that the analysis of the concrete oppressive reality calls for the key contributions coming from the social sciences rather than from philosophy, because at stake is not only the critical understanding of oppression but the social-scientific vision and implementation of specific models of liberation as well.

For Sobrino and others, theological method derives from the epistemological break consisting of the actual following of Jesus Christ: " 'Method' as road traveled is not found in critical reflection on the road traveled to reach understanding, but in the traveling itself. . . . It is the real following of Jesus that enables one to understand the reality of Jesus, even if this understanding must then be explicated by using a plurality of methods, analyses, and hermeneutics. In its deepest meaning method is understood as content."[14] In other words, Latin American liberation theology conceives a theological method as a real journeying, a contextualized recapitulation of the praxis of Jesus, as it were, rather than merely thinking about that praxis. A number of dualisms are thus ovecome, such as the separation of process and content and, most importantly, the radical dualism between theory and praxis, between faith and history.

"In light of the Word." The Bible plays an indispensable role in liberation theology whose main concern is, precisely, the relationship between the gospel—and especially God's Word as recorded in scripture—and present historical praxis.[15] Several specific considerations about the place and the function of the Bible in the process of theologizing will be included below. Therefore, at this point a few introductory remarks will suffice.

In liberationist theologizing a dialectical process takes place whereby new historical awareness (e.g., awareness of domination and oppression) becomes associated with new religious experiences, with new understanding of God, and with a new form of faith. This dialectical process generates a rediscovery of several interrelated dimensions of the biblical message as we have been indicating throughout this book. Some of these interrelated dimensions include the metaphor of God (and, therefore, Jesus

Christ) as liberator; the paradoxical symbol of the kingdom of God, the prophetic-utopian vision and the political-eschatological dimensions of the gospel; the praxis way of knowing and the epistemology of obedience and doing justice; and the privileged situation of the poor and oppressed (chapter 5). Indeed, these biblical themes recur consistently in liberation theology. The scriptural message has contributed substantially to reshaping both religious faith and theological understandings.

DOING THEOLOGY AS A KIND OF RELIGIOUS EDUCATION

The liberation of theology and the mode of theological reflection advocated by liberationists take on a more specific shape when described in terms of the actual experience of the grassroots Christian communities.[16] In fact, "critical reflection on Christian praxis in the light of the Word," becomes one special design for religious education which is strikingly analogous to the pastoral approach—and, in Brazil, the Catholic Action methodology[17]— characterized by three movements—*observing, judging,* and *acting.* In connection with this observation, Leonardo Boff asserts that the Medellín Episcopal Conference (1968) endorsed and appropriated the methodology of the emerging liberation theology. The starting point is always the critical analysis of reality ("observing") in the context of actual involvement on the part of the Christians. The next movement consists of the effort to illumine Christian praxis in the light of the resources provided by revelation and theological reflection ("judging"). In the third and completing movement, the lines of appropriate pastoral action ("acting") are discerned and decided.[18] An explanation of this liberationist approach follows, including a simple illustration of doing theology in the confrontation of a common "limit-situation" facing Latin American Christians, the problem of the land and related issues such as agrarian reform.

Observing: The Socioanalytic Mediation

Before any process of theological reflection per se may take place, liberation theology presupposes a prior commitment on the part of the theologian, the pastor or pastoral agent, to the people actually and existentially confronting the question of the land as a priority so defined by the people themselves. This assumed commitment may take different forms such as some kind of actual concrete participation by the theologian in the grassroots peasant community or the rural workers' associations, and the like. In other words, there is no such thing as starting from the theoretical stance of a given "theology of the land" to be applied, adopted, or contextualized somehow in a certain setting. Rather, that theology will be developed along the way.

The first phase in this process consists of an analysis of the local situation in light of the people's own experience. In the case of our example, this would mean simply that the issue of work and the land will be carefully observed, discussed, and further problematized from the perspective of the rural workers' predicament. The actual struggles of the peasants and their families in the area, the law of the land, the behavior of the landowners, and government action or lack of action will have a prominent place in the agenda for sharing and discussion. This will happen especially by focusing on the people's perception of their problems and ways they have attempted to deal with them. The "socio-analytic mediation" (i.e., mediation in the sense of means or instrument for theological construction) involved in this method-ological movement consists of a critical look at the world of the oppressed. The goal is to understand the nature, the sources, and the implications of the oppression that is taking place, which is another way of reiterating that liberation theology starts with the here-and-now concrete historical situation. In other words, before questioning the meaning of oppression from God's perspective, as it were, the pastoral agent or the theologian, together with the people, need to come to grips with the real world of oppression and its causes. Hence the emphasis that at the root of the method we find the synapse linking faith with concrete practice. In the words of the brothers Boff, liberation theology acts within this principal dialectic of theory (faith) and praxis (of charity): liberation theology is always a second act, the first one being "faith that works through love" (Galatians 5:6).[19] Therefore, critical awareness vis à vis the real world of oppression and suffering in terms of specific limit-situations (such as that confronted by disenfranchised peasants) is an essential dimension of the overall theological process.

It is obvious that this approach calls for major infusions from the social sciences. The task involved in the process of observation, analysis, and critical reflection includes the discernment of alternative explanations. Thus, Latin American liberation theologians have rejected the superficial, do-goodism understanding of poverty as a *vice* (i.e., the product of ignorance, indolence, or mere human malice) and the corresponding pseudosolution of "assistance-ism" (from almsgiving to divers aid programs that make the "unfortunate" poor the object of charity). They have also rejected the functionalist explanation of poverty and oppression in terms of socioeconomic underdevelopment and the prescribed palliative of "reformism" that ignores the conflictive nature of oppression and fails to address the unjust social structures. The socioanalytic mediation has led liberationists to adopt some form of historical-structural or dialectical explanation of poverty, precisely in terms of *oppression* whereby the former is understood in light of society's fundamental political and economic organization. The poor and oppressed are thus considered as subjects emerging in a process of societal transformation.

Another reference to Marxism is in order at this point, given the frequent charge that liberation theology *uncritically* adopts Marxism and socialist views and that liberation theology manipulates the gospel to justify a priori political options.[20] Liberationists have been careful to qualify their use of Marxist analysis. Thus, in authentic liberation theology: 1) Marxist analysis is subject to the judgment and the cause of the poor (and not the other way around); 2) Marxism is to be used instrumentally and selectively by applying useful methodological indicators such as attention to economic factors, class conflict, and the mystifying power of ideology; 3) the theologian is to maintain a critical relationship with Marxism as a companion and helper along the way but never as the ultimate guide for the journey.[21]

Judging: The Hermeneutical Mediation

The transition toward the second methodological movement occurs when the focus of the agenda becomes correlating the people's Christian faith with the concrete problem of the land.

The religious belief that the land is a gift of God for everyone to enjoy and to share; the divine promise of blessing associated with physical work and cooperation with God; the hope of a "new earth" in the coming kingdom; and the responsibility expressed in commitment to faithful stewardship of natural resources and personal gifts—these are but a few of the faith claims to be reappropriated in light of the gospel. "Judging," then, takes place in the process of that kind of critical interpretation which affirms the normative, guiding function of the Word of God, especially as recorded in the Bible. Obviously, the teachings of the church may also be taken into account in this process (e.g., teachings concerning the land and mercantilism, private property and social justice and the common good.)[22]

Once the real situation of oppression has been duly grasped ("observed") from the perspective of the oppressed, the question is then raised: How does the Word of God speak to this situation and illumine our reflection and action? In other words, at this point the issue of oppression and liberation is to be dealt with in light of the Christian faith as anchored in the Holy Scripture. The Bible is approached not in a neutral fashion—which would be a psychological impossibility anyway—but from the concrete existential stance of the actual suffering and the hope of the oppressed. Hence a new interpretive reading is called for, namely the *hermeneutic of liberation,* to which we will refer in more detail in the next section. Liberationists acknowledge that this new hermeneutic of liberation is not the only possible and legitimate reading of the bible. However, this new interpretive mode is the *privileged* hermeneutic for the Third World. The new hermeneutic highlights such biblical motifs as God as the parent of life and the advocate of the oppressed; liberation from the house of slavery; the prophecy of the new world; the kingdom given to the poor; and the church of the total communion. Even though the whole Bible is reclaimed as the text of the church and the book of the people, it is obvious that the liberationist approach requires a certain hermeneutical selectivity. In fact, the "judging" involved in the second methodological movement betrays a preference for the following biblical documents: 1) The *Exodus,* with the story of political-religious liberation from slavery and freedom for becoming the people of God in the promised land and in the context of the covenant.[23] 2) The *prophets,* with their compelling defense of God the liberator, their vigorous denunciation of injustice and the announcement of the messianic reign. 3) The *gospels,* with the central, normative presence of Jesus and his overall ministry of liberation together with his cross and resurrection which establish the absolute or definitive meaning and purpose of history. 4) The *Acts of the Apostles,* with the portrait of the ideal of a free and liberating Christian community. 5) The *Revelation* or *Apocalypse,* with the symbolic description of the struggle of the people of God confronting all the monsters of history. The liberation hermeneutic meshes the pertinent and urgent questions in the agenda of the poor and oppressed who yearn for the promised "abundant life" (John 10:10) on the one hand with the transcendental issues of conversion, grace, and resurrection on the other hand.[24] This is to take place in the process of *hermeneutical circulation* involving three elements: the people, their context, and the biblical text.

A few additional comments about the liberationist hermeneutical mediation are in order in the face of our present interest. *First,* since orthopraxis is the main concern, the liberationist hermeneutics employed in the "judging" movement will tend to emphasize one's understanding of practical application rather than simple explication. Therefore, beyond the possible analyses and explanations concerning the limit-situations of disenfranchised peasants or rural workers, what matters most is the question of interpreting and understanding the "text" of the real life of those people in light of the scripture. Textual meanings should correlate with existential and practical meanings. *Second,* the fundamental goal of the judging moment is to reactivate creatively the enabling and transforming energy elicited by the biblical texts. Thus critical interpretation is meant in its own way to foster conversion, empowerment, and transformation. The end result is to maximize the common good and to correct injustice by assessing and even devising guidelines and directions regarding the current oppressive situation in which the poor are exploited or deprived of the possibility to work in the land. *Third,* critical interpretation underscores the social context of the biblical message at the point at which exegesis (or the study of the text within its historical context) can become translated into the here-and-now historical context of the people. *Fourth,* the liberationist hermeneutical mediation stresses a christological key, that is, the actual following of Jesus Christ as the way of knowing the truth and choosing and realizing life itself (John 14:6), as indicated in chapter 3 in the discussion of praxis epistemology. Hence, by affirming the gospels as the highest level of divine revelation, the vision of the poor and oppressed is situated within the greater vision of the Lord of history.[25]

Acting: The Practical Mediation

It can be said that socioanalytical mediation is oriented toward the world of the oppressed in order to understand it critically *(observing),* whereas the hermeneutical mediation *(judging)* attends to "God's world" in order to discover the divine plan with regard to the oppressed. The practical mediation *(acting)* in turn informs the third methodological movement which consists of exploring, implementing, and evaluating operational approaches consistent with both the people's hopes for liberation and the revealed divine will for justice and peace. In the case of our recurrent example of the land, a variety of alternatives will be carefully considered such as the value and feasibility of the organization of the rural workers in unions and associations for special projects such as requests for changes in the law or its implementation, the defense of squatters, and establishing cooperatives. A major action-oriented plan could propose redistribution of the land in the context of agrarian reform and divers forms of social and political mobilization at the local, regional, or national level. Discernment of effective ways of action may suggest the utilization of existing structures such as governmental agencies, political groups, or divers forms of civil disobedience.[26] In sum, in Freirean terms, "limit-situations" are confronted with "limit-acts" thus realizing "untested feasibilities" in the search for freedom and justice.

Liberation theology thus emerges from Christian praxis—"faith that works through love"—and leads to further praxis. The return to action and critical reflection is characteristic of this theologizing which defines and shapes religious and theological education at the level of the faith community. Obviously, the closer to a given local setting, the more specific the practical mediation will tend to be, including a more definite appreciation of concrete events and here-and-now circumstances, and a more precise prediction of consequences. At any rate, several method- ological principles have to be taken into consideration: 1) Deter- mining what is possible or historically feasible through careful identification of the contours and structures of social reality, in- cluding potential resistance and opposition to change. This ap- plies particularly to the exploration of creative alternatives (e.g., local networks of moral and material support for workers and families) in the face of oppressive and unjust situations. 2) Dis- cernment of strategies and tactics with special consideration for nonviolent means and methods such as dialogue and persuasion, application of moral pressure, and peaceful resistance. Such dis- cernment includes deliberation about additional resources in light of Christian ethical concerns, such as popular mobilization in marches and strikes, together with other active confrontational approaches which express protest and point to alternative social projects. 3) Articulation of the praxis of the people of God with other historical forces present in society such as branches and levels of government, political parties, and unions. This includes the careful examination of action taking place in the local setting of the faith community in correlation with the larger social, eco- nomic, and political system. 4) Ongoing assessment of objectives and means together with evaluation of results and discernment of possible consequences and ramifications for further action and reflection. This assessment is to be done, again, in light of the gospel and the church's understanding of its special nature and mission.

This liberational method of theologizing does not function in a linear manner as if each movement could be neatly separated from the rest in actual practice. Rather, the method operates in an inductive and dialectical fashion whereby each movement is closely related to the other two.[27] The *socioanalytical* mediation involved in "observing" already includes some indications rel- evant for the "judging" to be carried out in terms of a *hermeneu- tical* mediation as well as preliminary suggestions or guidelines for "acting," the *practical* mediation. Action in turn further elic- its and informs both interpretation and observation, and so on. In sum, we are dealing with specific references pointing to the very definition of liberation theology as a process of *"critical reflection* (i.e., observing—socioanalytical mediation) on Christian *praxis* (i.e., acting—practical mediation as starting and arriving point) in the light of the Word (i.e., judging—hermeneutical mediation)." In the articulation of this methodological process it is possible to observe various levels of specificity, abstraction, sophistication, and comprehensiveness. Such a diversity correlates, mainly, with particular settings for theologizing (e.g., local faith communities, centers for leadership training, pastoral institutes, seminaries, and universities) and with the gifts and vocations of the protagonists (grassroots lay people, pastors, religious and pastoral agents, professional theologians).

On the level of the common people gathered in the context of ecclesial communities, "doing theology" in a liberation key contributes much to religious education. Its contribution lies in the fact that its main thrust, content, and purpose is the conscientizing religious education of youth and adults. To this topic we will return in the next chapter.

On the level of leadership training and ministry development, "doing theology" in a liberation key revises and restructures theological education in a creative fashion. Theological education is seen, essentially, as one special form of the teaching ministry of the church. Its reason for being is to reflect on ways in which the faith community can work toward the realization of Christian mission in light of God's reign and equip persons for that purpose.[28] Further, the traditional separation between "theological education" (as clergy or pastoral education associated with theological schools) and "Christian religious education" (for the lay people in the church) tends to be blurred deliberately.[29] Religious education needs the appropriate infusion of theology. The need to effectively reconcile and integrate those two dimensions of the church's educational ministry and to reshape theological education and to somehow bridge the existing gap between *academia* and *ecclesia* is also keenly addressed by Thomas Groome. Groome asserts that his "shared praxis" approach to Christian religious education is at its heart a process of bringing people to do theology in a mode fully consistent with the liberationist understandings. And those understandings have to do with the privileged subjects, locus, and purpose of theology and, especially, the emerging paradigmatic shift toward a dialectical unity between praxis and theory.[30]

THE LIBERATION OF THE BIBLE

The liberationist "new way of doing theology" assumes the special status of the scriptures in the life, in the struggles of the people, and finally in the theological task. What is remarkable is the forceful affirmation by liberationists that the Bible is God's textbook for the people—a new conviction among Latin American Catholics—and, more importantly, the fact that the Bible is being read as never before.[31] In the words of Carlos Mesters, the Bible, which was taken out of the people's hands, is now being taken back by them. The people are "expropriating the expropriators," as they realize that the Bible is their book, written for them and which speaks to them here and now; in short, the Bible is again the people's book.[32] Once more in the history of the church, the scriptures are playing a crucial role in ecclesial, religious, and theological renewal. However, from a liberationist perspective, the key function of the Bible depends on its being put in second place, as it were, relative to concrete here-and-now human life itself which takes the first place. In other words, the "hermeneutical mediation" involved in critical reflection and interpretation for transformation focuses on understanding, on liberating, and on enhancing here-and-now human life rather than on interpreting the Bible per se. The hermeneutical axis has shifted to trying to interpret life with the indispensable help of the Bible.[33]

The liberationist view and use of the Bible may also be considered in terms of the interest in sociological awareness pertaining to the worlds of the text and the interpreters.[34] The social analysis of the world of the interpreters becomes a prerequisite to biblical interpretation. Thus, in the liberationist hermeneutic, the biblical text must be viewed in light of the socioeconomic reality of the present historical context.[35] Furthermore, the stress on the analysis of the present situation (i.e., the "socioanalytical mediation") intersects with the emphasis linking praxis and knowing. For liberation theologians, the authentic meaning of the scriptures is grasped and appropriated in light of the challenges emanating from Christian praxis.

In the following three sections we will expand these introductory comments on the purported liberation of the Bible and will consider some ramifications especially relevant from the perspective of religious education.

Dimensions of the Liberation of the Bible

The crucial question of the liberation of the Bible may be considered in terms of both emancipation—liberation *from*—and enablement or empowerment—liberation *for.* The main concerns in the liberationist approach to scriptures are the related issues of *who* reads and interprets the Bible, and *whose interests* are served in biblical scholarship. Closely connected with those concerns is the question of liberation from ideological captivity.

People, Teachers, and Scholars. The liberation of the Bible is considered, first of all, in terms of the persons involved in reading and interpreting the scriptures. In his presentation of an inductive theology, Georges Casalis discusses several dimensions of biblical hermeneutic as "the science of Hermes." He contends that the most vital and indispensable constituent of biblical hermeneutic is to reclaim possession of the text and its meaning from those who have unwarrantedly locked them away.[36] This dimension of hermeneutic requires, then, a certain breakaway and conversion to the people on the part of the Bible scholars because hermeneutic is always partisan and it is authentic only by being really popular. Casalis adds that his conviction is basic to Paulo Freire's "political conscientization by alphabetization."[37]

The Bible's own message encourages its liberation from the control of the academicians, theologians, and Bible scholars, and even from the church magisterium. As Mesters puts it, in the past "we members of the clergy expropriated the Bible and got a monopoly on its interpretation. We took the Bible out of the hands of the common people, locked it with a key, and threw the key away. But the people have found the key and are beginning to interpret the Bible."[38] For his part Paul Lehmann asserts that, while the Protestant Reformation put the Bible in the hands of the people, the "new Reformation"—ushered in by liberation theology and the base communities—expresses and exposes what the people have found.[39]

By adopting a liberation hermeneutic, the experts or specialists in biblical interpretation—scholars, pastors, and teachers—are also emancipated from prejudice and privilege and are freed to become useful and faithful resources for the sake of God and the people. The "teachers of the Word" thus become facilitators and servants (rather than rulers and controllers); they become co-learners and co-pilgrims together with the people. The main question about the role of experts and specialists is to what an extent they encourage or promote conscientization and creativity, as explained in the first chapter of the present volume. In the words of David Lockhead the intuition of what the text means in context is ultimately not a matter of expertise but, rather, a matter of creative insight.[40] We look to the specialist not for an exposition of the biblical text but for background information which will help to listen to the text in its own context. Lockhead goes on to say that our experience in entering the world of the text should be a form of consciousness raising. And he adds that, even though no method can automatically provide creative insight into the reading of the Bible, without creativity it is difficult to see how any reading of the scriptures could be considered as liberated and liberating.[41]

Overcoming Ideological Captivity. The expression "ideological captivity" evokes first of all the negative and even pejorative meaning of ideology that is associated with the thought of Karl Mannheim, especially when "ideology" is contrasted with "utopia."[42] In this sense, ideology refers to the mental mechanisms that serve a certain group or class, or other interests, by concealing or sacralizing a given situation. Thus, ideology consists of rationalizations of self-interest and a means by which a group seeks to justify social control. To the extent that ideologies fulfill that functional role, to that extent do they become a powerful force in the direction of conformity and maintenance of the status quo. The prophetic and utopian vision espoused by liberation theologians is clearly focused on exposing, denouncing, and replacing prevailing ideologies supportive of current oppressive and alienating social conditions. It is the hypothesis of Juan Luis Segundo that those ideologies unconsciously control and guide our theological notions and our pastoral practice. On the basis of that hypothesis, Segundo adopts from Paul Ricoeur the key concept of *suspicion,* that will be discussed briefly below.[43]

A somewhat more neutral meaning of ideology denotes the

sociocultural and political-economic dimensions of one's point of view, also associated with perspective and even "prejudice." In this more general sense of "viewpoint" the term ideology may be used to underscore the fact that reality is always known from the unique perspective of the knowing subject. What we understand reflects not only the reality which is understood but the viewpoint from which it is understood as well. As Robert McAfee Brown explains, our "ideological captivity," consists of the failure to acknowledge that 1) all of us have certain ideological assumptions (i.e., nobody thinks in disinterested or pure categories); 2) we tend to use our ideologies to rationalize keeping things as they are, especially when things are working to our convenience (and, we detect this tendency more easily in others than in ourselves); and 3) our reasons for affirming what we affirm are thus always open to (ideological) suspicion.[44] Being challenged or confronted by a different or contrasting viewpoint—so that we are forced to take seriously the other view—is essential for recognizing our ideological captivity. We are thus led to examine our own positions.[45]

Critical awareness concerning social and personal ideologies is essential not only for our own liberation but also to avoid making the Bible captive to our prejudices. Our perennial temptation is to force the scriptures to fit our perspectives and frameworks. As Lockhead states, our task is to read the Bible in such a way that it is liberated from our blindness to the relativity of our own point of view. Put another way, we have to read the Bible so that it is able to liberate us from the bonds of our perspective.[46] In other words, our own personal, group, or class ideologies should not control or dominate the text; rather, the text should be allowed to expose and illumine the prejudices we bring to it. As a result, a true "dialectical hermeneutic" can emerge, a hermeneutic which consists of a mutually liberating interaction engaging the reader and the biblical text. It is in light of this realization of the richness and complexity of the "hermeneutical mediation" and the "politics of understanding"[47] that the role of the experts as resource can be redefined and reaffirmed. And that reaffirmation includes the indispensable participation of the ecclesial community that anticipates a faithful response of discipleship ("orthopraxis") to the gospel of the coming reign of God. Ultimately, the twofold liberation of the Bible and its various dimensions with respect to both emancipation and enablement and empowerment must include faith commitment in terms of lifestyle and communal and societal transformation.

Learning Through Hermeneutical Circulation

The question of the liberation of the Bible is central in the key issue of theological method raised by liberation theology. Such centrality is implied in the very definition of theology as "critical reflection on Christian praxis *in the light of the Word,*" and is explicitly dealt with by Juan Luis Segundo. In fact, Segundo's fundamental methodology, as spelled out in *The Liberation of Theology,* consists of a "hermeneutic circle" involving the continuous change in the interpretation of the scriptures in function of the continuous changes in our present reality.[48]

Before describing the transformational learning process of hermeneutical circulation, we must note that, for Segundo, the Bible must be perceived primarily as the record of an educational process directed by God. Indeed, according to his basic hermeneutical principle, the Bible itself must be seen as a religious and biblicotheological educational process rather than as fixed or static message. Related to Segundo's emphasis on method is the notion that dealing with the Bible invites a learning-how-to-learn rather than teaching a given scriptural content per se. Although we welcome this proposition in principle, we must indicate the error involved in positing a sharp dichotomy of content and method (while suggesting, as Segundo does, that the liberating nature of a theology and the best hope of theology for the future lies not in its content but in its method).[49] The problem of alienating or domesticating encounters with the Bible is not a question of method/process versus message/product, as implied by Segundo. The question is rather, and simply put, to what extent the teaching-learning process encourages prescription and indoctrination, or dialogue, critical reflection, and creativity.

Hermeneutical Circulation. Segundo defines the process of hermeneutical circulation as the continuing change in our interpretation of the Bible which is conditioned or dictated by the continuing changes in our present-day reality, both individual and societal. In other words, hermeneutical circulation consists in the interplay between the scriptural text in its historical context and the ecclesial community reading the text in light of the current historical situation. The circular character of this interpretation stems from the fact that each new reality compels us to discern and interpret God's Word afresh, to transform reality accordingly, and then go back and reinterpret the Word of God again. The operation of this process and the successful completion of the "circle" depends on two conditions: 1) profound and enriching suspicions and questions about the real-life situation; and 2) an equally enriching new interpretation of the scriptures.[50]

The sequence of hermeneutical circulation includes four distinct movements from faith to faith, so to say, through ideological, theological, and exegetical suspicion. The four movements are succinctly described by Segundo as follows. First, our new way of experiencing and seeing reality leads to *ideological* suspicion. Second, we apply our suspicion to the entire ideological superstructure in general, and to theology in particular (i.e., *theological* suspicion). Third, as we begin to experience reality differently an *exegetical* suspicion is generated: we begin to suspect that traditional and current biblical interpretation do not take into account important biblical data. Fourth, we arrive at a *new hermeneutic*—that is, at a new way of interpreting the scriptures with the new elements we now have at our disposal.[51]

The sense or the perception of definite problems or conflict situations and the commitment to confront them are essential for setting in motion the process of hermeneutical circulation formulated by Segundo. Frustration and dissatisfaction with present reality leads to raising "suspicions" and challenging questions on the road to effectively changing that reality. In other words, the hermeneutical process engages conflict "in the context of rapport" and "problematizing" in a manner strikingly reminiscent of Freire's conscientization approach as seen in light of creativity. Indeed, it can be argued that the hermeneutical circle is analogous—and, in fact, a special version of—conscientization as creativity, as explained in the first chapter of the present volume.

In Latin America, the flow of the hermeneutical circle can be further described as follows. Poor and oppressed persons experience reality in a way that leads them to suspect that the dominant classes are supported by an ideology which conceals the reality of their situation. This in turn leads to a theological suspicion and from that to an exegetical suspicion suggesting that representatives of the dominant classes and culture do theology and reinterpret the Bible to support their own privilege and domination. The poor and oppressed thus have an opportunity to reread and reinterpret the scriptures and discover the biblical message within their own context. Through the transformational learning process of hermeneutical circulation, the poor and oppressed can reaffirm their faith by unmasking the ideologies of vested interests which traditional theology enshrines. Hence the claim stated above that our experience of reality compels us to reinterpret the Word of God. This creative reinterpretation may in fact help to change our own reality which, in turn, requires a new interpretation of the gospel. Consequently, the process of hermeneutical circulation becomes a continual essential ingredient of the theological task, at one level. At another though related level, the hermeneutical circle becomes integrally incorporated into the ongoing biblicotheological and religious education. In sum: we have the ideological suspicion, the theological suspicion, and the exegetical suspicion; these three interactive suspicions lead us to a new way of reading the Bible and interpreting Christian faith itself.

As they long for and seek for structural change, Latin American Christians may participate in the process of hermeneutical circulation as an important tool for nurturing and strengthening their faith. Paradoxically, the poor and oppressed enjoy what Hugo Assmann has called an *epistemological* (and, therefore, hermeneutical) *privilege*.[52] This privilege results from the fact that the situation of the poor and oppressed is nearer to the situation of those to whom the biblical message was originally addressed. For that reason, liberation theology proposes that we look more closely at the place and role of the Bible for the common people and at grassroots hermeneutic in particular, in the search for liberating clues relevant for both theology and religious education.

The People's Text and Grassroots Hermeneutics

The centrality of the Bible in the Latin American Christian communities, together with its essential role in the life, work, and struggles of the people can hardly be exaggerated. Interestingly enough, the *relocation* of scripture—i.e., the Bible becoming central and taken seriously at the grassroots level—involves some dramatic *dislocations* regarding the more traditional ways of dealing with the sacred text. We will discuss briefly some of those dislocations first. Then, we will refer to grassroots hermeneutics in the cases of the popular church in Solentiname (Nicaragua), and the "Bible circles" in Brazil. Finally, we will indicate further key features of liberationist grassroots hermeneutics from the perspective of religious education.

Creative Dislocations. When the common people reappropriate the Bible and its message, a number of situations change substantially, and we can underscore the following three.

1) The first creative displacement consists in the very *deliberate repossession of the Bible on the part of the lay people.* Countless stories point to the fact that the people experience the Bible as their book, addressed primarily to them, and that they have the right to read it in their own special way and enjoy it on their own terms.[53] By the same token, the place and role of the "doctors"—scholars and theologians mainly—must undergo a fundamental change. Their existential "location" changes because they are required to place themselves not only within the academic and scientific circles but in the company of the "reading people" as well. Thus, the privileged place where the scriptures are read becomes the location of the poor and oppressed. It is the location where new and different things can be discerned and discovered.[54] The people set the agenda for biblicotheological reflection by formulating the key questions as main "interlocutors" in biblical hermeneutics. Scientific exegesis must concern itself with the questions that the people are raising.

2) The second creative dislocation, simply put, lies in the *emphasis placed on the meaning of the Bible for the people reading here and now* rather than in the text's meaning in itself. This dislocation is obviously a corollary of the liberationist position that we must move from the focus on the biblical text to the real life situations. In the words of Carlos Mesters, the Bible is not the one and only history of salvation but a kind of "model experience." Every single people has its own unique history of liberation and salvation.[55]

3) The third creative dislocation advanced by liberation theology and the base communities consists in the shift from abstract cognitive understanding to an *affirmation of faith, community, and history in the process of biblical interpretation.* Liberationists claim that the common people—especially the poor and oppressed—are helping other Christians to realize that "without faith, community, and reality we cannot possibly discover the meaning that God has put in that ancient tome for us today."[56] The necessity of faith and religious experience, and the recovery of the "sense of the church" *(sensus ecclesiae)* in biblical interpretations are also essential in the shift from the often proclaimed (pseudo) neutrality in biblical exegesis, to taking sides in tune with the project of the reign of God. This is indeed a major tenet of liberationist hermeneutic and—together with the other dislocations mentioned—needs to form the backdrop of the two cases of grassroots hermeneutics which will be treated in the next few pages.

The case of Solentiname. Solentiname is the name of a thirty-eight island archipelago on the southern part of the Lake of Nicaragua, in the Central American Republic of Nicaragua. Solentiname is also the name of the archipelago's largest island where Ernesto Cardenal and two colleagues established a little community or lay monastery for contemplative retreat in 1965.[57] A number of projects related to the welfare and the sociocultural development of the broader Solentiname community were soon started such as a school, a clinic, a public library, and the collection of pre-Colombian art. In other words, the disciplines of spiritual contemplation were integrated with service and action as expressions of "faith that works through love."[58] By 1970 the contemplative community and the people of Solentiname associated with it chose to support the Sandinista movement against the United States-backed dictatorship of the Somoza dynasty. Solidarity with the peasants and fishermen of Solentiname now included the risks and pain of political commitment for radical change. The community was in fact destroyed by the Somoza army in 1977. The testimony of the popular church and the grassroots hermeneutics recorded in *The Gospel in Solentiname,*[59] a direct biblical commentary from the oppressed, correspond precisely to that period of time of ferment and turmoil.

We must underscore several observations regarding the case of biblical hermeneutic in Solentiname,[60] beginning with the fact that reading and interpreting the Bible took place in the *context of worship* and *celebration of community.* The Sunday Mass and communal meals provided an ideal framework conducive to dialogue and critical reflection. Second, together with the affirmation of equality and mutuality, we observe that people developed a *profound trust and respect for the leadership* of Ernesto Cardenal as teacher of the Word. He was thus able to function as the "servant-expert" we described above, by explaining the historico-cultural context of the text, the theological perspective of the writers, or the meaning of certain words and expressions in the original language.[61] This sense of trust and respect is essential, among other things, for people to be open to the resources of the critical methods that often challenged cherished preconceptions and beliefs regarding the Bible. A third observation underlines *active solidarity* on the part of the ecclesial community with the larger social context of Solentiname. That solidarity became effective in a number of projects and in actual cooperation with the inhabitants of the archipelago. Thus an action-reflection dynamic was concretely established. Fourth, future-oriented *political commitment* in the form of concern for and involvement in the transformation of the broader political-economic structures constituted another presupposition of grassroots hermeneutics.

In sum, in Solentiname, the worshiping and working ecclesial community approached the biblical text very much aware of the community's historical reality. Participants understood that the scriptures spoke to them and they in turn dialogued with the gospel. Interpretation leading to further action and reflection (i.e., praxis) followed in an ongoing transformational learning process.

"Bible Circles" in Brazil. For several years now, Brazilian Christians have gathered in the context of liberation-thrusted Bible study. The purpose of these "círculos bíblicos" is to assist ecclesial communities to find pertinent responses to their existential challenges, including both questions and real life struggles. The creative dislocations discussed above find very concrete expressions in the *círculos* which have also produced popular incisive biblical commentaries with the guidance of Carlos Mesters[62] and other leaders.

Mesters reports that grassroots hermeneutics consists of a community of people who, while studying the Bible, inject concrete reality and their own existential situation into the process. Three major dimensions in the common people's interpretation of the scriptures during this liberationist scripture study are, then: the Bible itself, the Christian community, and the reality of the surrounding world. We have adapted Mesters' picture of this multiway conversation[63] (which resembles our own discussion of agendas of biblicotheological reflection)[64] as follows:

THE TEXT

of the Bible

$\updownarrow$

Hearing (and responding to)

the Word of God today

$\nearrow$ $\nwarrow$

THE PRE-TEXT   THE CONTEXT

of the real life situaton   of the ecclesial community

Each of those three dimensions or factors—text, pre-text, and context—is deemed indispensable for authentically hearing and responding to God's Word today. Furthermore, it does not matter whether the group starts with the reality of the surrounding world, with the Bible, or with the church community they represent. What is crucial in biblical interpretation, in light of the base communities and the Bible circles in Brazil, is to include all three dimensions while assisting participants to make their own discoveries in creative fashion.[65] The interpretation of the scriptures makes no real progress, and even becomes distorted, whenever one of those three factors is missing. The dynamic integration of Bible, real-life situation, and ecclesial community facilitates a process of transformational learning focused on an existential conversation with the very Word of God.

For Latin American grassroots people, the gospel message or "Word of God" involves much more than the scriptural text itself. The Bible, the ecclesial community, and their real life situation—all together and in concert—constitute the whole gospel message. God's Word is to be discerned and listened to in the community itself and in reality as much as in the scriptures. Read in the context of the ecclesial community, the role of the Bible is to assist the faithful to discover where God is calling them in the hubbub of real life.[66] This is the significance of putting the Bible in second place, as mentioned above. The focus is not so much on interpreting the scriptures but on interpreting and transforming life with the indispensable help of the Bible.

Three Principles from Grassroots Hermeneutics. The gospel quotation of Mark 4:11—"You have been given the secret of the kingdom of God"—has a special meaning when appropriated by grassroots Christians in Latin America. We have spelled out the implications and ramifications of such an appropriation in the preceding pages. At this point we can indicate three specific contributions of grassroots hermeneutics in liberationist perspective which are specially relevant for religious education—prophetic contextualization, the primacy of orthopraxis, and the integration of worship, community, and mission. These contributions stem from the existential stance of people looking at the Bible as one looks at a mirror, as Frei Betto states, to see a reflection of their own reality (rather than looking at the Bible as though looking through a window, curious to see what is happening outside).[67] Further, these principles are based on the application of two intersecting approaches in fruitful tension, as highlighted by Guillermo Cook—"higher criticism" (at the service of faith and a "theology from below") and the "wisdom of the people" in communal dialogue and critical reflection in the light of the Word.[68]

1) *Prophetic contextualization* in grassroots hermeneutics is much more than contextualization on the level of language or biblical imagery in order to achieve a better cultural adaptation.

Prophetic contextualization seeks to transform traditional biblical theology into political theology.[69] The Bible is seen as the story and the written record of God's dealing with the people in diverse historical contexts, which invites further contextualization in the present situation. Prophetic contextualization, therefore, provides biblical grounding for fashioning the *countercultural consciousness* of the church as God's alternative community (as explained in the second chapter of the present volume). Prophetic contextualization involves a disruptive and dysfunctional confrontation ("denouncing") of oppression and injustice as well as the search for creative alternatives ("announcing") illumined by the Bible in dialogue with the ecclesial community in the real life situation.

2) The principle of the *primacy of orthopraxis* in biblical interpretation points to the claim that the truth of God's Word must be actually incarnated in our own concrete history. Efficacious truth involves both correct belief ("orthodoxy") and faithful action ("orthopraxis"). Indeed, faithful action is not only the validation of correct belief or orthodoxy but it is the only way to arrive at truly correct belief in the bibilical sense of the term. Put in other words, truth must be verified in concrete action rather than rationalistically.[70]

3) The principle of the *integration of worship, community, and mission* includes and expands the other two. This principle assumes the essential role of biblical interpretation as a special form and instance of religious education in light of the main facets of the life of the church, namely worship, community, and mission. According to liberationist pastoral theologians, Bible study must take place within the context of worshipful (though not necessarily liturgical) celebration. Thus reading and discussing the scriptures may often become a form of prayer and praise, a unique means for eliciting religious experience in the mode of *worship*.[71] Simultaneously, the ecclesial community gathered around the Bible seeks for the nurturing of faith as growth in discipleship in *community* life as well as in all forms of witness and service, or *mission*. The three dimensions of worship, community, and mission are obviously interconnected. Whenever the purported integration does take place we have a revealing illustration of the very centrality of the task of religious education in the church, as represented below in the diagram.[72] In this light, religious educa-

tion has a crucial *discipling*[73] role: *it must enable for worship, equip for community, and empower for mission.* That being the case, grassroots hermeneutics in a liberation key represents a special manifestation of the assumed (and not often explicitly stated) centrality of the educational task.

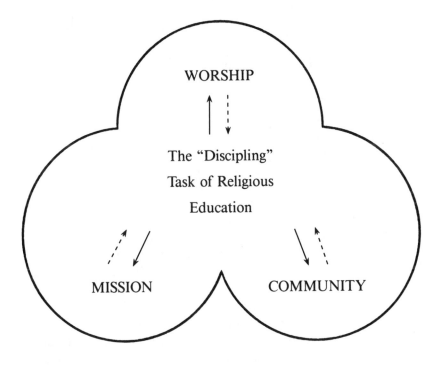

With this observation in the background we will complete the discussion of faith seeking understanding vis à vis the encounter of liberation theology and religious education.

LIBERATION AND RELIGIOUS EDUCATION

In the Preface of this book we indicated that Latin American liberation theology presents a pedagogical structure and orientation which so far has not been duly recognized and evaluated by either theologians or religious educationists. That structure and orientation indeed becomes apparent in a number of liberationist tenets and emphases such as those regarding the normative import of the teachings of Jesus, the view of the Bible as the text of the church and the book of the people, the dynamics of faith and discipleship (i.e., the committed following of Jesus Christ), and doing theology as, essentially, an educational task for the ministry and mission of the ecclesial community. The content of the present chapter further illumines this pedagogical structure and orientation. It also lends support to the claim that liberation theology may provide both a background and a clue for the educational ministry, as indicated in chapter 2.[74]

Several religious educationists have welcomed liberation theology, and some of them have proposed a liberationist approach to religious education.[75] For instance, in the mid-1970s, John Westerhoff contended that "liberation theology provides the most helpful theological system for Christian education today."[76] Westerhoff asserts that liberation theology makes possible a creative new synthesis of two historic theological movements, namely, neo-orthodoxy (with its concern for the historic Christian tradition) and liberal theology (with its concern for justice and the social order). He also underscores the liberationist contribution in terms of method (action-critical reflection), perspectives on the experience of God in history, and the uniting theme of humanization of persons and institutions.[77] Writing on the topic of liberation and the future of Christian religious education, Allen Moore asserts that liberation theology calls into question the very understanding of theology and its function in Christian religious education. He goes on to say that liberationists propose "an educational process which involves living from and reflecting on the deeds of faith. The implication here is that one thinks and talks about faith, not for the sake of knowing about faith, but for the sake of faith itself."[78] For our part, in the following section we will indicate other strengths as well as weaknesses of liberation theology from the perspective of religious education in general and in connection with the agenda of the present chapter in particular.

Contribution and Limitations of the Liberationist View

In the course of this book we have made numerous observations concerning strengths and weaknesses of liberation theology both in itself and with respect to its encounter with religious education. As the discussion moves forward, previous critical remarks about liberation theology can be further indicated and expanded.[79]

Strengths and Contributions of "Faith Seeking Understanding." Our review of liberation theology with focus on its approach to theologizing calls for the reaffirmation of some key insights and principles already underscored in chapter 1 concerning cognitive restructuring and development. This review also highlights the liberationists' contributions in terms of educational process and biblical interpretation.

Enhancing the Cognitive Dimensions of Human Emergence. As a special version of Freire-inspired conscientization, the liberationist methodology encourages a process of *awakening* via dialogue, critical reflection, and the "hermeneutics of suspicion." Participants in the theological task (and, additionally, in liberation-oriented religious education) may thus be able to understand far more critically 1) the perennial risks of oppression-directed forms of instructional manipulation (structural content) and 2) oppressive and alienating ideologies (substantive content). Further, the transformation of vision, perspective, or paradigm becomes a primary objective in the learning to *see,* judge, and act inherent in the theological task of the ecclesial community. It can also be claimed that the liberationists' "faith seeking understanding" implicitly fosters *cognitive development* and explicitly promotes a *postconventional morality;* further, it deliberately provides a critical-cognitive base for the promotion of *faith development.*

Affirming the Learning-Teaching Process. Because of its emphasis on methodology and critical interpretation and understanding for transformation, liberation theology provides a theological foundation for sustaining the unity of process and product in the educational task. The liberationist view can thus contribute further foundation material for a *hermeneutical approach* to religious education theory and practice. Such a contribution could indeed strengthen the proposals to see religious education as, primarily, an interpretation or hermeneutical process, as suggested from different perspectives.[80] The liberationist-hermeneutical approach underscores the centrality of *meaning* (together with *justice)* seen as necessary substantive process content for liberation and humanization.

Two religious educationists who demonstrate the potential value of the liberationist-hermeneutical approach are Thomas Groome and Mary Elizabeth Moore. Interestingly, in Groome's case the very definition of his "shared praxis" approach reveals the strong and direct influence of liberation theology not only in terms of theological base but also as the structuring core for the educational process. Not surprisingly, Groome's definition includes the three "mediations" discussed at the beginning of this chapter. For Groome, "Christian religious education by shared praxis can be described as *a group of Christians sharing in dialogue their critical reflection on present action* [i.e., 'observing'] *in light of the Christian Story and its Vision* [i.e., 'judging'] *toward the end of lived Christian faith [i.e.,* 'acting'].''[81] For her part, Mary Elizabeth Moore describes her approach as a "traditioning model" of Christian religious education. Traditioning is defined as "a process by which the historical tradition is remembered and transformed as the Christian community encounters God and the world in present experience and as the community is motivated toward the future."[82] Moore explicitly identifies the traditioning model as having two dimensions, namely, the hermeneutical and the transformative. Added to this is her three-pronged methodological approach: transmission, reflection, and transformation. These pedagogical methods deal respectively with what?, why? and how? questions, and they are analogous to the observing-judging-acting liberationist-hermeneutical paradigm.

Reclaiming the Centrality of the Bible. Together with the restatement of the question of theological method, liberation theology makes a distinct contribution regarding the centrality of the Bible as the textbook of the church. Indeed, in the preceding pages we have established a number of principles concerning the Bible and biblical hermeneutic that are directly relevant from the standpoint of religious education. Therefore, two additional comments will suffice.

First, liberation theology strongly supports a *process* approach to the Bible as indicated in the discussion of liberationist hermeneutic. Such an approach translates mainly into a twofold emphasis on hermeneutical circulation (i.e., the interplay between the text in its context and the community reading the text in light of its here-and-now real-life situation) and dialectical hermeneutic (i.e., mutual critique and illumination between the biblical text and the interpreting community). Thomas Groome illustrates the relevance of this liberationist contribution with respect to religious education.[83] Further, liberationist hermeneutic suggests theological criteria for critiquing common weaknesses in religious education curriculum and instruction, for instance, regarding the very meaning of learning and teaching the Bible. In that light, the often-stated objective of "biblical literacy" via memorization (i.e., a "banking" approach, in Freire's educational terms) must be corrected with the emphasis on learning to perceive, love, and live "biblically," as James Michael Lee contends.[84] Also, the Bible needs to be taught biblically, that is by effecting "a synapse between the lifestyles recorded in the Bible and the lifestyles of the here-and-now learners, and between the lifestyle which *is* the Bible and the lifestyles of the here-and-now learners."[85]

Second, by focusing on the situation of the poor and oppressed, liberation theology invites nonpoor and nonoppressed persons to exercise the spiritual discipline of humble receptivity in connection with bibilical learning, nurture, and transformation. The challenge of liberationism to the non-poor and non-oppressed is that such persons become open to the potentially mediating role of the poor and oppressed who are deemed to have a certain epistemological-hermeneutical privilege in the encounter with the scriptures. The eyes and ears metaphors are appropriate for conveying the significance of this challenge. We are invited to read the Bible with the eyes of the poor and oppressed, as far as possible.[86] Additionally, we are encouraged to listen to the voice and cry of the poor and oppressed in order to grasp more fully the whole Word of God in the study of the Bible.[87] For example, a liberationist reading of the Emmaus narrative (Luke 24:13-35) that sees the turning point of the story when the disciples put their faith into action by inviting the stranger to share a meal with them (thus becoming their *companion*),[88] nicely supplements other complementary meaningful readings on the part of religious educationists.[89]

Weaknesses of "Faith Seeking Understanding." Several issues evoke our attention as both limitations and lacks of balance in the methodological approach of liberation theology. Among those issues we can mention the following three: the overemphasis on the cognitive, verbal, and rational dimensions of "understanding," the insistence upon critique and suspicion, and the sparse attention to tradition and continuity.

On Critical Reflection and Understanding. The first critical observation we can make from the standpoint of religious education in a sense restates previous comments (chapter 1) on the question of ultracognitivism in the liberationist approach. Our discussion of doing theology as an educational task as well as the question of biblical interpretation, shows that *critical reflection* is considered the principal mode of learning and knowing. Yet, the development of critical consciousness, while necessary, still is not a sufficient condition for holistic liberation and humanization. The heightened awareness and critical understanding made accessible in those cognitive processes may or may not effectively inform faith decisions; likewise, they may or may not correlate with lifestyle transformation and structural change. Indeed, the relevant empirical research shows that there is very little direct correlation between cognitive knowledge and understandings, on the one hand, and lifestyle activity, on the other. Verbal rationality can be easily overemphasized while underestimating noncognitive registers of behavior. As Mary Elizabeth Moore proposes, critical inquiry and reflection must be integrated with "depth reflection" which includes affective imagination.[90] Overemphasis on the cognitive dimensions also imposes severe and indeed crippling limitations on the range of available teaching procedures.

In order to correct this serious unbalance, the liberationist view must take more consistently into account the remarkable holistic flesh-and-blood experience of the base communities for further redefinition of the theological task per se and the possible role of liberation theology in religious education. To this question we return in the next chapter.[91] One final related comment is that the very notion of *understanding* in liberation theology can be challenged as well as enriched from a religious education perspective.[92]

Beyond Critique and Suspicion. There are decided risks in the political-confrontational stance of liberation theology. This is in fact a problem recognized by Clodovis and Leonardo Boff among what they call "temptations" of liberation theology. The Boff brothers mention the risks of neglecting or overlooking the mystical and spiritual roots of Christian faith and praxis by unduly overvaluing political action. The Boffs also warn against the "inflation" of the political dimension in analyzing and dealing with oppression and poverty and subordinating the "discourse of faith" to a "discourse of society" which underestimates the specifics of religion and the Christian life in particular.[93] These warnings obviously apply to theological reflection as well as biblical hermeneutics. Thus, for example, in the case of hermeneutical circulation Beatriz Melano Couch has challenged liberationists to move beyond suspicion to a hermeneutic of hope and engagement.[94]

Another related observation concerns James Fowler's suggestion that "ideological" liberation theologies need to be supplemented with liberation theologies of "balance." This is crucial for Fowler in order to sponsor faith development beyond stage 4—"individuative-reflective faith."[95] In other words, Fowler contends that "ideological" theologies address stage 4 faith which is characterized by critical awareness and "demythologizing," on the one hand, and a tendency to see things in terms of dichotomies and either/or choices, on the other hand. Liberation theologies that focus on stage 4 faith strive to establish and maintain firm and clear boundaries, use intentionally passionate language, and appeal to commitment and action for transformation. In contrast, a theology of "balance" sees the line between oppressor and oppressed, for instance, as passing through people and groups rather than merely between two groups or social classes. That is to say that the dichotomies typical of stage 4 are rejoined and viewed as complementary and polar tensions in stage 5, "conjunctive" faith. Fowler goes on to compare the two sets of theologies regarding the task of theology, the view of God's relation to history, perspectives on time, and notions of sin and evil. He concludes by affirming the need to maintain both positions—"ideological" and "balance" theologies—in dialectical tension and conversation.[96]

On Transformation and Tradition. A third critical observation, partially related to the previous comments, pertains to the question of limited attention which liberation theology accords to tradition and continuity. Obviously the liberationist view raises to a privileged position radical change on all levels, including personal, communal, and societal transformation. This liberationist stance corresponds in turn to the prophetic and utopian vision of hope, promise, and orientation to the future—in short the political-eschatological dimensions of the gospel. A problem of lack of balance arises, however, whenever tradition and continuity are not adequately taken into account. And it is indeed ironic that, in spite of the liberationist emphasis on history, the past dimension of the historical process tends to be underestimated together with the substantive content and process dynamics of tradition. Religious educationists influenced by liberation theology, such as Thomas Groome and Mary Elizabeth Moore, however, have proposed a more balanced approach to timing and history particularly. The correctives proposed by Groome and Moore affirm both the integrity and the integration of continuity and transformation for the discipling task of religious education. These correctives strive to keep in dialectical tension and bring into a creative new synthesis the strengths and contributions of both a socialization/enculturation model and the reconstructionist model in religious education.[97] Such modification of liberationist contributions imply an affirmative response to the question whether the dichotomy of "handing on tradition" and "changing the world" can be overcome in religious education. In the words of Letty Russell, "both are what God's Tradition is all about."[98]

Timing Principles for Religious Education

Our discussion of the encounter between religious education and liberation theology has been focusing on the main principles intersecting these two arenas of human activity. In chapter 1, our comprehensive review of Paulo Freire's work and thought led us to conclude that his contribution inspires a religious education approach that is *dialogical* in spirit, *prophetic-eschatological* in vision, *praxis* oriented, *hermeneutical* in character, and *communal* in shape. More specifically, in the first chapter we refer to the teaching-learning process in terms of conscientization and creativity. In chapter 2 we suggest that the liberationist theme of the prophetic and utopian vision helps both to define the mission of the church and to appropriately inform the guiding principle of religious education. We also consider the overall aim of religious education in a liberationist perspective—"to enable people to appropriate the gospel of the reign of God"—and spell out four general objectives in light of the guiding principle and the overall aim. In chapter 3 we review the praxis-centered epistemological base in liberation theology and religious education, which strongly defines much of the encounter between the two fields. In chapter 5 of this volume we deal more pointedly with the questions of context and persons involved in the task of religious education.

Together with the key questions pertaining to substantive process and product content as well as structural content, our discussion in chapter 4 is also helpful to illumine the educational category of *timing* in religious education. Simply put, this category refers to the questions of *when* religious education occurs. Timing includes several interrelated dimensions.[99] Obviously, learning and what we have called human emergence happen continually and, on the personal level, in divers but related registers of human behavior engaging cognition, affectivity, and lifestyle. Furthermore, a given learning sequence such as that described in terms of conscientization and creativity can occur in various time frames. Yet learning may be fostered and assessed more carefully when it is guided in an intentional and deliberate way in those specific instances and contexts agreed upon by the people involved. Thus, assuming as we do the centrality of the educational task vis à vis worship, community, and mission, a major challenge becomes apparent in light of our ongoing discussion. This major challenge consists in making accessible the experience of religious education so that learning and personal emergence may continually occur in the best possible ways.

There are several aspects to consider in the question of timing in religious education. These aspects include issues of personal development, personal maturity, and communal and societal change. In light of our discussion in both chapter 2[100] and in the present chapter, we can refer briefly to educational timing in terms of the four agendas of biblicotheological reflection on the reign of God and the fourfold overall purpose of religious education. Our summary statement of purpose indicates that, in a liberationist key, *the overall aim of Christian religious education is to enable people to appropriate the gospel of the reign of God by existentially responding to the call of conversion and discipleship in the midst of the ecclesial community which is to promote social transformation for the increase of freedom, justice, and peace; make accessible knowing and loving God; and foster human emergence, wholeness, and fulfillment.*[101]

One dimension of the educational question of timing must be seen in terms of the actual present *experience of the faith community,* its *past* (history and tradition, especially as enacted in its living story), and its *future* orientation (promise and hope, anticipation of God's will and expectation of the coming kingdom utopia). The discernment of the "times" of the church must be done in connection with the discernment of time in the sociocultural and historical context, and God's time *(kairos).* The goal of this comprehensive discernment process of reflection and interpretation is to discover educationally appropriate—i.e., "timely," pertinent and faithful—responses to the gospel of the reign of God.

A second dimension of the timing ("when") question of religious education pertains to what we have called the *agenda of the surrounding world.* Discernment and appraisal of current events and emerging trends in the social, cultural, and political milieu constitute an essential component of the educational program and curriculum of the ecclesial community. Obviously discernment and appraisal do not focus exclusively on the presence of alienating and oppressive situations and factors in the wider society. They also include attending to those dimensions that enhance life and promote humanization and community as well as the movement and work of the Spirit of God outside the church. Thus by "testing the spirits" of the age in both church and society ("to see if [those spirits] are from God," 1 John 4:1) the sense of timing may be heightened and the historical and eschatological consciousness may be augmented. Further, this process may foster motivation for learning and transformation and may provide relevant subject matter along the way.

A third dimension of the question of timing that must be addressed refers to the admittedly elusive issue of the *time or kairos of God.* What we mean by this reference is the sensitivity and responsiveness to the activity of God in the midst of history—in both church and society as well as in the whole creation—as a central concern in the educational task. The challenge to be met is how to develop awareness of the free movement of the creative and liberating divine will, in tune with the eschatological view of the gospel of the reign of God. The educational program and process must thus affirm hope and expectance in the face of mystery.

A fourth dimension of the question of timing focuses on *the learners' timing* (their readiness and the schedule and sequence of personal growth conditioned by their motivations, plans and choices, and so on) in terms of what we have called the "agenda of human emergence." Religious education must be especially sensitive to the question of personal self and development, that is, the actual existential situation of the persons involved in the educational task. Hence personal timing exerts significant influence on subject matter as well as on the process and structural content of religious education whenever life stages and social relationships and context are effectively taken into account. In fact, the time factor can also be assessed explicitly in light of subjective manifestations of timing such as haunting memories, the paralyzing presence of certain oppressive situations, the pulling forward movement of liberational longings, visions, and dreams, or the sense of challenge and opportunity, to name a few. A corollary principle in this regard is that religious educators must be especially careful when engaging in assessment of the needs of the people.[102]

The four dimensions of timing must be considered together and in close relation to one another. Just as we indicated with regard to the four agendas that inform the task of religious education, the four timing dimensions are also in a certain dynamic tension with each other. In actual practice, opportunities and problems in personal and communal development must be approached in light of the challenges of the times—i.e., the real-life situation of the surrounding world—together with the historical perspective of the faith community and the search for revelatory clues about God's timing. In sum, the whole process of religious education must be "timed" in such a way that the persons who are involved in learning and emerging together in the context of the faith community may actually appropriate the gospel of the reign of God.

So far, the liberationist tenets of conscientization, prophetic and utopian vision, praxis knowing, and critical interpretation for understanding and transformation have all illumined the task of religious education in various ways. With the treatment in the next chapter of a fifth liberationist motif—base community and the oppressed—we will complete our discussion of the encounter of religious education and liberation theology. We will thus also complete from our perspective the restatement of foundations and principles for the practice and theory of Christian religious education in a liberationist key.

Notes

1. Mark 4:11.
2. Juan Luis Segundo, *The Liberation of Theology,* trans. John Drury (Mary-knoll, N.Y.: Orbis, 1976), pp. 8-9.
3. Mary Elizabeth Moore, *Education for Continuity and Change: A New Model for Christian Religious Education* (Nashville: Abingdon, 1983), pp. 77, 81, 132-133.
4. In his reference to the witness of Mark's gospel and to the importance of the political hermeneutical key, Segundo emphasizes the special place that Mark gives to those theological debates and controversies, which embody Jesus' active opposition to the religious and ideological apparatus responsible for oppression within Israel. He calls attention to the fact that Jesus associates his disciples with the religious-political task of unmasking the mechanisms of ideological oppression, giving them an assignment as hazardous as his own. Hence, it is typical for Mark to indicate that Jesus repeatedly insisted his disciples must *understand* those mechanisms. It is in light of this concern that Jesus is bothered by the fact that his disciples do not seem to grasp the *general* (anti-ideological) theology underlying all the parables (see Mark 4:13). For Segundo, the parables were not meant to convince and convert the opponents of the kingdom but to accentuate the wide chasm between two different, opposed value-worlds structured by equally opposed and irreconcilable premises of both an ontological and epistemological nature: "They sensitize us precisely because they unmask and stress the conflict that gives the kingdom its power and its impact. Discipleship under Jesus cannot be imagined if one does not have a basic, overall understanding of that root conflict. One must understand 'the secrets of the kingdom'." (Juan Luis Segundo, *The Historical Jesus of the Synoptics,* vol. II of *Jesus of Nazareth Yesterday and Today,* trans. John Drury [Maryknoll, N.Y.: Orbis, 1985], p. 138.)
5. Various critical assessments of traditional academic theologies from liberationist perspectives appear in the following books: Hugo Assmann, *Theology for a Nomad Church,* trans. Paul Burns (Maryknoll, N.Y.: Orbis, 1976), pp. 43-125; Leonardo Boff, *Jesus Christ Liberator: A Critical Chris-*

tology for Our Time, trans. Patrick Hughes (Maryknoll, N.Y.: Orbis, 1978), pp. 1-48; Gustavo Gutiérrez, *A Theology of Liberation,* ed. and trans. Caridad Inda and John Eagleson (Maryknoll, N.Y.: Orbis, 1973), pp. 3-19; José Míguez Bonino, *Doing Theology in a Revolutionary Situation* (Philadelphia: Fortress, 1975); Segundo, *The Liberation of Theology,* pp. 3-38; Samuel Silva Gotay, *El Pensamiento Cristiano Revolucionario en América Latina y el Caribe* (Salamanca, España: Sígueme, 1981), pp. 29-181; Jon Sobrino, *The True Church and the Poor,* trans. Matthew J. O'Connell (Maryknoll, N.Y.: Orbis, 1984), pp. 1-38.

6. There is an interesting and complex relationship between political theology and liberation theology, the latter affirming in principle the hermeneutical, prophetic, and eschatological thrusts of the former. In fact many key theological themes discussed by the leading European political theologians such as Johannes B. Metz, Jürgen Moltmann, and Dorothee Sölle have been taken up also by liberation theologians. However, underneath those similarities there exist profound differences stemming from the liberationists' methodological approach to doing theology which is more grounded in concrete experience and praxis, more specific in analyzing socioeconomic realities, and more committed to action and transformation. Further, the special nature of the Latin American setting, and the close connection with the church and with grassroots ecclesial communities particularly, account for the unique character and contribution of liberation theology. For a succinct presentation of the differences between these two theological movements, see Francis P. Fiorenza, "Political Theology and Liberation Theology: An Inquiry into their Fundamental Meaning," in *Liberation, Revolution, and Freedom,* ed. Thomas M. McFadden (New York: Seabury, 1975), pp. 3-29. Rebecca S. Chopp, in *The Praxis of Suffering: An Interpretation of Liberation and Political Theologies* (Maryknoll, N.Y.: Orbis, 1986) includes helpful interpretive studies of Gustavo Gutiérrez, Johannes B. Metz, José Míguez Bonino, and Jürgen Moltmann. She rightly affirms that a most significant area of both agreement and disagreement between German political theology and Latin American liberation theology is the vision of faith (and the church) acting in a critical relationship to the world and the germane question of the nature of theology as a political activity: "Locating the critical activity of the church through its political, educational, and social activity with the poor, Latin American liberation theology committed itself not only to interpreting critically the world, in the tradition of its German counterpart political theology, but also to transforming that world" (p. 20).

7. Dennis P. McCann, *Christian Realism and Liberation Theology: Practical Theologies in Creative Conflict* (Maryknoll, N.Y.: Orbis, 1981), p. 150. These words fittingly allude to the challenge faced by liberation theology in regard to its method: "Criticism in theology must engage in a form of methodological reflection because the task is to account for the tradition's theoretical incoherence and practical irrelevance in a way that will open up plausible alternatives. If greater coherence and relevance can be achieved thereby, the results of such criticism eventually will be regarded as constructive rather than subversive and in time will become part of the tradition. This eventuality represents the difference between prophets and heretics" (Ibid.).

8. Gutiérrez, *A Theology of Liberation,* p. 13.
9. All major liberationist contributions include converging references to the challenge for revolutionary societal change in light of the objective conditions of oppressive structures and injustice (see note 5 above).
10. Gutiérrez explains that sin is at the base of all forms of alienation, and, thus, it is never adequately contained in any one expression of alienation. Further, sin demands a radical global liberation (which in turn necessarily implies practical particular liberations). By the same token, salvation cannot be reduced or identified to any one specific instance of human transformation, fulfillment, or liberation. However, in relation to sin, salvation involves radical and practical, redemptive mediations through partial fulfillments in the midst of history. The intimate connection between salvation and liberation is further illumined by Gutiérrez in his reference to the *three levels of liberation,* including: 1) particular or political liberations; 2) the process of liberation of humanity throughout history; and 3) liberation from sin into the freedom of solidarity with God and humanity. In other words, liberation entails particular events and is intrinsic to salvation (but no single act of liberation can ever be fully identified with the depth and comprehensiveness of salvation). Consequently, liberation is understood as inherent in the nature and purpose of history as the continual transformation of the new humanity. Liberation in concrete situation pertains to the fullness of salvation which is, ultimately, God's gift, as the very gift of the kingdom. (*A Theology of Liberation,* pp. 36-37, 152ff.) See also Leonardo and Clodovis Boff, *Salvation and Liberation,* trans. Robert R. Barr (Maryknoll, N.Y.: Orbis, 1984) for an expanded explanation of these fundamental notions in liberation theology.
11. The "hermeneutic of suspicion" constitutes the critical dimensions of Juan Luis Segundo's contribution to the question of method, in his *The Liberation of Theology.*
12. Sobrino, *The True Church and the Poor,* pp. 10-29.
13. Chopp, *The Praxis of Suffering,* p. 134. Chopp presents an insightful constructive reformulation of method for liberation theology whose various aspects are distinguished and related through six theses as follows: 1) the two sources for liberation theology are human existence and Christian tradition; 2) the source of human existence is interpreted politically, utilizing, among other disciplines, all the social sciences to reflect on the full concreteness of historical existence; 3) theology employs a hermeneutics of liberation, including a project of deideologization in relation to the source of Christian tradition; 4) the method of liberation theology can be characterized as a critical praxis correlation, wherein praxis is both the foundation and the aim of theological hermeneutics; 5) this method of critical praxis correlation is, by its nature, a form of ideology critique; 6) liberation theology must develop an adequate social theory to attend to the full meaning of praxis (pp. 134-148). See also Matthew L. Lamb, *Solidarity with Victims: Toward a Theology of Social Transformation* (New York: Crossroads, 1982). Lamb discusses the paradigmatic shift toward a dialectical unity between praxis and theory in doing theology and, especially, the "critical praxis correlation" type of the relationship between theory and praxis, as reflected in the method of liberation theology (pp. 86ff.).

14. Sobrino, *The True Church and the Poor*, p. 23. In religious education, James Michael Lee has contended from a different perspective that method is content in its own right—structural content, in Lee's terms.

15. A helpful collection of representative essays is included in Norman K. Gottwald, ed., *The Bible and Liberation: Political and Social Hermeneutics* (Maryknoll, N.Y.: Orbis, 1983).

16. The character of the grassroots or "base ecclesial communities" will be discussed in detail in chapter 5, especially in terms of the question of persons-in-context in religious education.

17. Catholic Action is a movement which began in Italy in the 1920s and 1930s. Its purpose was to mobilize lay people to engage in sociopolitical action under the aegis of the Vatican. (It must be remembered that since the absorption of the papal states by the newly formed Italy in the early 1870s, the Vatican had been bereft of effective political influences, and the clergy of Italy were suspect when they tried to extend political power; Luigi Sturzo was the exception). Catholic Action—always under Vatican and episcopal control by definition—spread to Spain, France, Belgium, and after World War II to the United States. Catholic Action central leaders were heavily influenced in their philosophy and theology by scholasticism. They adopted, naturally, as their threefold modus operandi the procedure proposed by the greatest of the scholastics, Thomas Aquinas: 1) observe, 2) judge, 3) act. This threefold method gained its greatest prewar fame in the Jocist movement founded in Belgium by Joseph Cardijn. In Brazil, Acâo Católica became the action arm of the Conferencia Nacional dos Bispos do Brasil, and these two institutions represented the church's response to newly perceived social challenges in the early 1960s. For detailed accounts of the emergence and development of new social awareness, involvement in the arena of the socioeconomic reality of the poor, and changing pastoral strategies, see: Charles Antoine, *Church and Power in Brazil* (Maryknoll, N.Y.: Orbis, 1973); Thomas C. Bruneau, *The Political Transformation of the Brazilian Catholic Church* (London: Cambridge University Press, 1974); Emmanuel de Kadt, *Catholic Radicals in Brazil* (London: Oxford University Press, 1970); *The Church at the Crossroads: From Medellín to Puebla* (1968-78) (Rome: IDOC, 1978).

18. Leonardo Boff, *Teología Desde el Lugar del Pobre* (Santander, España: Sal Terrae, 1986), p. 33. Actually, Pope Paul VI seems to echo an analogous approach in his *Octogesima Adveniens* (1971), n. 4.

19. Leonardo Boff and Clodovis Boff, *Cómo Hacer Teología de la Liberación* (Madrid: Ediciones Paulinas, 1986), p. 34.

20. For example, the Vatican's "Instruction on Certain Aspects of the 'Theology of Liberation' " (September, 1984) in general endorses both the values of commitment to the poor and oppressed and also the reaction against the existing social structures in Latin America. But the document emphatically rejects any objective and systematically understood Marxist worldview as incompatible and inimical with a Christian worldview. See especially vii, "Marxist Analysis" and viii, "Subversion of the Meaning of Truth and Violence." For a response to the Instruction on this point, see Leonardo Boff and Clodovis Boff, *Liberation Theology*, trans. Robert R. Barr (San Francisco: Harper & Row, 1986), pp. 65-72. Some of the most ideologically motivated and articulated criticisms of liberation theology

appear in most of the essays edited by Ronald Nash, *Liberation Theology* (Milford, Mich.: Mott Media, 1984). For an unabashed defense of capitalism and the presentation of a "North American liberation theology" supposedly embodied in the "liberal society," see Michael Novak, *Will It Liberate? Questions About Liberation Theology* (Mahwah, N.J.: Paulist Press, 1986).

21. Boff and Boff, *Cómo Hacer Teología de la Liberación,* pp. 40-41. For a well-balanced discussion of Marxism in liberationist perspective, see José Miguez Bonino, *Christians and Marxists: The Mutual Challenge to Revolution* (Grand Rapids, Mich.: Eerdmans, 1976). Arthur F. McGovern helpfully summarizes the impact of Marxism on Christianity and specifically in Latin America, in chapter 5 of his excellent book, *Marxism: An American Christian Perspective* (Maryknoll, N.Y.: Orbis, 1980). In response to the question of how much liberation theology's praxis and call for liberation is based on Marxist analysis, McGovern rightly indicates the following: 1) Liberation theology itself contains relatively little socioeconomic analysis as such, and the explicit references to Marxist writings are rather infrequent. 2) The Latin American bishops (Medellín, 1968; Puebla, 1979) are also convinced about the failure of capitalism (i.e., we could say that there is agreement about *observing* the situation as one of unjust dependence, *judging* it as "sinful" in light of the gospel; and affirming the challenge for Christians to *act* in the direction of overcoming this situation and working for justice and peace). McGovern concludes his assessment by affirming that liberation theology is not grounded in Marxism but in the experience of the peoples of Latin America and in faith reflection. Marxism is used "heuristically," in that certain insights (e.g., into the relation of theory and praxis, the political-economic causes of "underdevelopment," and the relation between ideology and social structures) are utilized for illumining both specific social situations and Christian faith itself. Finally, some specifically Christian counterparts to Marxist contributions can also be identified in this context, such as the commitment to living the faith and reflection on religious experience, biblical denunciations of injustice, criticisms of the church in every age for failing to act on justice and liberation demands, and so forth.

22. A twofold attitude of critique and recovery or reclaiming is observable on the part of Catholic liberation theologians with regard to the church's theological tradition in general and to the magisterium particularly. On the one hand, the targets of criticism are the theoricist, dualistic, elitist, and ahistorical tendencies of traditional theology, tendencies which are devoid of sensitivity for the social situation of the poor and oppressed and their (historical) liberation. A case in point, for example, would be much of scholastic theology and some directions of classic spirituality. On the other hand, contributions such as the unitarian conception of salvation history, the underscoring of the social demands of the gospel, and the realization of the prophetic dimension of the mission of the church are affirmed and incorporated together with the paradigmatic witness of saints, prophets, and martyrs.

23. The significance of the Exodus motif for liberation theology can hardly be overstated. A foundational work in the Latin American liberationist hermeneutics is J. Severino Croatto, *Exodus: A Hermeneutics of Freedom,*

trans. Salvator Attanasio (Maryknoll, N.Y.: Orbis, 1981). Croatto, influenced by Paulo Freire and Paul Ricoeur among others, seeks to develop a method of rereading the Bible from the perspective of his own Latin American situation, a situation that finds a focal point and a source of interpretation in the book of Exodus. The message found there is a symbol of a liberation theology which, for Croatto and many others, represents the core of the whole biblical message. For a liberationist biblical commentary on Exodus, see George V. Pixley, *Exodus: A Liberation Perspective* (Maryknoll, N.Y.: Orbis, 1987). Pixley proposes an "evangelical" and "popular" reading of Exodus on the basis of scientific exegetical work on the text and in light of actual contexts of oppression where the Bible is read, discussed, and interpreted.

24. Boff and Boff, *Cómo Hacer Teología de la Liberación,* pp. 46-50.

25. Ibid., p. 50.

26. Some interesting cases of popular mobilization with the participation of grassroots ecclesial communities in Brazil can be found in the booklet by Clodovis Boff, *Comunidades Eclasiales de Base y Prácticas de la Liberación* (Bogotá: Indo-American Press Service, 1981) pp. 9-19. The examples supplied in this book include situations of active resistance and solidarity in the face of injustice perpetrated by rich and powerful landowners.

27. Good descriptions of the method of liberation theology as operative on the grassroots level appear in Fray Betto, *Lo que son las Comunidades Eclesiales de Base* (Bogotá: Indo-American Press Service, 1981) and Joao B. Libânio, *Formacao Consciencia Crítica,* 3 vols. (Petrópolis, Brasil: Vozes, 1979-1980).

28. The liberationist redefinition of theology suggests a major revision in the field of theological education. Thus, we can identify a number of principles or guidelines pointing to new directions, as indicated in Daniel S. Schipani, "Pautas Epistemológicas en la Búsqueda de Alternativas para la Educación Teológica en América Latina," *Boletín Teológico* 20 (julio a septiembre 1985), pp. 32-60: 1) The theological task of the church belongs to the total family of God. Therefore, the search for new alternatives in theological education should start with the effective recognition of the people's participation and contribution. This in turn obviously calls for considerable restructuring and expansion of the theological curriculum, including radical reorientation in epistemology and methodology.

2) The recognition of multiple subjects in the theological task suggests a twofold responsibility: on the one side, various levels of theologizing should be distinguished and appreciated in their peculiar richness and complexity; on the other side—simultaneously—the divers theological contributions should be duly integrated. In this regard, Pablo Richard asserts that professional theologians need to be liberated by the evangelizing potential of the poor and need to develop their theological creativity in the context of ecclesial base communities and in their service: "The theologian must also develop a *professional theology* by starting with the *spiritual theology* of the poor and believing people and with the *organic theology* of the church of the poor." "Para Entender la Teología de la Liberación," *Teología de la Liberación—Documentos sobre una Polémica* (San José, Costa Rica: DEI, 1984), p. 105. The idea, then, is for theological education to develop means and resources to stimulate, recognize, evaluate, and

reappropriate the "spiritual theology" of the believers and the "organic theologies"—more or less explicit and coherent—of local, grassroots faith communities. On this point see also Boff and Boff, *Cómo Hacer Teología de la Liberación,* chapter 2.

3) Ecclesial communities have an immense potential for developing their theology as expression of maturing faith and also at the service of that faith in the light of God's reign. Actually, there are no such things as faith communities without "theology" (or, even, more or less complementary or conflicting "theologies"). Hence, a special challenge for theological education is to participate in the construction and re-creation of local theologies according to contextual models. It is assumed that the whole community plays a protagonic role in the development of local, "organic" theologies and that these theologies (as all authentic theology) must be at the service of the church itself in the framework of the global project of the reign of God. Concerning an appropriate methodology to face that challenge, see Robert J. Schreiter, *Constructing Local Theologies* (Maryknoll, N.Y.: Orbis, 1985). Schreiter proposes a systemic model that combines a careful consideration of factors related to the faith community, the gospel, and the sociocultural reality.

4) Theological education is to be inspired by an "ecclesiocommunity paradigm" rather than by a "clerical paradigm." Curriculum dispersion and fragmentation as well as the risks of "professionalization" and the individualistic conception of ministry, among other problems, need to be corrected. Thus, instead of focusing on the ministerial formation of leaders that will function in a professional manner, the *key guiding principle for theological education and the integrating image of ministry becomes the formation and transformation of the faith community.*

An additional note of clarification is fitting here. The transplantation of patterns and structures from the North Atlantic region to Latin America seems to account for the analogy observable in North and Latin America with respect to the discussion and critique of theology and theological education, as formulated by Edward Farley, for instance, in *Theologia: The Fragmentation and Unity of Theological Education* (Philadelphia: Fortress, 1983). Of particular interest for us is Farley's view of the "clerical paradigm" of ministry. See also Edward Farley, "Theology and Practice Outside the Clerical Paradigm," in *Practical Theology: The Emerging Field in Theology, Church and World,* ed. Don S. Browning (San Francisco: Harper & Row, 1983), pp. 21-41. Other helpful discussions connected with this topic are James F. Hopewell, "A Congregational Paradigm for Theological Education," *Theological Education* 21:1 (Autumn, 1984), pp. 60-70; Joseph C. Hough and John B. Cobb, *Christian Identity and Theological Education* (Chico: Scholars Press, 1985); and James N. Poling and Donald E. Miller, *Foundations for a Practical Theology of Ministry* (Nashville: Abingdon, 1985).

5) The adoption of the ecclesiocommunity paradigm in theological education presupposes that, as far as content is concerned the consideration of the rich and complex reality that is the life and mission of actual faith communities passes to the forefront. Among other things, this calls for dialogue and cooperation between theological institutions and local churches and parishes as well as the development of interdisciplinary

perspectives. By focusing on the grassroots faith community, theological reflection attends to the actual Christian story and vision as manifested in the midst of particular historical-cultural situations by representative microcosms of both church and society.

6) The ecclesiocommunity paradigm calls for radical curricular and methodological reformulations around so-called "practical theology" or "theology applied to ministry." For one thing, the dissociation between "theoretical" and "practical" components whereby "theological disciplines" (Bible, theology, history) merely inform and translate into ministry (e.g., religious education in the church) can no longer be supported. For another thing, since the theological task and ministry become essentially the responsibility of all of God's people, leadership training will be reoriented and reshaped; for example, such training will concentrate more on the formation of the healing and interpreting community rather than on the professional development of the pastoral leader's therapeutic and hermeneutical skills per se.

7) The ecclesiocommunity paradigm presents a particular challenge for the school and other institutions of theological education in the sense of substantial change in their character and self-definition. Two aspects stand out in this regard, and they must be seen as intimately related. First, those institutions are called upon to be "faith communities" themselves (although not necessarily in the sense of the local, ecclesial congregation). Second, theological education within this perspective must be carried out in the context of community formation and transformation. Ideally then, there would be a substantial analogy between ministry and community formation within theological schools and outside (in the parish or elsewhere).

29. Doing theology at the level of the local faith community can become a liberating pedagogical process in terms of reflection and action, including of course liberation from alienating and domesticating structures and models of religious education. This question relates directly to the problem of the "clerical paradigm" of ministry and theological education referred to in the previous note. The distance and gap between theological education and religious education is not a superficial phenomenon but part of the profound structures of the church's self-understanding, including basic assumptions about faith, theology, learning, and education. Edward Farley illumines this discussion in "Can Church Education be Theological Education?" *Theology Today* 42:2 (July, 1985), pp. 158-171.

The ecclesiocommunity paradigm alluded to above suggests that the theological task must be effectively integrated with the process of growth and maturity of the faith community, not as an end in itself of course, but for the sake of the fulfillment of Christian mission. Therefore, the educational ministry, particularly in the case of the religious education of youth and adults, can be seen as integrating a truly transforming and enabling (i.e., *conscientizing*) biblicotheological education within the larger framework of *worship, community,* and *mission* (see note no. 110 in chapter 2 and p. 183 in the present chapter). The educational processes and the biblicotheological re-creation occurring in base ecclesial communities are paradigmatic in this regard, as we will observe in chapter 5. Negatively speaking, we have here the rejection of the common assumption that church education cannot be also "theological education." The challenge, therefore, is to discover ways of placing the rich and varied resources— theological and otherwise—at the disposal of the church, resources that facilitate, for example, biblical exegesis and hermeneutics as well as other tools for historical, literary, social, and psychological analysis and critical interpretation, in line with the affirmed centrality of the educational ministry. In other words, what we have here is another facet of the liberationist challenge to take education in the church very seriously.

30. Thomas H. Groome, "Theology on Our Feet: A Revisionist Pedagogy for Healing the Gap between Academia and Ecclesia," in *Formation and Reflection: The Promise of Practical Theology,* ed., Lewis S. Mudge and James N. Poling (Philadelphia: Fortress, 1987), pp. 55-78.

31. In the last two decades, there has been a proliferation of translations and increased promotion and distribution of Bibles, including the production of "popular versions" in today's vernacular. This phenomenon correlates in turn with the growth of biblical scholarship in the Latin American continent.

32. Carlos Mesters, "The Use of the Bible in Christian Communities of the Common People," in *The Challenge of Basic Christian Communities,* ed. Sergio Torres and John Eagleson, trans. John Drury (Maryknoll, N.Y.: Orbis, 1981), p. 205.

33. Ibid.

34. Sociohistorical and sociological analyses of the world of both the biblical text and the interpreter provide foundation material for a significant and influential approach in biblical interpretation, as illustrated in the variety of contributions in the collected essays by Gottwald, ed. *The Bible and Liberation.* Together with the contributions stemming from Latin American theology, two other major streams of liberationist hermeneutic must be taken into account:

1) The *materialist exegesis*—which originated in Latin Europe, especially in Portugal and France, combines historical materialism with structuralism—and shares several emphases of the Latin Americans. Representative writings from this exegetical school stress (a) that the poor are a primary concern of the Bible, who must be rescued from the hands of the powerful, and (b) that the scriptures must be read in order to discern political praxis. See Fernando Belo, *A Materialist Reading of the Gospel of Mark,* trans. Matthew J. O'Connell (Maryknoll, N.Y.: Orbis, 1981) and Michel Clèvenot, *Materialist Approaches to the Bible,* trans. William J. Nottingham (Maryknoll, N.Y.: Orbis, 1985).

2) The *feminist liberationist hermeneutic,* which represents mainly North American scholarship, shares the overall liberationist feature of "seeing from the underside of history." However, this feminist liberationist stream does not correlate directly with materialist/Marxist socioeconomic philosophical orientation as do the other two (Latin American liberation theology and the materialist exegesis approach). The feminist perspective in exegetical work has contributed fresh insights that male interpreters of the Bible failed to grasp. See for example, Phyllis Trible, *God and the Rhetoric of Sexuality* (Philadelphia: Fortress, 1978): Elisabeth Schüssler Fiorenza, *In Memory of Her: Theological Reconstruction of Christian Origins* (New York: Crossroads, 1983); and Letty M. Russell, ed., *Feminist*

Interpretations of the Bible (Philadelphia: Westminster, 1985).

Both the Latin European hermeneutic and the feminist hermeneutic of the Bible affirm the value of the sociology of knowledge. They demonstrate that the interpreter's social situation affects substantially the reading of the text; hence *both* the text and the interpreter together must come under close scrutiny. For a helpful discussion of these and related topics, see Willard M. Swartley, "Beyond the Historical-Critical Method," in *Essays on Biblical Interpretation: Anabaptist-Mennonite Perspectives,* ed., Willard M. Swartley (Elkhart, Ind.: Institute of Mennonite Studies, 1984), pp. 248ff.

35. See the pioneering study by José Porfirio Miranda, *Marx and the Bible: A Critique of the Philosophy of Oppression,* trans. John Eagleson (Maryknoll, N.Y.: Orbis, 1974). Unfortunately, Miranda's book tends to present a one-sided and over-simplified biblical interpretation. He often imposes a Marxist framework on the scriptures with an approach vulnerable to the critique of political-economic reductionism.

36. Georges Casalis, *Correct Ideas Don't Fall from the Skies: Elements for an Inductive Theology,* trans. Jeanne Marie Lyons and Michael John (Maryknoll, N.Y.: Orbis, 1984), p. 62.

37. Ibid., p. 63. "Political conscientization by alphabetization" refers to the transforming process of learning to "read" (i.e., critically interpret) reality and to "write" one's story (i.e., fashioning the future) while becoming literate.

38. Mesters, "The Use of the Bible in the Christian Communities of the Common People," pp. 202-203.

39. Paul Lehmann, "Forward," Richard Shaull, *Heralds of a New Reformation: The Poor of South and North America* (Maryknoll, N.Y.: Orbis, 1984), p. x.

40. David Lockhead, "The Liberation of the Bible," in *The Bible and Liberation,* p. 83.

41. Ibid., p. 88.

42. Karl Mannheim, *Ideology and Utopia* (New York: Harcourt, Brace and World, 1936). For Mannheim, the concept of ideology refers to a discovery stemming from political conflict, namely, that ruling groups can in their thinking and view of reality become so intensively interest-bound to a situation that they are blinded to certain facts which would undermine their sense of domination: "There is implicit in the word 'ideology' the insight that in certain situations the collective unconscious of certain groups obscures the real condition of society both to itself and others and thereby stabilizes it" (p. 40).

43. It should be noted that the relation of faith and ideology is dealt with throughout Segundo's *The Liberation of Theology* as a dominant theme of the book in a nuanced fashion. See also Segundo's *Faith and Ideologies,* vol. i of *Jesus of Nazareth Yesterday and Today.* Segundo discusses a more neutral meaning of *ideology,* and he asserts that faith and ideology cannot be separated in practice, although they can be distinguished. Thus, for instance, faith can be recognized 1) by a pretension to an objective absolute value, whereas an ideology lacks this pretension, and 2) by the fact that faith entails a stronger association with the *goal* (signification), while ideology points more directly to the *means* to achieve the goal (efficacy).

See Alfred T. Hennelly, *Theologies in Conflicts: The Challenge of Juan Luis Segundo* (Maryknoll, N.Y.: Orbis, 1979), pp. 123ff. Hennelly's book is an excellent introduction and interpretive study of Segundo's theological contribution until 1979. He suggests that the real, though unexpressed, major thesis of Segundo's *The Liberation of Theology* is that "the entire millennium and a half of Constantinian Christianity has involved a gradual and massive ideologization of the gospel in favor of powerful and privileged interests in Western society" (p. 135).

44. Robert McAfee Brown, *Theology in a New Key: Responding to Liberation Themes* (Philadelphia: Westminster, 1978), pp. 79-80.

45. The confrontation with a radically different perspective as an opportunity for perspective transformation and liberation from "ideological captivity" is trenchantly demonstrated by Robert McAfee Brown in *Unexpected News: Reading the Bible with Third World Eyes* (Philadelphia: Westminster, 1984).

46. Lockhead, "The Liberation of the Bible," p. 80. Lockhead also discusses the "liberation" of the Bible in a public sense (i.e., how the Bible is presented in the media, for instance). Furthermore, he deals with the connection between liberating the Bible from its various captivities and the process of personal liberation. Lockhead asserts that the mechanisms that allow the Bible to be put in ideological captivity are built into the very nature of understanding. Says Lockhead: "We have found that self-criticism and consciousness-raising are absolutely necessary in any attempt to engage in a liberated reading of the Bible" (p. 87).

47. Ibid., pp. 80ff. Understanding is political in the sense that what we "know" or "understand" always takes place in a social context constituted by a complex system of social relationships, including *power* relationships. In Lockhead's words, "There can be no escape from this kind of politics of understanding . . . relations of dominance and submission arise at every stage. *Who selects the text? Why is this text chosen? What interests are reflected in the resources which the group is using? In whose interests is it to read the text the way we do? Why do we analyze our contemporary reality the way we do? Why do we apply the text in one way rather than another?* In relation to all our questions we need to ask, *Whose interests are being served?*" (p. 86).

48. The term "hermeneutic circle" has been previously applied to the exegetical approach of Rudolf Bultmann. However, Segundo contends that his own theological method corresponds more adequately to the strict sense of the "circle." For our part, we prefer the expression *hermeneutical circulation* utilized by Casalis in *Correct Ideas Don't Fall from the Skies,* pp. 67-70. "Circulation" connotes a dynamic hermeneutical process, which is precisely what Segundo proposes.

49. For a reference to the question of content and process, see chapter 1, note 114, in the present volume.

50. Segundo, *The Liberation of Theology,* pp. 8ff.

51. Ibid., p. 9. Segundo goes on to describe how key critical thinkers and their works such as Harvey Cox *(The Secular City),* Karl Marx *(The Communist Manifesto),* and Max Weber *(The Protestant Ethic and the Spirit of Capitalism)* began the circle but, upon reaching a certain level of suspicion, interrupted the process without pressing on to a new hermeneutic and to a reaffirmation of their faith. In contrast, Segundo proposes that

James Cone *(A Black Theology of Liberation)* successfully completed all four phases of the hermeneutical circle. Obviously, we may also pose the challenging question as to whether all liberation theologians always effectively complete the circle.

52. Hugo Assmann, "Statement by Hugo Assmann," in *Theology of the Americas,* ed. Sergio Torres and John Eagleston (Maryknoll, N.Y.: Orbis, 1976), p. 300. We will discuss in detail the epistemological/hermeneutical privilege of the poor and oppressed in the next chapter.

53. José Míguez Bonino, "Reading the Biblical Text from a Liberation Theology Perspective: Implications for the Church, Christian Education, and Ministry." Lecture at the Associated Mennonite Biblical Seminaries, November 3, 1986. See also Guillermo Cook, *The Expectation of the Poor: Latin American Basic Ecclesial Communities in Protestant Perspective* (Maryknoll, N.Y.: Orbis, 1985), chapter 7.

54. The question of transformational learning in light of the epistemological/hermeneutical privilege of the poor and oppressed is also dealt with in the next chapter.

55. Mesters, "The Use of the Bible in Christian Communities of the Common People," p. 208.

56. Ibid., p. 209.

57. Ernesto Cardenal who, at the time of this writing is the Minister of Culture in the Nicaraguan national government, received spiritual direction from Thomas Merton at the Trappist monastery of Our Lady of Gethsemani, in Kentucky.

58. Together with Merton, Cardenal embraced a spirituality and a view of the gospel which integrate social and spiritual redemption. Furthermore, according to Cardenal, Merton told him that in Latin America the contemplative person could not be detached from political struggle. Ernesto Cardenal, "Lo que fue Solentiname (carta al pueblo de Nicaragua)," *Nuevos estilos de vida* (Lima: CELADEC, CCPD núm. 5), ii (1978), p. 22.

59. Ernesto Cardenal, *The Gospel in Solentiname,* vols. 1-4, trans. Donald D. Walsh (Maryknoll, N.Y.: Orbis, 1976-1981). See also Philip and Sally Sharper, eds., *The Gospel in Art by the Peasants of Solentiname* (Maryknoll, N.Y./Dublin: Orbis/Gill and Macmillan, 1984).

60. For these observations concerning basic presuppositions in the grassroots hermeneutic of Solentiname, I am partially indebted to Héctor Rubén Sánchez Fernández, my former professional colleague at Seminario Evangélico de Puerto Rico.

61. For example, when studying the lesson "Jesus Teaches How to Pray," Cardenal explains that Matthew uses the Greek word *battalogein* which is like saying "don't go *blah, blah, blah, blah* like the pagans" (Mt. 6:7). Cardenal also states that Jesus really used the familiar word "Papá *(Abba)* rather than the more formal "Father." A number of interesting comments by the Solentiname participants deal with the meaning of communion with and simple spontaneous love for God, fearless closeness to God, etc. Those comments are later supplemented by keen observations about genuine spirituality, community, and justice. What we can observe, then, is a blending of *biblicotheological* and *religious* education, as people learn about the Bible and they are challenged also to learn the Bible (i.e., learning to see, feel, and act biblically). (Cardenal, *The Gospel in Solentiname,* pp. 208ff.)

62. Carlos Mesters is a Catholic pastor and theologian of Dutch origin working in Brazil. A biblical scholar and a philologist, he has dedicated his
considerable knowledge and skills to serve the Brazilian people by helping
them to enter into a fruitful dialogue with the scriptures. Unfortunately,
his numerous essays on the Bible—including commentaries, teachers'
manuals, and related materials—are not available in English. For instance, an interesting case is a popular commentary on the book of Ruth:
Carlos Mesters, *Rute: Uma História da Bíblia* (Sao Paulo, Brasil: Ediçóes
Paulinas, 1985). This little book has the following catchy subtitle: "Pao,
Famíla, Terra! Quem vai por aí nao erra!" (or, "Bread, Family, Land!
Whoever takes that road will not err!"). For those of us who associate the
biblical story of Ruth mainly with an ancient family situation—including
a few clues on getting along with one's mother-in-law!—Mesters' commentary is disarmingly revealing. Materials like that originate in the lively
dialogues, reflections, and insights promoted in the *círculos bíblicos*. Mesters and his colleagues then rearrange the observations more systematically
and include needed background information and a few additional exegetical handles adopted from "scientific" exegesis and hermeneutics. The
material is then ready to be returned to the people, as it were, for further
processing and illumination.
63. Mesters, "The Use of the Bible in Christian Communities of the Common
People," p. 199.
64. Review our discussion of biblicotheological reflection in the second chapter (pp. 95-98 and note 110). Notice that this representation of grassroots
hermeneutic in Brazil can also be nicely correlated with our stated assumptions about the centrality of the educational task in the church.
65. Mesters, "The Use of the Bible in Christian Communities of the Common
People," pp. 200, 203.
66. Ibid., p. 205.
67. Frei Betto, "Church Born of the People," LADOC 12:3 (January-February
1982), pp. 1-19.
68. Cook, *The Expectation of the Poor,* pp. 110-111.
69. Ibid., p. 123.
70. Ibid., p. 125.
71. Mesters, "The Use of the Bible in Christian Communities of the Common
People," p. 206. Ecclesial communities encourage the creation of popular
renditions of significant biblical texts in the composition of songs for
worship, proclamation, and edification.
72. Religious education is seen, then, as a unique and essential form of ministry, as a facilitating servant, as it were. Religious education does not exist
for its own sake but rather for the sake of worship, community, and
mission, which are the main facets of the life of the church and the
church's very reason for being. The inverted arrows represent a reciprocal
relationship: worship, community, and mission. The last-mentioned three
themselves include educational dimensions which can in turn be integrated, reshaped, and redirected during the very enactment of religious education itself.

These and related notions have been developed in the context of the
Task Force on Future Models of Congregational Education, an Inter-
Mennonite project in process. For their articulation I am indebted to that
group and, especially, to my colleague and friend Marlene Y. Kropf.

73. "Discipling" here simply means the process of formation, transformation, and empowerment of Christian disciples on both personal and communal levels. It is another way of referring to the awakening and nurturing of faith understood in light of the scriptures (i.e., faith as, essentially, lifestyle) and carried out in and through the educational ministry of the church.

74. See p. 94 and notes 98 and 99 in the second chapter.

75. Together with the writers mentioned in chapter 2—especially Thomas Groome, John L. Elias, and William Bean Kennedy—we must include Malcolm L. Warford, *The Necessary Illusion: Church, Culture and Educational Change* (Philadelphia: Pilgrim, 1976).

76. John H. Westerhoff III, *Will Our Children Have Faith?* (New York: Seabury, 1976) p. 31.

77. Ibid., pp. 30-32. Westerhoff was in search of a theological framework for religious education and foundations for the development of an alternative to the "schooling-instructional paradigm." However, thus far he has not spelled out either that theological framework or the educational contours for the alternative paradigm. Implicitly, Westerhoff seems to incorporate several dimensions of a liberationist approach later for instance, in his *Living the Faith Community: The Church that Makes a Difference* (Minneapolis: Winston, 1985). In this book Westerhoff discusses, among other things, the question of the church as a base community, its alternative prophetic consciousness, and its passion for the stranger and oppressed.

78. Allen J. Moore, "Liberation and the Future of Christian Education," in *Contemporary Approaches to Christian Education,* ed. Jack L. Seymour and Donald E. Miller (Nashville: Abingdon, 1982), p. 117. Moore proposes that religious education become a prophetic education that challenges oppressive social structures from the perspective of Christian eschatology. Thus a major issue to be addressed is lifestyle, defined as a pattern of beliefs, values, and attitudes which can be described and which are manifested in the way people choose to live. Moore concludes that, as Christians, we must learn to see the world through the eyes of faith, as Jesus would see it (p. 121).

79. It may be useful for the reader to review the sections with explicit discussions of contributions and limitations of liberation theology in the previous chapters and also in chapter 5.

80. For example, from the perspective of the field of biblical hermeneutics, a hermeneutical approach to religious education is proposed by H. Edward Everding, "A Hermeneutical Approach to Educational Theory," in *Foundations for Christian Education in an Era of Change,* ed. Marvin J. Taylor (Nashville: Abingdon, 1976), pp. 41 ff. From the perspective of the field of religious education, an interpretation approach is presented by Jack L. Seymour and Carol A. Wehrheim, "Faith Seeking Understanding: Interpretation as a Task of Christian Education," in *Contemporary Approaches to Christian Education,* pp. 123 ff.

81. Thomas H. Groome, *Christian Religious Education: Sharing Our Story and Vision* (San Francisco: Harper & Row, 1980), p. 184.

82. Moore, *Education for Continuity and Change,* p. 121.

83. See Groome, *Christian Religious Education,* pp. 195-197, 217-223. Also, Mary C. Boys and Thomas H. Groome, "Principles and Pedagogy in Biblical Study," *Religious Education* 77:5 (September-October, 1982), pp. 486-507.

84. James Michael Lee, "Process Content in Religious Education, in *Process and Relationships: Issues in Theory, Philosophy, and Religious Education,* ed. Iris V. Cully and Kendig Brubaker Cully (Birmingham, Ala.: Religious Education Press, 1978), p. 27. See also Lee's essay "Religious Education and the Bible: A Religious Educationist's View," in *Biblical Themes in Religious Education,* ed. Joseph S. Marino (Birmingham, Ala.: Religious Education Press, 1983), pp. 1-161.

85. James Michael Lee, *The Content of Religious Instruction* (Birmingham, Ala.: Religious Education Press, 1985), p. 641.

86. Brown, *Unexpected News,* Introduction.

87. Edesio Sánchez-Cetina, "Listening to Other Voices," in *Always Being Reformed: The Future of Church Education,* ed. John C. Purdy (Philadelphia: Geneva, 1985), pp. 87 ff.

88. Brown, *Unexpected News,* p. 27.

89. Different scholars approach the Emmaus narrative differently. Thus, Thomas Groome discusses the example of the risen Christ as teacher in the Emmaus story, in *Christian Religious Education,* pp. 135-36. He also includes the story among the illustrations supplied when spelling out his "shared praxis approach," pp. 207-223. For a profound epistemological analysis of the Emmaus event from the perspective of creativity and transformation, see James E. Loder, *The Transforming Moment: Understanding Convictional Experiences* (San Francisco: Harper & Row, 1981), pp. 96-121. Loder discusses the story as paradigmatic of "convictional knowing," defined as "the patterned process by which the Holy Spirit transforms all transformations of the human spirit." And James Michael Lee refers to the example of Jesus as teacher in light of the Emmaus narrative in *The Content of Religious Instruction,* pp. 742-43; Lee underscores the ultimate success of the Emmaus pedagogy as being strongly correlated to Jesus' deliberate introduction of multidimensional substantive content in the teaching situation.

90. Moore, *Continuity and Change,* pp. 129-30. Moore's own approach—the "traditioning model"—includes the comprehensive goals of knowledge with understanding, together with the transformation of persons' actions, beliefs, and values. Further, she explicitly includes creativity, curiosity, awe, and hope and the integration of thought, feeling, and action among the characteristics of her model.

91. See note #28 in the present chapter and also, in chapter 5, the discussion of religious education and theologizing, pp. 226-228, 239.

92. Seven *meanings* and four *modes* (sensorimotor, emotional, analytic, and synthetic understanding) of understanding are discussed in Charles F. Melchert, " 'Understanding' as a Purpose of Religious Education," *Religious Education* 76:2 (March-April, 1981) pp. 178-86. In his response to Melchert in the same volume, Craig Dykstra adds some helpful comments on the *dynamics* of understanding. Dykstra also deals with the crucial question *what* do we want people to understand if the purpose of religious education is realized? Dykstra then discusses the issue of calling into question patterns of human understanding on the part of biblical faith. Dykstra views "understanding" finally as a penultimate, necessary purpose of religious education whereas "the kind of understanding that is at the center of religious education is an understanding of what leads to the mysteries at the depths of human life and into the encounter with the

realities that show up the limits of our understanding." (Craig Dykstra, "Understanding the Place of 'Understanding,' " p. 194.)

93. Boff and Boff, *Cómo Hacer Teología de la Liberación*, p. 83.

94. Cited in Brown, *Theology in a New Key*, pp. 88, 97-100. Beatriz Melano Couch has written one of the best introductions to the contribution of Paul Ricoeur, in *Hermanéutica Metódica: Teoría de la Interpretación Según Paul Ricoeur* (Buenos Aires: Docencia, 1983).

95. James W. Fowler, "Black Theologies of Liberation: A Structural-Developmental Analysis," in *The Challenge of Liberation Theology: A First World Response*, ed. Brian Mahan and L. Dale Richesin (Maryknoll, N.Y.: Orbis, 1981) pp. 69-90. Although focused on black liberation theologies, Fowler's essay is very relevant for our discussion, as already suggested in chapter 1 (note no. 45).

96. Ibid., pp. 87-88. It can be argued, in fact, that many liberation theologians have moved significantly beyond the early "ideological" liberationist stances. For instance, the brothers Boff briefly address other "temptations" of Latin American liberation theology such as these: 1) absolutizing liberation theology to the detriment of due consideration of other theologies; 2) failing to duly appreciate dimensions of oppression other than socioeconomic poverty; 3) excessive emphasis on confrontation and discontinuity, while neglecting the potential of dialogue and mutual enrichment with other theological positions, including the official Catholic magisterium. Boff and Boff, *Cómo Hacer Teología de la Liberación*, pp. 83-84.

97. The purpose of the "traditioning" model of Christian religious education is to maximize both continuity and transformation. See Moore, *Continuity and Change*, pp. 17-18, 121ff. Thomas Groome also deals with explicitly balanced views of time, tradition and change, and continuity, in his *Christian Religious Education*, pp. 5-19, 185-187, 198-199.

98. Letty M. Russell, "Handing on Tradition and Changing the World," in *Tradition and Transformation in Religious Education*, ed. Padraic O'Hare (Birmingham, Ala.: Religious Education Press, 1979), pp. 73-86. Other chapters in this volume deal with the same topic—chapters by Mary Boys, Maria Harris, C. Ellis Nelson, and Dwayne Huebner.

99. In this discussion I follow closely my comments on the subject of timing in Daniel S. Schipani, *Conscientization and Creativity: Paulo Freire and Christian Education* (Lanham, Md.: University Press of America, 1984), pp. 138ff.

100. See especially pp. 95-100.

101. P. 100.

102. On the topic of need assessment, see Maurice L. Monette, "Paulo Freire and Other Unheard Voices," *Religious Education* 74:2 (September-October, 1979), pp. 543-554. Monette discusses the ethical and political assumptions of the need-assessment approach to program planning in adult education. He argues convincingly against different ways of unilaterally prescribing the "needs" of others and of merely catering to their wants and indiscriminate felt needs, thereby promoting an individualistic ethic which fails to promote social awareness and responsibility. He concludes that a religious education designed to promote justice will administratively and programatically be based on a listening process which will encourage a *critical* analysis of needs both as perceived by the educator and by the educatees.

Chapter 5

The Oppressed and the Base Community

"Blessed are you who are poor . . ."[1]

JESUS

"Faith comes alive in the dynamism of the good news that reveals us as children of the Father and sisters and brothers of one another and creates a community, a church, the visible sign to others of liberation in Christ.

"The proclamation of the gospel . . . takes place from within an option of real and active solidarity with the interests and struggles of the poor, the exploited classes. The attempt to situate oneself in this locus . . . demands a conversion to another world, a new way of understanding the faith—and it leads to reformulation of the gospel message."[2]

GUSTAVO GUTIÉRREZ

"The converted life is a revolutionary existence over against the status quo, a life committed to a vision of God's coming community of liberation, justice, peace, whole community, and the well-being of all people . . .

"God calls his people to be the signs of Shalom, the vanguard of God's coming community, a community of cultural change . . .

"The people of God are called to live for this vision and the church's educational ministry is given the responsibility of transmitting and sustaining that vision and enhancing its understanding."[3]

JOHN H. WESTERHOFF III

INTRODUCTION

There is a very close relationship between the previous chapter and the present one as suggested by the two gospel quotations—"you have been given the secret of the kingdom of God" and "blessed are you who are poor"—when seen in liberationist perspective. We have just discussed the question of critical reflection and biblical interpretation by focusing mainly on the educational categories of product content and process content. Now we turn our attention to the principal subjects of liberation theology, the people oppressed, the poor.[4] How is the beatitude uttered by Jesus according to Luke 6:20 to be interpreted? Two interrelated insights are possible when that teaching is perceived from a liberationist vantage point and with the eyes of actual believing poor.[5] First, when Jesus declares that the kingdom belongs to the poor, he is calling our attention to the fact that the poor can reveal more adequately what is happening around us. Thus the poor are channels of divine revelation and facilitators of transforming learnings such as a re-visioning of social reality in the direction of God's reign of justice and peace (*shalom*). Second, the beatitude affirms, not so much the internal spiritual inclinations of the poor, but rather God's inclinations, that is to say the way in which God is predisposed on behalf of the weak, the victim, the marginal, the oppressed. This insight is, therefore, a reference to the mercy and justice which typifies God's reign. The teaching of Jesus does not leave room for a moralizing or spiritualizing exegesis, not even in Matthew's version—"poor *in spirit.*"[6] In fact, the same biblical texts which speak about the poor mention the hungry, the imprisoned, the blind, and other unfortunates and rejects of society, not to mention the explicit curses for the rich that Luke includes after the beatitudes.

In light of this kind of biblical grounding liberation theology presents a compelling twofold call for transformation and community. And such a call, explicitly registered in the quotations from Gustavo Gutiérrez and John Westerhoff which opened this chapter, will be discussed mainly in terms of the persons-in-context category of religious education.[7]

The interface between liberation theology and religious education at this juncture will lead us to recapitulate in a sense the whole discussion of this book. Historically, an interesting connection can be established between the rise and growth of the base (or basic) ecclesial (or Christian) communities (BECs) and the Base Education Movement inspired by Paulo Freire in Brazil. In both instances, progressive Catholic leaders, and especially several bishops, endorsed and promoted pedagogical work with and among the people, including conscientization-orientated religious education programs. So here we underscore again the striking association between a pedagogical approach and practice—both in general "popular" education as well as in "religious" education—and ecclesial and theological renewal, including reformulation and revitalization of catechesis, especially since the Medellin Bishops' Conference in 1968.[8]

Before proceeding with the discussion, a point of clarification is in order. Today the association between liberation theology and the BECs is taken for granted. However, it can be argued that the confluence of these two movements—as far as an explicit, consistent, and systematic object of theologizing is concerned—goes back only to the Puebla Bishops Conference in 1979. Before that it is possible to identify distinct bodies of literature, separate thinkers and institutional streams, and even separate sources in Medellín. The base community movement, which emerged mostly in Brazil, and the significant expansion across Central America of the ministry of the lay Catholic religious educators (*delegados de la palabra*) arose under the impetus of creative thinking in pastoral theology and religious education specifically, even as liberationists were themselves pastorally active also. Puebla officially sanctioned the central theme of liberation theology—the "preferential option for the poor" (although liberation theology was not endorsed as such)—as well as the BEC movement.[9] In this light and with that qualification, one can agree with Harvey Cox's observation that ecclesiology is the key to understanding liberation theology because "its view of the church is derived in considerable measure from the empirical reality of the base communities."[10]

We will explore first the stated privileged position of the poor from the liberationist perspective. Then we will focus on the transforming potential of the faith of the oppressed. Finally, there will be a description of the character of the prophetic church as modeled in the BECs, and the question of the faith community as context of religious education. Our dialogical and critical approach to the interfacing between religious education and liberation theology will be employed throughout this chapter, including specific references to the limitations of the liberationist perspective.

THE PRIVILEGED POOR

The association between the poor and Latin American liberation theology can hardly be overstated. This theology has been articulated in light of and in response to the sufferings of the poor and it continues to mesh with their struggle for liberation and justice. In order to present the liberationist perspective on the poor we need to discuss briefly its connection with the church's official teaching and pastoral work, the biblical base, the poor as theological locus, and the meaning of poor as "base."

Medellín, Puebla, and Beyond

The Latin American bishops have declared: "We affirm the need for conversion on the part of the whole church to a preferential option for the poor, an option aimed at their integral liberation." This option is spelled out in detail in the Final Document of the Puebla Conference, including a consideration of aims, means, and commitment.[11]

The fact is that the poor have been consistently the *objects* of concern and mercy on the part of the church.[12] In Latin America that kind of privileged situation of the poor has been dramatically emphasized and specified in terms of the social, economic, and political setting, after Vatican II, as registered in the official teachings and documents. Leonardo Boff alludes to five theological-pastoral lines of reflection and action assumed by the church since Medellín and Puebla: 1) Priority given to the plight of the poor who constitute the vast majority (roughly 80 percent) of the Latin American population by becoming not just a church *for* the poor and *with* the poor, but rather a church *of* the poor. This identification happens especially to the extent that the hierarchy and the leadership become better acquainted and more identified with the world of oppression and—simultaneously—when the poor become more active participants in the life and ministry of the church. 2) Directly related to the previous point is the understanding of salvation as comprehensive liberation rather than spiritual redemption only. This implies an actual search for socioeconomic and political justice as well as for cultural and religious freedom and creativity. Hence salvation involves a process perceived as a necessary historical mediation, realization, and advancement of the reign of God. 3) The proliferation and growth of the BECs. BECs are understood as representing the rebirth of the church in terms of the faith of the common people, especially the poor and oppressed. Furthermore, BECs provide the existential context in which the poor actually practice freedom and creativity and organize for further liberation in light of the gospel. 4) Involvement in the cause of human rights, especially as a "preferential concern to defend and promote the rights of the poor, the marginalized, and the oppressed" (Puebla, 1217). 5) An option for the adolescent (more than 50 percent of the population in Latin America), again a Puebla guideline as a "preferential concern for young people on the part of the church which sees in them a force for the transformation of society" (1218).

What is new (or at least more radical) in the liberationist perspective is that it goes one step further than the church's official teaching in spelling out the privileged status of the poor. It assumes that the poor are also, and primarily, *subjects*, indeed "the principal historical subjects in the realization of the project of the poor of Nazareth," in the words of Boff.[13] The active irruption of the poor in the social and ecclesial scenes while confronting oppressive structures is thus seen to be a manifestation of the power of faith and the relevance of the gospel. Indeed, Gustavo Gutiérrez testifies that those who were working for the evangelization of the poor and exploited people came to realize that they were being evangelized by the oppressed, thus validating the Puebla reference to "the evangelizing potential of the poor." The poor were recognized not just as the privileged receivers of the gospel message but its bearers also.[14]

A Biblical View

Bible study and biblical reflection play a major role in both the theological method and the religious education processes fostered by liberation theology, as already suggested in chapter 4. It is not surprising, then, that the understanding of poverty as well as the identification with the poor on the part of liberation theologians (including living with and among them) assume a strong biblical foundation. These theologians affirm a biblical perspective toward the poor and poverty which strengthens the case for the "preferential option" and substantiates the understanding of the privileged status of the poor.

In the Old Testament, God is the God of the poor and the oppressed who sides with the victims, taking their part and identifying with them. In the New Testament, the same God becomes incarnate, not in a wealthy, influential man with a good name, but in a Jew who belongs to the lower, working class and who consistently casts his lot with the poor until the powerful manage to kill him. Further, in the biblical documents, poverty is not simply a fact of life but the result of the sin of the powerful. Being poor is determined by oppression, and it is a cause for the wrath of God.[15] Hence a kind of conversion takes place when the believing poor and oppressed—and those who identify with them— pass from acquiescence to a cry for justice and to some form of resistance and work for transformation. Accepting poverty as the will of God or as a kind of natural phenomenon therefore becomes a manifestation of unfaith. Moreover, in the dialectical reinterpretation of the biblical texts in light of the historical context and liberating praxis, the discovery is made that the poor are the special locus of divine presence and action. The poor are seen as playing a singular and privileged part in the fulfillment of God's plan and dream for humankind and creation (i.e., cosmic reconciliation and recreation through Jesus Christ: Ephesians 1:10; Colossians 1:20). The oppressed have a mediating role, as it were, in the coming of God's reign. This is the reason why, after restating the notion that every genuine theology stems from one or another concrete spirituality (that is to say, an existential encounter with God within history), liberationists can affirm that their theology "has found its cradle in the confrontation of faith with injustice perpetrated against the poor."[16]

The Poor as Theological Locus

Meeting the poor, identification with and commitment to them, is the first and indispensable moment for theological inquiry and reflection. The poor constitute not only the necessary context and starting point but they are also the privileged inter-locutors of the theologians, as Robert McAfee Brown indicates in his discussion of the "challenge to established harmonies" on the part of liberation theology.[17] The theological commitment pre-supposes the "epistemological privilege" of the oppressed already alluded to in our brief reference to the interpretation of the beatitude ("blessed are you who are poor") in the sense that the poor's perception of the world is closer to the reality of the world than the way the rich and powerful view it. Further, theological reflection must respond to the questions raised by the oppressed peoples themselves and enter into dialogue with them.

Several factors support the contention that the poor have be-come the primary context or "place" for doing theology. Gustavo Gutiérrez emphasizes that their actual presence and proactive role is being felt in the historical process of Latin America, prin-cipally in the struggles of the common people for liberation and in the new historical awareness associated with those struggles.[18] The simple fact that the great majority of people are poor—and most of them even poorer than before after decades of failed political-economic policies—can no longer be underestimated. Further, if the poor and oppressed had been somehow "absent" or "silent" before, they are now confronting the exploitation and despoliation produced by an unjust social order at home and the effects of imperialism and its allies. The change from passive acceptance of their fate to divers forms of challenge and resis-tance has been brought about in part by the process of modern-ization. Modernization disrupts the poor's traditional way of life, and their eyes are opened to structural and global realities, main-ly through participating in the grassroots basic Christian commu-nities which foster Freire-style conscientization endeavors. Their resistance has often provoked, in turn, further violent reaction and divers forms of repression by right-wing groups and United States supported regimes. This "irruption of the poor," which is seen dramatically in their active participation in the life and ministry of the church, takes the form of alternative projects for renewal and transformation in different contexts (church, society) and on diverse levels (neighborhood; and local, state, national political structures). The affirmation of the poor and oppressed as privileged theological locus, then, needs to be seen in light of that complex and dynamic social reality.

Liberation theologians understand that to assume the "place" of the poor is, mainly, to recognize and support their interests and cause, the struggle for justice, and for new ways of realizing life in community. So this theological relocation is primarily a movement of *solidarity*[19] which defines both praxis and reflection. In other words, the locus or context of theological inquiry and discussion correlates with involvement and participation in the actual historical settings of alienation, marginalization, and oppression within which the church is to adopt a new shape and orientation. Says Boff: "In Latin America the following question has been raised: 'Which is the world where the church is to be preferently situated as sacrament of salvation? And the answer is: it is the world of the poor, the 'subworld' where the vast majority of our people live."[20] In solidarity, this involvement in historical liberation praxis constitutes the "first act" in liberationist perspective; actual theologizing is the "second act." Consistent with our discussion of praxis knowing in chapter 3, Gutiérrez clarifies that here we are dealing with much more than methodology in a narrow sense: "When we speak of 'first act' and 'second act' . . . [we] are talking lifestyle—a way of living the faith. In the last analysis we are talking spirituality in the best and most authentic sense of the word. . . . In liberation theology, our methodology is our spirituality—a life process in the way to realization."[21] One could say, then, that both the first and the second "acts" are to be played on the same stage, that is, the concrete situation of the poor and oppressed.

A final comment is in order on the main implications of the statement that the poor constitute a special theological and religious locus, a privileged context for Christian praxis and reflection.[22] First, there is the implication that the poor and oppressed constitute the place where the God of Jesus is especially present with a twofold challenge to illumination and conversion. God's special presence in the poor and oppressed is initially hidden, or unattractive and disturbing and disconcerting, like the historical Jesus himself. Divine presence in the poor is both a prophetic (i.e., denouncing-announcing) and an apocalyptic presence which ushers in a new era. Second, "theological locus" also conveys the idea of the most appropriate and conducive situation for the religious experience of faith in Jesus and the corresponding praxis of discipleship. And third, it follows that the position of the poor is the most fitting place for reflecting on Christian faith, for doing theology. Thus the liberationist principle is restated: The optimum locus of revelation and faith is also the optimum locus of the liberating salvific praxis and theological praxis.

"Base" Are the Poor

Before describing briefly the striking phenomenon of the *base communities* as a new configuration of the church in Latin America, we need to make clear that "base" primarily refers to the "popular classes"—the poor, oppressed, believing Christians and their ties of class, race, and culture. Gutiérrez insists that the main point of reference for understanding "base" has to do with the world within which the church is present and in which the church gives testimony to the love of God. "Base" means, then, the lowest rungs of society—the whole range of exploited classes, marginalized races, and despised cultures. The "base" refers also to the "evangelical poor," that is, those people who, by solidarity and commitment, make their own the life, the interest, and the aspirations of the poor and oppressed.[23]

In his excellent study of grassroots communities, Guillermo Cook includes Roger Garaudy's dialectical definition of *base* (understood as people denied their own future) as the result of four interrelated factors: *social* oppression (people deprived of ownership, power, and knowledge); *economic* manipulation (lack of power to determine the orientation of their labor and the distribution of its fruits); *political* disenfranchisement (lack of effective participation in political decision making); and *cultural* alienation (lack of cultural self-determination: the ideology of the dominant class, which legitimizes the established order, determines the culture of the *base*). Cook rightly challenges this last point by demonstrating that the culture of the base is not totally determined by the dominant class and that the poor are refusing to give up their own future.[24]

Together with those mainly *sociological* connotations indicated, João B. Libanio has suggested two additional sets of interrelated dimensions included in the Portuguese and Spanish word *base*, namely the *psychosocial* and *cultural* meaning in the sense of "nuclear" and "cellular," or "fundamental," on the one hand, and, on the other hand, the *theological* meaning, associated with

Christian *koinonia*—communion or the "elemental Christian fabric" of lay people.[25]

Further, we should not underestimate the fact that oppressed and believing people gather in relatively small, mid-communities, thus facilitating primary relationships and the experience of equality, mutuality, and participation. These considerations are included too in the understanding of base. The emphasis here is on the affirmation of the privileged status of the poor and oppressed whose evangelical faith inspires ecclesial and communal contexts with a unique experience of worship, care and support, education, social action, and mission.

THE OPPRESSED AND TRANSFORMATIONAL LEARNING

The transformation of theological reflection postulated by liberation theology assumes the priority of an epistemological conversion. The first movement in this process consists in listening to the manifestations of the faith of the common people, especially the poor, the oppressed, and the marginal. Biblically speaking, the epistemological conversion assumes not only the gospel declarations "You have been given the secret of the kingdom of God . . . Blessed are you who are poor," but the Pauline dictum also: "It was to shame the wise that God chose what is foolish by human reckoning. . . .Those whom the world thinks common and contemptible are the ones that God has chosen—those who are nothing at all to show up those who are everything" (1 Corinthians 1:27-28). We will discuss this central idea, starting with compassion as a source of theological knowledge vis à vis the suffering of the oppressed. From there, we will consider the theological and educational authority of the faithful oppressed and some implications and ramifications for religious education.

Suffering, Conversion, and Understanding

The reality of human suffering is obviously an essential component of any given situation, and particularly in the case of Latin America. Therefore, it also becomes a fundamental motivation for theological reflection, for the process of understanding faith. Thus liberation theology starts where human pain is locat-

ed. That suffering provides an indispensable analogy for understanding God and the divine historical project. The present history of our world is considered as the ongoing history or the continuation of God's own suffering. The culminating moments of
revelation have been accompanied and characterized by intense
suffering as evidenced from the cry of the oppressed in Egypt to
the cry of Jesus on the cross—suffering that is projected in the
pain of birth of the whole creation eagerly longing for its final
liberation (Romans 8:19-23). Consequently, the cry of the oppressed acquires a privileged place for liberation theology, first of
all as a motivation and stimulus for the theological task. Jon
Sobrino states that in the epistemological break brought on by
suffering, a practical and ethical orientation to theological comprehension is revealed. In fact, liberation theology claims to present a pattern of response to the generalized suffering of people.[26]
It is by asking and facing the question of massive historical human suffering that liberation theology can claim to make a
unique contribution to the speech and knowledge of God. Rebecca Chopp rightly points out that liberation theology rethinks
human existence, Christian tradition, and present Christian experience by bringing suffering into the midst of reflection. New
understandings, new interpretations, and indeed a whole new
paradigm are thus proposed by the liberationists who argue that
suffering ruptures our categories, our experiences, and our history. In other words, suffering relocates theology: The knowledge of
God is to be discerned essentially in the midst of the anguish of
history.[27]

It must be emphasized that the reflection stimulated by suffering is not merely an effort to explain the nature of suffering, to
justify it, or to investigate its compatibility with the facts of
divine revelation. It is more an effort to confront and eliminate
human suffering. In other words, even though analysis of the
causes of suffering is imperative (hence the importance of the aid
of the social sciences, for instance) the epistemological perspective leads us in the direction of attacking suffering itself. The
main point here is that theological reflection and comprehension
is inspired and oriented by a profound human *compassion* (from
the Latin, *pati* and *cum*, "to suffer with") which is but one of the
faces of love. "Compassion asks us to be where it hurts, to enter

into places of pain, to share in brokenness, fear, confusion, and anguish. . . . Compassion requires us to be weak with the weak, vulnerable with the vulnerable, and powerless with the powerless. Compassion means full immersion in the condition of being human."[28] It is love-from-God and love-of-God aimed at social re-creation and transformation according to the justice and peace of the reign of God. In tune with the gospel demands for conversion, compassion thus understood becomes a special source of theological knowledge. Further, to the extent that reality contradicts the project of the reign of God, conversion implies that even the very knowledge of that reality is to be transformed. We can thus notice again the parallel between epistemological and ethical dimensions in the liberationist perspective. Theological knowledge for learning and transformation is not interested so much in the language used when discussing God and divine action but rather in the concrete historical mediation of the God of Christian faith. The mediation of the absolute Other, then, takes the form of those who are really the "other," namely, the poor and oppressed. The Other is discovered dialectically and through the suffering of the oppressed. As Sobrino suggests, the necessary rupture required to have real access to the Other comes from the break caused by the presence and suffering of the oppressed. They challenge us concerning our own identity. And the rupture happens not merely at the level of self-understanding and feelings but at the level of concrete historical reality. Therefore, "conversion" comes—as in the gospel—through those who are historically "the other" in relation to ourselves, the oppressed. It is through them that we discover what is characteristic of the God of Jesus: a free disposition to make himself an "other," immersed in history.[29] Besides, as a concrete mediation of God, the poor and oppressed "other" not only causes the rupture of our identity but their own existence is a call to liberating action. The "other" is there to be liberated, re-created so that genuine communion and community are made possible, not only now in the midst of suffering, but in celebration and joy as well. The question that immediately arises is: How do we go from compassion with the suffering of the oppressed to the liberating action in solidarity? How does the demand of the presence of the "other" become effective? The answer is that it is by an act of obedience.

Truth understood in light of biblical faith, as emphasized in our discussion of praxis epistemology in chapter 3, is personal and communal and therefore requires commitment and obedience. Etymologically, the word obedience means "listen from below." Hence, the word "obey" comes from listening and hearing; it presupposes attention and responsibility. Both understanding and obeying imply submitting to something bigger or greater than ourselves, something on which we depend. Both terms imply submission to the truth of the gospel, to the greatness of God, and the seeming "lowness" of the poor and oppressed. This is what Henri Nouwen testifies to having relearned in Latin America. During a Sunday experience of worship and reflection on Hebrews 5:7-9, it became clear to him that Jesus, through his struggles and sufferings, came to listen more perfectly to God, came to know God, and could respond to his call. Nouwen suggests that perhaps there are no better words than those to summarize the meaning of the option for the poor: "Entering into the suffering of the poor is the way to become obedient, that is, a listener to God. Suffering accepted and shared in love breaks down our selfish defenses and sets us free to accept God's guidance."[30]

The Teaching Authority of the Oppressed

The integration of the expectations of compassion and obedience in solidarity corresponds to the recognition of the authority of the common people of God and, particularly, the oppressed. The concept of the "doctrinal authority" of the poor and oppressed people of God in Latin America is especially relevant for discussion from the vantage point of religious education. The question liberation theologians raise is whether the common people have an *educational authority* within the church and, if so, what kind of authority is it, in light of their objective poverty and marginality.

In the first place, it is emphasized that the people have an *indirect* but effective *authorship* in the teaching ministry of the church. This is so particularly to the extent that theologians and ecclesial leaders read the signs of the times adequately and put into theological terms (as "voices of those who have no voice") what already exists at a level of historical reality as an expression of the faith of the people. Furthermore, this clear reference to the so-called "epistemological privilege of the poor" has another dimension. Besides possessing indirect authorship, the oppressed people of God are also *authors* of their own reflections, visions, and dreams. This is especially so when grassroots Christian communities grow and develop around Bible study and the religious education processes of reflection and action centering on their situation and their search for creative ways to articulate and express their faith. In other words, faith is celebrated, shared, and reflected upon while new perceptions arise together with new questions and challenges. The reason why people "do theology" in this way is simply because faith is present and it has vigor and relevance in an atmosphere of hope and gratitude. The goal pursued in such a popular theologizing is to cultivate and strengthen faith in order to "put the spirits to the test" (1 John 4:1) in society and in the church itself, to give meaning and direction to their hope, to confront evil and death with courage. Sobrino claims that these poor and oppressed Christians have intuitively rediscovered two important presuppositions of God's self-revelation in the Bible and therefore of how the scriptures should be read. The first presupposition is that God's revelation is directed to all persons and its purpose is to create a new people (hence the importance of the communal context and framework for reading and reflection). The second presupposition is that because the Bible has been handed down or bequeathed to us its reading necessarily assumes and includes a tradition to be creatively reappropriated in the present while generating new spaces for future-oriented action.

The important point made in the preceding paragraph is not only a rereading of the sacred text, but a re-creation of God's text in the process of the human search for divine will for today, including the practice of putting that will into effect. The people's perception and comprehension involved in this process point to certain basic and central structural themes such as the Exodus, the prophets, the symbol of the kingdom, the gospel as the good news for the poor, the liberating God and the supremacy of love, the commitment to justice and peace, and the resurrection motif. In other words, this perception and comprehension is another reference to the "hermeneutical privilege" of the poor and oppressed and the rediscovery of the partiality of God's revelation. It is in this way and in this sense that the poor and oppressed also become agents or channels of further revelation and transformational learning.

The poor and oppressed as theological subjects are important in two respects. First, they are direct and indirect authors in the theological task. Second, they possess a special *authority* to elaborate their comprehension of faith from the ground of their own faith. To substantiate and explain that claim, two theological principles can be adduced.

The first of these theological principles is the *correlation between God and the poor*. God's revelation contains in itself a partiality in favor of the weak, the victim, the oppressed. Therefore there is no substitute in the theological task for the poor and oppressed or the "little ones" on the road to encountering and knowing the God of Jesus. Hence theology must acknowledge that the poor and the oppressed show theology what God wills— and what God does not want—in this world. The imprints of evil and sin are revealed with utmost clarity. Poor and oppressed peoples reveal that God demands conversion first of all, the way to life and the rejection of death. Also, the desire and the need for liberation and re-creation are made manifest through the here and now experience of the poor and oppressed.

The second theological principle presupposes the first and is the *correlation between the offer of God's revelation and the response of faith* that is formed and grows. The response of faith— to the extent that it becomes analogous to the response of the faithful poor, receptors and privileged agents of God's revelation and love—will comprise a better way for understanding God. God will be perceived, preferably, through the faith of the oppressed, their desire to follow Jesus, and their communal commitment in hope, prayer, and work. This is, then, the clue of "the evangelizing potential of the poor" (Puebla) and the key to their educational authority. In other words, the theological authority of the poor and marginalized consists *a priori* in the fact that it is God who grants them authority by divine predilection toward them; *a posteriori*, their authority stems from their faith, experienced and formulated, nurtured, tested, and witnessed through suffering. It is God who demands that we listen to the faith of the oppressed in our search for truth and light.[31]

The foregoing paragraph suggests that the task of the magisterium and the theological community is to contribute to a more explicit articulation of the people's faith, including the tasks of completion and correction.[32] What is called for, then, is a deep conviction that God's presence as well as faith itself will be found among the poor and oppressed. It also demands an examination to see if we really know how to listen to the expressions of their faith and if we are willing to hear and obey from the stance of solidarity with and compassion for the poor and oppressed.

At this point we need to move beyond the liberationist discussion of the faith of the poor. In other words, our treatment should be broadened to include other non-poor oppressed and marginalized peoples and groups. Gregory Baum has provided an illustrative historical case on this subject in connection with the Radical Reformation of the sixteenth century. He anlayzes the forced marginalization and persecution of the Anabaptists as a regrettable and costly loss of the opportunity for mutual religious and theological enrichment. That loss was due mainly to the lack of disposition or the incapacity of the established churches—both Catholic and Protestant—to listen to the faith of those oppressed and marginalized believers. The point is, again, that there is divine revelation in the encounter with the other, and particularly with the marginal other. Baum contends that the word of God is present in the human word and that there is a significant transformation of our awareness-revelation in the other brother or sister in the faith. He concludes that "what we are discovering today and in particular . . . when we reflect on the history of the Anabaptists is that there is even more divine revelation as we listen to the other oppressed . . . revelation which is so powerful that usually we can't accept it at all."[33]

The importance of encountering the other is a key epistemological principle which has a theological dimension as well as a pedagogical dynamic and structure. Hence we have here a foundational principle for religious education. We rediscover that suffering and compassion reach a special intensity and depth as we appropriate not only the suffering of the oppressed but also our own, motivated by the transformation of conscience. The claim is that we are challenged to a greater extent when the oppressed express themselves than when somebody else speaks to us. This is so because, potentially, our own sin—or the complicity with sin and evil—is manifested to the point of threatening our personal and vocational identity. In other words, conversion and liberating and re-creating action are all necessary and simultaneously called for. The theological lesson is, then, that there is divine revelation by way of encountering the oppressed. The pedagogical lesson is that attentive listening and obedience can foster transformational learning.

In sum, a certain pedagogy of the faith of the oppressed is being sketched here, the centerpiece of which is the epistemological conversion implied in the oft-quoted expression "looking at the world from below."[34] Obedient attention to that faith facilitates the special learning associated with the perspective of those who suffer. And learning of this kind is complex because it includes substantive cognitive content (i.e., new insight and perspectives) as well as skills and tasks involved in the very "looking," not to mention the affective and other dimensions engaged in such a human transaction (i.e., attitudinal changes, values transformation). In fact, it can be argued here that the tendency to overemphasize the cognitive dimension—rather than a comprehensive and balanced view of "perspective transformation," as indicated in chapter 1—does not do justice to the richness and depth of the conversion that is advocated. With this in mind let us consider now some ramifications arising from our discussion.

IMPLICATIONS FOR RELIGIOUS EDUCATION

Religious Education and Theologizing

The preceding discussion indirectly supports the observation that liberation theology tends to deliberately blur the distinction between "theological education" and "Christian religious education," as indicated in chapter 4.[35] The pedagogical process of action and reflection in which people's religious experience—and especially, the faith of the oppressed—is taken seriously into account can amount to both doing theology and training for all forms of ministry, including religious education at the level of the local faith community. In fact, once the special role of the people and the poor or marginal is reaffirmed as a key to the theological task as comprehension of faith, the foundation for ministry *of* and *by* the people is also further strengthened.[36] "Theological task" and "ministry" are thus held to be distinct yet inseparable dimensions in the life and mission of the church. Thus religious education—especially in the case of young and adult people—may be seen as playing a crucial mediating role. It can build bridges between the engagement of local people in the theological process—which is essential for theology as such and their involvement in ministry for the mission of the church. For one thing, the fact that religious education mediates between theology and life in concrete historical reality, as James Michael Lee has convincingly asserted, is here further confirmed. In fact, from a liberationist vantage point there is no question that "religious instruction pushes forward the boundaries of theological science per se . . . [it] plays a uniquely prophetic role relative to theology inasmuch as its very work consists in a here-and-now, deeply existential theologizing."[37] However, since facilitation of Christian living cannot be separated from the Christian vocation for service—especially in the context of a base ecclesial community—it must be added that *religious education also mediates between theology and ministry.* Further, religious education may facilitate that both the theological task and the practice of ministry be undertaken with full participation of the people in every local context. In other words, *grassroots participation* and *contextualization* are two interrelated principles to be underscored in this regard.[38]

A note of caution is in order here. We must keep in mind that people's concerns normally revolve around their faith and overall religious experience as such, rather than around "doing theology" (particularly as professional theologians understand and do theology). Therefore, utmost respect and prudence ought to be exercised when assessing the people's manifold and multiform expressions of faith and spirituality. Otherwise, we run the risk of imposing foreign theological patterns and agenda, even in the name of freedom and liberation. Actually, this problem is frankly acknowledged by some leaders of the BEC movement under the categories of "vanguardism" and "political discourse." Vanguardism refers to the elitist tendency on the part of the pastoral agents to set the pace and the direction of the people's theological reflection. The related problem is that of attempting to impose a political-theological discourse while disregarding or underestimating the religious discourse.[39] The difference between traditional theological language and religious language needs to be recognized in connection with this. The characteristics of religious language as deeply personal, subjective, affective, sensuous, metaphoric, and allegoric[40] need to be appreciated anew.

We can go a step further in light of that concern. The epistemological restatement proposed by liberationists regarding the privileged perspective of the people, especially the poor and oppressed, calls for revising the very definition of theology as "critical reflection on Christian praxis in light of the Word." Such critical reflection would continue to be acknowledged as necessary for the theological task but by no means sufficient. The theology which emerges from the people's faith will have to include a variety of expressions: linguistic and nonlinguistic, artistic and musical, testimonial narration and celebration, dreams and visions that not necessarily allow for a translation into the logical-systematic, lineal, analytic-reflective, propositional language of tradition theology, which liberation theologians still generally adhere to. Also, a rediscovery and new appreciation for spiritual values and virtues such as humility, patience, and purity can be integrated and reappropriated. A true liberation of the imagination for theological creativity may then take place inasmuch as those and other expressions of religious faith have been postponed, subordinated, underestimated, or even suppressed in mere "theologizing." This could signal another facet of the educational authority of the common people and the poor and oppressed, not only in the sense of revelation content, but also in terms of providing alternative ways, means, and processes for comprehending faith creatively and living Christian spirituality more faithfully.

Religious Education, Countercultural Consciousness, and Marginality

The epistemological conversion that liberationists propose is essential for understanding the formation and transformation of the *countercultural consciousness* of the church as an *alternative* community. That conversion leads to the enriched and strengthened ecclesial version of Freire's "critical transitivity" (i.e., critical or *transforming* consciousness, as opposed to "magical" or *con-*

forming and "naive" or *reforming* consciousness) as discussed in
the first two chapters in reference to the prophetic ministry of
religious education. That prophetic and utopian stance of liberation theology nurtures and evokes a consciousness and a perception alternative to the consciousness and perception of the dominant culture around us. Religious education thus partakes of the
overall prophetic endeavor of consciousness formation and transformation. The alternative (or, rather, *countercultural*) consciousness serves to critically dismantle the established, dominant consciousness and to energize and empower the community and its
members in the promise and hope for a better world toward
which they may move. A "better world" for the church means
liberation and re-creation in tune with the coming reign of God.
It includes the gift and also the promise, the expectations and the
demands of a *new humanity* under the lordship of Jesus Christ.
This is why, as liberationists insist, the faith community is to
attend to every aspect of human life and to seek the integration of
the religious, social, political, and economic dimensions on behalf of justice and *shalom* (or fullness of life) for all people. It is in
light of this shared conviction that John Westerhoff, after discussing the common life to support the alternative consciousness,
concludes by affirming that the church is called to be an alternative way of seeing life (faith) and an alternative way of being
(identity), especially as a "community that displays a biased passion for the outsider, the stranger, and the estranged and gives
people what they need, not what they deserve."[41]

Our current discussion is carried out mainly in terms of the
religious education category of persons-in-context. By correlating
the biblical canon—especially the prophetic texts—and the community of the marginal ones (i.e., a community not fully contained by the "royal rationality," in and from which the prophets
speak), Walter Brueggemann assists in envisioning religious education context in a liberationist key. He suggests that this is a
most important resource for education which may require that
we reexperience "that kind of marginality both in terms of social
power and in terms of rationality."[42]

This notion has been taken up by Craig Dykstra in a provoca-
tive essay on education, the gospel, and the marginal. He suggests
that the appropriation of the gospel will most likely take place in

contexts in which socialization processes—which foster accommodation and conformity—have broken down. Christian religious education, so oriented, would lead people to the culturally marginal in social and personal life, and it would also raise people's consciousness of the marginal in order for the gospel to elicit redemptive power. In other words, we must identify, not just the *what* (content) or *how* (process) of teaching and proclamation, but also a question of deciding on the *where* (context). The context, Dykstra argues, cannot be that of the predominant culture, but the margins of that culture and in the "cracks" of the enculturation process, ever upsetting, renewing, and transforming it.

Thus, the newness of the gospel emerges at points of marginality, not only in terms of association or involvement with the oppressed and socially outcast, but also on the level of personal existence in regard to those unsocialized areas and elements of our subjective lives. The dimension of resistance, conversion and confrontation, and countercultural consciousness for the alternative ecclesial community is thereby restated with focus on the question of context for religious education. In this perspective the teaching ministry of the church occurs "in contexts where we sense our inner 'strangeness,' where we make contact with others who are strangers to us by virtue of their social and cultural marginality, where we suffer with and for the other, and where we engage in resistance to the suffering that the dominating culture brings."[43]

At this point, in which we are expanding the reference to marginalization beyond the poor and oppressed, we are ready to identify critically a need for correction in the liberationist perspective.

Beyond the Idealization of the Poor and Oppressed

The following comments assume and supplement our successive indications of weaknesses in liberation theology from the vantage point of religious education in the preceding chapters as well as some critical observations already included in this one. Actually, the critical points underscored are interrelated and need to be considered together in light of our overall discussion. In this section, and in the end of the next section we refer briefly to some key problems observable in the liberationist perspective as particularly related to the persons-in-context category in Christian religious education. Once again, it will become apparent that the main contributions of liberation theology as foundational for religious education tend to become problematic. This is the case to the extent that those proposals betray a tendency to absolutization. By absolutization we mean an overemphasis in the direction of the corrective that those contributions supposedly provide. If the limitations and weaknesses of liberation theology remain unexposed and uncorrected, we are left with some misleading and distorting orientations for the educational work of the church. That is precisely the situation we are committed to avoid while engaging in a dialogical interface that is to be mutually enlightening for both religious education and liberation theology.

A case in point is the tendency to idealize the poor and oppressed in terms of a moral as well as cognitive superiority often implied when they are referred to as the primary source of revelation and transformational learning. In order to substantiate this critical observation, we need to take another look at the biblical basis and refer then to some of the main implications of the idealization.

The strong affirmation that God is on the side of the poor and oppressed has a definite biblical grounding, including of course the case for casting down the rich and oppressive. The problem with overstating this biblical truth arises when it is assumed that just because they are poor and oppressed people are to be considered automatically as part of the "people of God" and included as such in the church. The fact is that, biblically speaking, the "wretched of the earth" cannot simply be equated with the "people of God" in the tradition of Abraham and Jesus Christ. If the biblical texts are to be taken seriously, it would appear that the "people of God" are not any or every nation or any oppressed class of people, but those within the historical context of the Old and New Covenants, where God takes the initiative and sets the terms and the orientation. Further, the question of sin or disobedience applies to the poor as well as to the rest of us. Consequently, in principle it cannot be argued that God cares more about the salvation of the poor than the salvation of the rich, or that the poor have a special, inherent claim to the gospel. In the teaching of Jesus no one class of people is made a paradigm of virtue. In sum, there is no such thing as a *moral* privilege of the poor simply on the basis of their class status.

Given the centrality of the Bible in Christian religious education, this critical consideration is obviously important concerning the understanding of church, faith and Christian lifestyle, salvation, and evangelization. Consistent discernment is also obviously crucial in regard to potential distortions in the hermeneutical process including both Bible study and critical analyses concerning church and society.

The idealization of the poor and oppressed betrays a vision of humanity that fails to recognize the enormous human potential for evil. In spite of the acknowledgment of basic ambivalence and internal conflict, as discussed for instance by Freire in terms of the internalization of the oppressor, it is also clear that there is a great deal of liberationist optimism concerning the will and the power of the oppressed to attain the ideal of humanization and community once the oppressive social structures have been effectively confronted and removed. The liberationist affirmation regarding the privilege of the poor as especially privileged bearers of revelation and the efficacious vision of the new order seems to assume the following implication and expectation: the oppressed, once liberated, will somehow be different human beings, able and willing to use their freedom wisely and to avoid further exploitation and dehumanization. Many liberationists seem to believe *à la* Erich Fromm, that the pro-death ("necrophilic") tendencies will be essentially eliminated or neutralized in the context of some kind of humanistic socialism. There appears to be a flagrant contradiction between an inherently good human nature—idealistically assumed and historically recaptured by the liberated oppressed—and the reality of the present wicked socioeconomic predicament.

It is clear that this uncritical claim militates in several ways against the integrity of religious education as a task oriented towards liberation, creativity, and community. As already pointed out in chapter 2, the question of *purpose* tends to be narrowly focused in terms of emancipation and vindication of the socioeconomically oppressed which defines the mission of the church. Hence liberationists tend to collapse Christian eschatology into liberation projects. These projects suggest that the gospel is thereby reduced to politics.

The question of class conflict and struggle, including the problem of determinism, imposes some serious limitations and distortions on the educational *process*. Those limitations and distortions may include such things as the curtailment of dialogue and the mutuality principle and the forced "liberation" of the oppressors as is sometimes explicitly advocated.[44] The poor and oppressed are often treated by liberationists as beyond critique. The two-way street in the teaching/learning process of liberating religious education thus degenerates into a one-way track. As a consequence, authentic conscientization and creativity are severely compromised.

The idealization of the poor exacerbates the oppressed-oppressors dichotomy which thus becomes an oversimplification. It then appears unnecessary to discern, explain, and deal with divers forms and manifestations of poverty and oppression, alienation and marginalization, especially in the case of those who are not technically poor. For instance, a question that betrays a nagging fuzziness on the part of liberation theologians is the frequently discussed identification with the poor and oppressed. More clarity is needed in finding effective ways to achieve identification with the oppressed in solidarity, including the non-poor and, even more comprehensively, the marginal and the stranger.

In addition to these suggested corrections, another way to appropriate critically the liberationist contribution would be to extend its insights on the place and role of the poor and oppressed into a wider context. We already began to do this with the reference to marginality and strangeness above. It would seem, for instance, that the spatial imagery implied in "looking at the world from below" must be supplemented with "looking from the edges" or "from the outside." The poor and oppressed would still have a privileged and paradigmatic position among *strangers*. But we could thus grasp a more comprehensive picture of the human predicament as related to religious education for liberation, creativity, and community.

Parker Palmer is particularly helpful at this point. In *The Company of Strangers*[45] he discusses the stranger as *spiritual guide* in a way analogous to the educational process and model presented in liberation theology about the poor and oppressed and their epistemological-hermeneutical privilege. Through the stranger, our view of the world, of God, and of self, is expanded and deepened. Palmer reminds us that the stranger is a central figure in stories of faith and a bearer of truth that tends to shake common perceptions and assumptions. The function of the stranger—who often represents God—is grounded in the simple fact that truth is a large matter requiring various perspectives to be fully apprehended and appreciated. The intrusion of strangeness provides opportunities to look anew upon familiar things and thus to be open to divine restatements of truth and to re-creation of reality. Hence, in hospitably receiving the gift of the stranger, we not only perform an act of love but an act of faith and hope as well. And this is the case especially when we encounter and welcome the *suffering* stranger or the outcast who represent an entire class of oppressed people in our society. We may serve these strangers, but we also need them to guide us into deeper knowledge of Christ and to the service of God in truth and love, which sets *us* free.

Palmer echoes the liberationist claims that certain truths about life and about ourselves are more easily perceived when we are on the edge or when we take the view of those who are at the margin—poor, sick, hungry, or in prison (Matthew 25:40)—and can thus also grasp the direction which divine revelation assumes. In this perspective, fear and avoidance of the stranger betrays not merely a symptom of class conflict but also a deep existential struggle. The fact that we are also strangers to others and even to some extent to ourselves as well may be dangerously exposed. On the one hand, the stranger often gives us an opportunity to find ourselves.

This is what Craig Dykstra was alluding to in connection with the agenda of teaching ministry which includes those contexts where we can sense our inner strangeness. On the other hand, to welcome the external stranger hospitably (i.e., by making the space of "friendly emptiness" for them in our life) we must be comfortable with the stranger within. But, then, compassion and mutual redemption and liberation in terms of the wider social arena are also indispensable and, in fact, constitute inseparable dimensions in the relationship with the stranger.

This is a major realization experienced by Henri Nouwen after several months of journeying in Latin America. He met common faithful Christians in base communities; he saw multitudes of oppressed people, victims of exploitation, discrimination, and neglect; and he was confronted by liberation theology in action, including the teaching of Gustavo Gutiérrez himself. All of that, in the framework of an intense personal vocational search, led Nouwen to acknowledge with gratitude that a special transformational learning had taken place. This transformational learning is summarized at the end of his journal as an expression of "reverse mission," a movement from the south to the north[46]—a movement that corresponds, in the larger scale, to the conversion advocated by liberationists.

BASE COMMUNITY AS RELIGIOUS EDUCATION CONTEXT

In this final section of the chapter we will concentrate on the grassroots Christian community movement from the perspective of religious education. Having established the liberationist position concerning the poor and oppressed, together with its specific pertinence for religious education, we now move on to consider more precisely the question of the BEC as ecclesial context or medium for religious education. We will start with a brief, general characterization of the BECs and will focus on their nature and mission as locus for conscientization. After a critical reference to some assumptions of the "popular church," we will discuss in some detail the main principles of religious education context derived from the faith community model suggested by liberation theology and the BEC movement.

BECs as Locus for Conscientization

The emergence and growth of close to 300,000 grassroots Christian groups is one of the most striking phenomena in the social and religious landscape of Latin America.[47] The rapid proliferation of BECs is related to the radical reorientation of Christian belief and practice in the privileged option for the poor which has resonated in the lives of oppressed peoples throughout the continent in the last three decades. As Guillermo Cook demonstrates, the significance of the BECs has various dimensions which point to specific challenges to both Catholic and Protestant churches: 1) BECs are *historically* significant because they chal-

lenge the church's self-understanding, ecclesiastical institutional-
ism, lack of community, and centuries-old church-state alliances.
2) BECs are *sociologically* significant because they are a case of
grassroots creative protest against institutional fossilization. 3)
BECs are *ecclesiologically* significant because they confront traditional, pyramidal church structures. 4) BECs also challenge *missionary* theory and practice on the part of the Christian
churches.[48]

The BECs (or "popular" or "people's church," as they are
called in Central America) display a great variety of structures,
aims, and degrees of cohesion. However, they all fit into a single,
all-encompassing definition, as can be seen by examining the
terms—base, ecclesial, and community—which are represented
by the initials BEC (CEB, *comunidades eclesiales de base*, in
Spanish and Portuguese). "The groups are *communities*, because
they bring together people of the same faith who belong to the
same church and who live in the same area. They are *ecclesial*
because they have congregated within the church, as grassroots
nuclei of the community of faith. They are *base* because they
consist of people who work with their hands (the working
classes)."[49]

The communities are composed of a number of families—
usually not more than twenty—who come together on a regular
basis. There is a significant degree of lay participation and direction, even in the cases in which the BECs were initiated by clergy
and where priests and nuns continue to share in the leadership.
The strong communitarian spirit promotes equality, mutuality,
and intimacy. These are communities of religious celebration for
praying, singing, reading and reflecting on the Bible, sharing
meals and bread and wine—both eucharistically and informally.
The BECs foster mutual aid, charitable action, and service projects in a given neighborhood, as well as critical analysis of social
and economic issues leading to and reflecting on diverse forms of
political engagement. After centuries of silence, says Leonardo
Boff, God's people are beginning to speak: "They are no longer
just parishoners in their parish; they have their own ecclesiological power; they are re-creating the church of God."[50] Such an
"ecclesiogenesis" in fact covers a number of fronts, that is, not
only new ways of being the church and understanding social

reality and Christian mission, but also new ways of reading scripture and doing theology and a new practice of and reflection on spirituality.[51]

Grassroots Christian groups are a response to a number of problems, from atomization, anonymity, and new forms of oppression and exploitation and manipulation in the modern society to the crises confronting the church, such as the scarcity of ordained clergy. BECs proliferate where there is a yearning for more intense communal life and for deepening spirituality. In the Latin American scene one has to additionally take into account the bankruptcy of the dependent capitalist paradigm and the collapse of the Christendom model of Roman Catholicism. Poverty, marginalization and cultural alienation, and military repression are among the social variables present wherever BECs have thrived, especially, though not necessarily, with pastoral and hierarchical support. Some striking similarities between socioeconomic conditions at the close of the Middle Ages (e.g., feudalism; rudimentary forms of national and international capitalism; urbanization; the ravages of war; newer means of communication, etc.) and present-day Latin America can be established, thus providing further basis to the idea of a "new Reformation" in the making.[52]

Undoubtedly, Vatican II[53] and the Bishops Conference at Medellín provided definite impetus to the then fledgling liberation theology and BEC movement. In any case, from our vantage point it is crucial to underscore the fact that the emergence, the growth, and the very nature of the BECs are intimately related to religious education. In fact, in the pioneering case of Brazil, ecclesial communities were started around 1956 with an evangelization program carried out mostly by lay Catholic religious educators. The experiment of "religious education for the working class" included regular, small group meetings for prayer, Bible reading and other forms of religious instruction, and the building of a sense of ecclesial community. Hence Catholic religious educators became the center of grassroots communities and, eventually, meeting halls were built and used for religious instruction and broader education programs of general and specialized education such as trade schooling. Soon the community gathering included the agenda of common daily problems associated with family, health, work, and so forth. This in turn naturally led to considering the socioeconomic and political reality in a broader scale. Interestingly, this religious and ecclesial movement may be considered the beginning of the grassroots education movement (BEM, or Base Education Movement—MEB in Spanish and Portuguese) which, dialectically, provided a further foundation nationwide for the future of the BECs. Evangelization—which in this case consisted in taking the gospel to marginal and oppressed communities—was thus associated with grassroots literacy programs and conscientization with a view to effecting changes in the social, economic, and political structures.[54] As indicated in chapter 1, the work and thought of Paulo Freire has been thus a significant factor, influencing both "general popular" and "religious" education. Freire's work has also been an inspiration for theology, as well as for various forms of Christian ministry.

The BECs constitute a unique locus for conscientizing religious education. Purpose, process, and content converge in a "liberating education through conscientization and human advancement," in the words of Barreiro, in order that people may take a critical position toward reality and undertake a social change which will make possible the real experience of the gospel.[55] Awareness and interpretation of injustice and all forms of oppression in the light of faith and God's will take place as people gather to share and discuss specific problems and search for creative resolutions. Situations such as illness or unemployment and community problems involving water, electricity, sewers, paved streets, or schools become agenda items in the confrontation of gospel and life. The methodology assumes the familiar inductive-dialectical approach with three movements, already discussed in detail in chapter 4: *observing* (sharing, focusing; observation and description); *judging* (analysis and problematizing; interpretation in light of the gospel); *acting* (confronting the problem; planning, organizing, and carrying out of the plan or strategy).

One special setting for conscientizing religious education is the "*círculo bíblico*" (Bible circle) or small Bible study groups where BEC members gather for the "celebration of the Word" in prayer, singing, reading, and critical reflection. Historically, many original Bible circles have tended to evolve into BECs. Far from being passive recipients, the people take an active role in the process of hermeneutic circulation referred to in the previous chapter. Religious education in the BECs thus encourages popular and communal theologizing by focusing on the reality of church and society, especially in light of scripture (which tends to play a more important role than tradition and the magisterium). Pastoral and professional theologians in turn reflect theologically in light of their interaction with BECs and their popular theology. As the brothers Boff put it, these are three planes or levels of liberation theology that could be represented by a tree (the roots: BECs—popular theology; the trunk: pastors—pastoral theology; the branches: theologians—professional theology). Each level reflects the same phenomenon—faith confronting oppression in one global theological process.[56] Hence, *conscientizing religious education provides the setting for a threefold process of theologizing.*

Through conscientizing religious education, the BECs have created a milieu in which people develop an understanding of society as well as their commitment to transform it. Thus, the BECs present also a new understanding and practice of Christian mission—both denouncement and announcement—as proclamation in word and deed. It is a mission to be enfleshed in the ecclesial community itself as the new type of society is deliberately taught and learned within the community. Ideally, the BEC is to become society's *utopia* as well as an agent for social transformation.[57]

The central place and role of religious education in the BECs can hardly be exaggerated. We agree here with Maurice Monette that the rise of these "educative" communities represents a major shift in our understanding of religious education and the educational mission of the church. This is the case especially in the sense that conscientizing religious education in the BECs suggests a new way of conceiving social justice and peace education. These "educative justice communities" present a *radical* model which promotes, in Monette's terms: lay initiative; alliance with the poor and oppressed; a praxis methodology; interdependence and faith that does justice as a main purpose; community as context; and a social stance of transformation via paradigm shifting and systemic change.[58]

Another Look at the Messianic Church

There is no question that the base communities, especially in Latin America, have elicited admiration and even fascination as vehicles for both church renewal and societal transformation. In fact, not only do BECs assume the prophetic role of witnessing to the utopia of the reign of God, but they also strive to become historical actualizations of that human and divine utopia. We can certainly affirm this thrust together with the overall notion of the church as messianic community. It is clear that the BEC movement and liberation theology advocate a special model of faith community which is the locus for conscientizing religious education as we have just indicated. Furthermore, as a form of ministry, religious education always presupposes some understandings about the church. Therefore, at this point we need to pause in order to make two sets of critical observations before proceeding to spell out some relevant religious education principles stemming from that paradigm of faith community.

The Question of the True Church. The first and main observation is closely related to our previous discussion of the idealization of the poor. A correlation is established between the condition and status of the poor and oppressed and the postulated *normativeness* of the popular church or church of the poor as the true ecclesial reality.[59] Liberation theology assumes that the whole church is to follow the lead of the BECs in a reeducation process inspired by a conscientizing evangelization. The process is meant to be transformational, actually involving "conversion," "death and resurrection," "ecclesiogenesis," and "new Reformation." In this picture, the BECs often function as a kind of revolutionary vanguard in which poor and oppressed peoples become a new "chosen race." The expression "people of God" thus assumes a specific political reference.

Vatican II took up the biblical motif of the "people of God" to indicate the mission of the church throughout history. The concept and vision of the church as God's people then refers to the Christian global community, namely, a community of believers drawn from all nations and historical epochs, united in their faithfulness to the gospel. Liberation theology revises the seemingly too general and abstract ecclesiology of Vatican II. By way of conscientization and the political hermeneutics of the gospel, the meaning of the Council's use of the concept is translated into "popular church." The argument is that in Latin America the vast majority of the people are both Christian and poor; " 'church-people of God' means, therefore, 'church of the poor,' in the direct and empirical sense of church. Other Christians who are not poor have the duty of solidarity with the poor and thus become incorporated into the historical people of God that in that way actualizes today the suffering Servant."[60]

Obviously, this position tends to create problems at the level of ecclesiology, not to mention actual ecclesial tensions and conflict between "institutional church" versus "popular church." Liberationists argue, however, that no real conflict exists to the extent that a large part of the ecclesial institutions have joined the BECs including many cardinals, bishops, and pastors. The real tension, it is claimed, exists "between a church that has opted for the people, for the poor and their liberation, and other groups in that same church that have not made this option or who have not made it concrete or who persist in keeping to the strictly sacramental and devotional character of faith."[61] The suspicion of deep theological and ideological division and confrontation is not allayed, and this in turn compounds the issue of the church as context of religious education.

The liberationist view of the church of the poor is also vulnerable to the critique that such a view places itself, as well as the grassroots Christian bodies, in a position beyond critique while judging the rest of the church.[62] In the liberationist perspective, the church at large does not share the same plight and perspective as does the church in Latin America; hence it would follow that objections and critique from the First World, for instance, are to be disregarded on account of deficient credentials, credentials that accrue only to those who have the experience of being poor, or at least are in effective solidarity with the poor. The related problems of dogmatism and sectarianism thus become apparent, given the mood of absolute confidence and certainty of having found, without any further question, where Christ is present and active in history. In other words, not much room is then left for exploration and discernment and for the encounter and celebration of mystery.

Together with our rejection of reductionistic generalization whereby the Latin American ecclesial experience becomes normative for the church universal, we underscore again the mutuality principle in the global scale. Any attempt to universalize the BEC as normative popular church experience would become, ironically enough, a case of "reverse imperialism." A more modest and realistic expectation is that the Latin American contribution is indeed important for the whole church (Catholic and non-Catholic). But that contribution is important precisely as paradigmatic of the contextual embodiment of the gospel of the reign of God and of Christ's presence and mission in terms of and in the midst of *that* social and historical situation.

The Question of the Faithful Church. Another set of issues arises after having affirmed the church's call to be an alternative community with a countercultural consciousness while promoting direct involvement in the broad political arena. There is no question about the vision of an incarnate church that lives in mission in light of the carefully discerned politics of the reign of God which are pro-life, justice, and peace. Yet the capacity to maintain a faithful prophetic stance and messianic orientation necessitates on the part of liberationists the proper recognition of a certain dualism ("in the world—but not of the world," to paraphrase Jesus' prayer for his disciples in John 17). There is something radically unique in the revolutionary presence of the Christian faith community in the midst of history. This revolutionary character can be perceived by looking at the church as an original kind of community, different from other political alternatives. These other contemporary models are strikingly analogous in form and purpose to the political alternatives confronted and rejected by Jesus himself: 1) escape and isolationism (the Essenes); 2) sociopolitical compromising (the Herodians and Sadducees); 3) escape through separation—"purity"—within the system (the Pharisees); and 4) violent confrontation (the Zealots).[63] Jesus adopted a creative model in the formation of a faith community with a distinctive frame of reference consistent with divine incarnation itself. The new, utopian church society has some special features such as these: It is a voluntary association through repentance and commitment; it is mixed regarding its composition (sexes, races, cultures, social classes, religious backgrounds); it fosters a lifestyle characterized by sharing material possessions; it promotes the redemptive response of forgiveness and restoration for offenders; it countenances suffering in the face of violence; it is characterized by shared leadership and personal gifts. The new utopian church society is commissioned to confront oppression and injustice through building up a new order without the violent destruction of the old one, with a different model for interpersonal relations (between sexes, in the family, recreation, work, business, politics, etc.), with a special vision of the meaning and value of human life, and with a different attitude toward the state and the enemies in particular. At the center of this creative social experiment and paradigm lie solidarity and service over against the tendency to utilize power for domination and oppression. In this view, the foretaste of the reign of God is to be found primarily within the faithful Christian community whose involvement in the wider society is allegedly comprehensive enough to go even beyond the church's ministry to the economically oppressed.[64]

The main point of the preceding paragraph is that *the faithful church does not seek to get hold of the power structures and to replicate or mirror the political strategies and tactics of the "old order."* Hence the conscientization approach should include a more careful discernment in this regard, since process and content, goals and means, vision and character, are inseparable. The cross, or the suffering servant, becomes the central paradigm of obedience and power combined, not merely as a preferred political strategy, but as a way of life. That way of life is to be radical enough to embrace the "untested feasibility" of reconciling the irreconcilable ("Greek" and "Jew," slave and free, oppressed and oppressors . . .) which is at the core of the Christian story and vision. God's reign comes when we can consider *all* strangers as brothers and sisters and embrace those from whom we are estranged. As Westerhoff suggests, it is when we can unite in one congregation diverse social, ethnic, racial, political, and economic groups; when we can seek justice even for those who are least deserving or lovable; when we are liberated from private property, life, and commitment and are led into public property, life, and commitment; and when the needs and concerns of all the marginated are made our agenda for service and prayer.[65] The very existence of such a social reality constitutes a major (even threatening) change and alternative and is an inspiration for transformation. *The church is then called to live as a modeling, pedagogical community as a sign and instrument of the re-creative and liberating Spirit of God.* In this context, the absolutizing of any *proximate* mediation—including the church's own inclinations in this regard—is radically critiqued and rejected while the *ultimate* mediation of Christ is acknowledged and celebrated.

With these qualifications in mind, we can now consider some ramifications of the BEC liberationist paradigm specifically in terms of Christian religious education.

A Faith Community Context for Religious Education

The question of the community of faith as key metaphor or guiding image, together with a faith community model of Christian religious education,[66] highlights the crucial importance of the *context* or, as we prefer to call it, the persons-in-context category for the educational task. The resulting approach underscores the corporate nature of the human experience, views tradition as the springboard for the present and the future, and regards religious education as the responsibility of the whole people of God. It can be claimed that liberation theology and the BEC movement suggest a faith community model for religious education which further illumines the meaning and connotations of such a guiding image.

We assume that religious education partakes of the whole purpose and mission of the church. Therefore the key question is, what features and form should the ecclesial community have or strive for in order to serve as context for conscientization, nurture, and transformation in light of the reign of God?

The preceding foundational discussions assume the participation of God's Spirit in the midst of the worshiping, serving, and learning community that is called by God to embody the gift and the promise of a new creation. This affirmation involves the critique and rejection of prevailing pedagogical models which make rigid distinctions between "teachers" and "learners" on the basis of schooling, age, or official appointment. A consistent liberationist perspective challenges the assumptions and values in prevailing models, including indoctrinating and manipulative teaching styles. Even though special leading-teaching gifts and vocations are recognized (e.g., we need experts or specialists in Bible study and social analysis, especially), the emphasis is on learning together and from one another, in mutual service and celebration. There is a certain analogy in this regard between Freire's coordinators of the "culture circles" and the pastoral agents and religious educators in the BECs. Some clues are provided that illumine the question of the *people in context* educational category with implications also for *product content* and *process content* in religious education. The relationship between teachers and learners is one of equality, respect, and mutuality, precisely because everybody is committed to dialogical learning. The teacher's role is that of facilitator, avoiding both the imposition of ideas and the noncritical transmission of information. In other words, the authoritative (and often authoritarian) magisterial function of the religious educator is rejected. Educational goals and content are not to be determined, defined, and dictated from the top. The point is, again, that there must be space for conditions which foster and sustain nurture and transformation, freedom and creativity, in tune with the kingdom gospel as suggested by the following discussion of several key ecclesial context principles.[67]

The Ecclesial Context Promotes Mutual Support. This is essential to provide and sustain the necessary "context of rapport," as discussed in chapter 1, for persons, families, and groups to confront existential struggles and conflict situations. By "rapport" we mean that other persons are sympathetic to the situation and that they will somehow encourage, facilitate, interpret, celebrate, and benefit from its resolution. When this is the case, the social, religious, and cultural dimensions of rapport are clearly manifested in communal participation, both in the whole faith community and in smaller groups. And rapport is also expressed in the Christian language system that is utilized and which, concurrently, has the potential creative power to generate its social, ecclesial (*koinonia*) context.

Community is affirmed in liberationist religious education as the principal feature of being church as expressed in equality, deep commitment, and interdependence. As itself a local base ecclesial community, the church is concerned about every dimension of human life. We are thus referring to a particular historical realization of the Pauline metaphor of the body of Christ in which "each member belongs to all the others" . . . "serving individually as links and organs to one another" (Romans 12:5). And again, "if one member suffers, all suffer together and if one is honored, all rejoice together with it" (1 Corinthians 12:26). If this kind of organic context does not exist, people will lack the confidence and the freedom to engage themselves in the sort of social and existential struggles that become the conscientization agenda. Confidence to explore, to risk, and to change will be curtailed, and the utilization of denial and avoidance mechanisms will likely grow. Further, participation in a supportive ecclesial community is essential to generate vision and power. Such participation is also essential to sustain challenges against larger social, cultural, and political forces at work and to resist the threat or potential co-option from them.[68] Again, the idea of the alternative community with a countercultural consciousness surfaces. The key to the struggle for liberation, justice, and peace points to the formation and nurture of communities of support and confidence.

An additional point must be made concerning the essentially *religious* character of the base community as educational context. This important point pertains to the setting and atmosphere of worship. Worship is inherently educative and, in turn, religious education empowers people for and in worship. Prayer, singing, Bible study, and participation in the sacraments are essential. In fact, according to consistently concurrent testimony, if worship is weak or irrelevant, religious education is not only meaningless but the very existence of a BEC is in question. Worship provides the commonly appropriated and celebrated *authority* for Christian faith and life. This common authority is based on common liturgy which celebrates and makes present a common memory and vision, and it is necessary for God's gift of community in any given situation.[69]

The following three criteria for the church as an appropriate context for growth and religious education constitute principles in their own right, although they also qualify further what is meant by "ecclesial context of rapport."

The Ecclesial Context Fosters a Sense of Self-Worth and Affirmation. One of the striking things that happens in the BECs is the detectable radical change in the way people learn to look at themselves and to develop a sense of personal worth and self-confidence. The actualization of Christian community together with empowerment to "speak their word" and act together for creative transformation effectively breaks the grip of internalized oppression. A new vision of the world and a new sense of self (both as self-awareness and acceptance) thus may become apparent to both observers and participants in the BECs.

In Paulo Freire's view, a sense of self-worth is an indispensable subjective dimension in people's awareness of being subjects with an ontological vocation to make history and to shape their own destiny. For his part, James Loder refers also to positive self-regard as something "to be prized as a major personal premise for embracing and sustaining existential conflicts with persistence and expectance."[70] It is also essential for assuming openness, risk, and vulnerability in overcoming the temptations of control and achievement, and for a hospitable reception of the persons' own intuitions and insights.

Negatively speaking, this realization means that authoritarian and paternalistic instructional approaches and methods, so common in religious education, are to be avoided. First of all, the personal interaction involved and the kinds of content usually taught—narrow-focused, simplistic, stereotyped, or traditionalist—are designed to maintain given established frames of reference by means of a rigid, oppressive control. In terms of maternalistic stances—in general as well as in regard to specific groups such as women, youth, or the handicapped—there are similar unacceptable basic assumptions. Some persons need to be continually provided for and protected, otherwise they are not able to develop their potential. In other words, *interdependence* and the possibility of co-creation are to be affirmed as essential components of both Christian faith and religious education. In the ecclesial context there is a strong belief that human beings are called to be active, creative agents who participate with God in the ongoing liberation and re-creation of the whole world.

The Ecclesial Context Affirms Personal Differences and Vocational Ministries. This principle complements the previous comments, and it further illumines the body of Christ metaphor (Romans 12:3ff.; 1 Corinthians 12:14ff). Two interrelated dimensions need to be considered here.

In the face of our overall discussion, maintaining the integrity of each community member appears to be a basic authority principle. This is implied in the recognition and acceptance of personal differences between individuals, between persons and groups, and between diverse groups of people. Uniformity and conformity simply contradict and compromise the human creative potential and even distort the (apparent) peace which they supposedly make possible or preserve. The alternative is to promote interactional integrity, including respect for personal preferences and choices. Again, this relates to the principle of interdependence which assumes the sharing of power as well as responsibility. Interdependence connotes a mode of relating which leads to acting mutually in interpersonal relationships and also to affirm our solidarity with the oppressed.[71]

The second dimension to be considered refers to the claimed *apostolicity* on the part of the lay people which creates space for greater participation and balance in the various ministries. Apostolicity is the equivalent to the principle of the priesthood of all believers and the vocation of all Christians to use their particular gifts or talents for building up the church and advancing God's reign. Lay people are affirmed as successors of the apostles in that they have inherited the apostolic teachings and are co-responsible for the unity of faith and the community. Apostolicity is therefore shared in different ways, including the creation of many specific lay ministries (also called "services" and "charisms") related to religious education, worship, social action, mutual aid, and others. Specific examples include visiting and comforting the sick, family problems, orientation about human rights and labor laws, preparing children and parents for the sacraments, and so forth. Says Boff: "All of those functions are respected, encouraged, and coordinated in order that everything tend toward service of the whole community. The church, then, more than an organization, becomes a living organism that is re-created, nourished, and renewed from the base."[72] The whole community is to be involved in ministry, and all "services" are seen as gifts of the Holy Spirit to be cultivated as part of the agenda of religious education. Hence, our point above about religious education being also mediator between theology and ministry.

The Ecclesial Context Is Increasingly Open to the Wider Milieu. The experience of mutual support and confidence provided in the base Christian community is not an end in itself. In fact, the church is not to become merely a refuge in the midst of suffering or, even less, a ghetto for pious people. On the contrary, our foundational discussions emphatically point to the openness, outwardness, and service-mission orientation of the Christian vocation. First of all, this vocation is fulfilled to the extent that the church actually witnesses by its very presence and being to an alternative way of life as a partially and imperfectly realized utopia. And a key trait of this modeling pedagogical community is that it exists for sharing and service, in word and especially in deed. Such a community is open to the world and society, and especially to the oppressed, the marginal, and the stranger. It is therefore both a sign and an instrument for liberation, justice, and peace. In this light, religious education is to cover a wide variety of concerns in terms of substantive content for reflection and action. The community members share their problems and, in turn, social reality itself is "problematized." Diverse forms of social needs are discerned also as occasions for further involvement and cooperation. And the very process of interaction with the wider social milieu provides opportunities for further learning and transformation at the levels of both community and persons and in different areas pertaining to faith and life.

The following two principles have to do with the stance of the faith community regarding the complex nature of human and social reality and with the privileged status of conflict situations as agenda for conscientization and creativity in particular. These two basic principles represent criteria for religious education to fulfill its questioning, problematizing function as exemplified by Freire and liberation theology.

The Ecclesial Context Embraces Complexity and Engages Existential Conflict. Participation in the process of dialectical-hermeneutical religious education necessitates sensitivity to the complex nature of reality. Simplistic and prefabricated approaches and answers are to be avoided. Embracing complexity and engaging existential conflict is a special challenge given the Christian's search for meaning, direction, and purpose; for facing ethical dilemmas; and for the need to understand the seeming senselessness of massive human suffering.

Institutional religion and religious education in particular have tended to supply needed answers but quite often in simplistic, authoritarian, and dogmatic fashion. As we pointed out critically, this may happen even while professing a commitment to liberating truth. The alternative required in order that conscientization and creativity may be fostered calls for tolerance for ambiguity and ambivalence. The question of the church's mission in general and religious education in particular requires a careful consideration of interrelated agendas (e.g., the church's tradition, the cultural-political arena, scripture) converging in the ecclesial context at the service of people. And closely related to this emphasis on complexity and conflict engagement is the price of increased tension and anxiety which tends to characterize, at least in part, the task of religious education in the BEC. In other words, the "ecclesial context of rapport" is essential for confronting social and existential conflict situations on the part of individuals, families, groups, or the whole community, especially as part of the educational agenda. Religious education, for its part, makes an essential contribution to the formation and support of such an ecclesial context. Within this context, the contours, causes, and ramifications of people's concerns are to be discerned while a communal and linguistic-conceptual framework is provided for creative learning and liberating transformation.

As a prophetic and messianic faith community, the church is bound to encounter conflict in response to its enfleshment of the vision of God's reign. As an alternative way of seeing life (faith) and way of being (identity) the church necessitates a community fostering and nurturing educational ministry. The liberationist perspective, as historically embodied in the BECs, offers an appealing paradigm for the renewal of the church and for the revitalization of Christian religious education.

Notes

1. Luke 6:20.
2. Gustavo Gutiérrez, *The Power of the Poor in History*, trans. Robert R. Barr (Maryknoll, N.Y.: Orbis, 1983), p. 67.
3. John H. Westerhoff III, *Will Our Children Have Faith?* (New York: Seabury, 1976), pp. 41, 76.
4. "Poor" here means primarily the socioeconomic poor, people deprived of the necessary means for subsistence such as food, clothing, housing, basic health, education, and work. Hence, the reference is to something *collec-*

tive, involving classes, races, cultures, and the special condition of women. Although there is such thing as "innocent" poverty—a condition unrelated in principle to people's will—such as the case of natural disasters, drought, etc., liberation theology is interested in poverty determined and maintained mainly by the prevailing capitalistic system. Hence, the liberationist reference to the poor always points up the dimension of social and political *conflict*. The focus of critique is on unjust socioeconomic poverty as related to the process of exploitation of the worker (as denounced by Pope John Paul II in *Laborem exercens*, #8). This picture of privation of course further includes other forms of poverty, discrimination, and oppression that are also conditioned by the overall political and economic situation but include factors such as race (blacks, and mixed ethnic groups), sex (women), and culture (Indians). The poorest of the poor are often found in those groups. "Poor" and "oppressed" are therefore used interchangeably even though, to be sure, not everybody who is "oppressed" or marginalized in some form is necessarily socioeconomically poor. In any event, the liberation of the powerful and rich—the so-called alienated "above"—is predicated on the liberation of the weak and poor—those alienated "below." And the concept of "evangelical poor" in liberation theology refers specifically to Christian people who make an existential, practical decision to become poor on account of their solidarity with the socioeconomic poor and who opt for working for liberation and justice.

5. See Alvaro Barreiro, *Basic Ecclesial Communities: The Evangelization of the Poor*, trans. Barbara Campbell (Maryknoll, N.Y.: Orbis, 1982), pp. 14-45; Robert McAfee Brown, *Unexpected News: Reading the Bible with Third World Eyes* (Philadelphia: Westminster, 1984), pp. 11-17, 89-104, 157-161; Ernesto Cardenal, *The Gospel in Solentiname*, vol. I, trans. Donald D. Walsh (Maryknoll, N.Y.: Orbis, 1976), pp. vii-x, 170-189; Ignacio Ellacuría, *Conversión de la Iglesia al Reino de Dios* (Santander, España: Sal Terrae, 1984), pp. 129-151; Richard Shaull, *Heralds of a New Reformation, The Poor of South and North America* (Maryknoll, N.Y.: Orbis, 1984), pp. 1-4, 76-85; Elsa Támez, *Bible of the Oppressed*, trans. Matthew J. O'Connell (Maryknoll, N.Y.: Orbis, 1982).

6. Both Matthew and Luke had the same fundamental concept of the poor, which originated in the Old Testament, particularly in Deutero-Isaiah and the Psalms, through a long evolution. The poor—*anawim*—whom Matthew proclaimed as blessed were also socially and economically alienated and oppressed. The difference between Matthew and Luke lies in emphasis. Matthew stresses a total attitude of humility stemming from a state of economic and social humiliation, whereas Luke places more emphasis on the aspect of privation, oppression, and humiliation which the poor suffer because of their material poverty. Matthew is combating religious self-sufficiency, and Luke, worldliness. (Barreiro, *Basic Ecclesial Communities*, pp. 34-35, 77).

7. The concept "persons in context" alludes to the close association between the *who* and *where* questions in religious education such as the following: Who are the persons that are partners to the educational process and what are their roles? What kinds of interaction will be more conducive to learning tasks and experience? What are the proper environments or set-

tings for Christian religious education to carry on its work with integrity? Assuming as we do that religious education ministry partakes of the whole purpose and mission of the church, what characteristics should the faith community possess in order to serve as the privileged context for nurture and transformation?

8. See chapter 2, note no. 30.

9. See John Eagleson and Philip Sharper, ed. *Puebla and Beyond: Documentation and Commentary*, trans. John Drury (Maryknoll, N.Y.: Orbis, 1979), pp. 210-213, 263-267, and scattered references to both the poor and the BECs. Also, Gutiérrez, *The Power of the Poor in History*, part iii, "Puebla."

10. Harvey Cox, *Religion in the Secular City: Towards a Postmodern Theology* (New York: Simon & Shuster, 1984), p. 138. Cox argues that this view and experience of the church makes liberation theology an "empirical theology" because it is woven from both the ancient Catholic ecclesial tradition and from "consulting the faithful" in the basic communities. In the context of this book, tradition also means that theologians and pastors are obligated to make themselves aware of what the people believe and do as an essential element in formulating theology. This is an issue that we will explore in some detail in the section on the faith of the oppressed.

11. Eagleson and Sharper, eds., *Puebla and Beyond*, pp. 264ff.

12. For a study of the church's social teaching from the perspective of an option for the poor, see Donal Dorr, *Option for the Poor: A Hundred Years of Vatican Social Teaching* (Dublin: Gill and Macmillan/Maryknoll, N.Y.: Orbis, 1983). Dorr argues that two central themes lie at the heart of Catholic social teaching: a particular concern for the poor and powerless together with a criticism of the systems that leave them vulnerable; and a defense of certain personal rights against collectivist tendencies. He holds that recent developments in that teaching can be seen as a shift in emphasis from the second to the first. Clodovis and Leonardo Boff refer to the relationship between the social doctrine of the church and liberation theology, in their *Cómo Hacer Teología de la Liberación* (Madrid: Ediciones Paulinas, 1986), pp. 50-53. These two authors indicate that liberation theology attempts to integrate and explicate creatively the church's positive orientations to social action in light of the concrete context of the Third World, an attempt that is facilitated by the dynamic and open nature of the church's social teaching itself. The Boff brothers conclude by affirming that liberation theology and the social doctrine of the church complement each other for the benefit of the whole people of God. For a restatement of Vatican guidelines on this subject see the document "Instruction on Christian Freedom and Liberation," *National Catholic Reporter* 22:26 (April 15, 1986), pp. 9-12, 41-44.

13. Leonardo Boff, *Teología Desde el Lugar del Pobre* (Santander, España: Sal Terrae, 1986), pp. 42-43.

14. Gustavo Gutiérrez, "The Irruption of the Poor in Latin America and the Christian Communities of the Common People," in *The Challenge of Basic Christian Communities*, ed. Sergio Torres and John Eagleson (Maryknoll, N.Y.: Orbis, 1981), p. 120.

15. See, for instance, the well-documented essays by Elsa Támez, *Bible of the Oppressed*, and Thomas D. Hanks, *God So Loved the Third World: The*

Biblical Vocabulary of Oppression, trans. James D. Dekker (Maryknoll, N.Y.: Orbis, 1983).

16. Boff and Boff, *Cómo Hacer Teología de la Liberación*, p. 12.
17. Robert McAfee Brown, *Theology in a New Key: Responding to Liberation Themes* (Philadelphia: Westminster, 1978), pp. 60ff.
18. Gutiérrez, "The Irruption of the Poor in Latin America," pp. 107-123.
19. One of the most helpful descriptions of *solidarity* for our discussion is found in Jürgen Moltmann, *The Power of the Powerless*, trans. Margaret Kohl (San Francisco: Harper & Row, 1983), pp. 107ff. Moltmann affirms that neighborly love and solidarity are critically related and in fact actually complement one another. He points out that solidarity means at least three things: 1) Standing shoulder to shoulder and struggling together. In other words, solidarity is neighborly love in situations of social and political crises, such as liberating the oppressed and promoting equal rights for everyone. 2) Suffering for one another, or sharing one another's burdens. Solidarity moves beyond activism and embraces fear, anxiety, guilt, and grief. It requires a fellowship in impotence, in helplessness, and even in silence; it thus forms a "community in the depths." 3) Learning to live in fellowship and community with one another. The Christian principle of community is the messianic principle of hope. In sum, solidarity as a common struggle unites people who are alike in being oppressed; solidarity as community in the depths unite people who are alike in their suffering; and solidarity in hopeful love goes beyond those limits of oppression and suffering: By the power of creative love it becomes healing, re-creative, and reconstructive. (See also Moltmann's discussion of the liberation and acceptance of the handicapped, pp. 136-154).
20. Boff, *Teología Desde el Lugar del Pobre*, pp. 32-33.
21. Gutiérrez, *The Power of the Poor in History*, pp. 103-104.
22. Here we will follow closely the discussion of this topic by Ellacuria, in *Conversión de la Iglesia al Reino de Dios*, pp. 153-178.
23. Gutiérrez, "The Irruption of the Poor in Latin America," p. 116.
24. Guillermo Cook, *The Expectation of the Poor: Latin American Basic Ecclesial Communities in Protestant Perspective* (Maryknoll, N.Y.: Orbis, 1985), pp. 6-7, 253-254.
25. Joao B. Libanio, "A Community with a New Image," *International Review of Mission* 68:272 (July 1979), pp. 243-265.
26. Jon Sobrino, *The True Church and the Poor*, trans. Matthew J. O'Connell (Maryknoll, N.Y.: Orbis, 1984), pp. 28-30.
27. Rebecca S. Chopp, *The Praxis of Suffering: An Interpretation of Liberation and Political Theologies* (Maryknoll, N.Y.: Orbis, 1986), p. 151. Chopp's thesis is that *liberation theology is indeed a new paradigm of theology, with a substantial shift in basic assumptions, categories, and ordering of issues.* Four interrelated reasons are presented to account for the distinctive contribution of liberation theology as new paradigm: 1) Its basic claim about human suffering and the quest for liberation; 2) its orientation toward transformation demanded by suffering and facilitated by the very ontological structure of human existence and by God as liberator; 3) its emphasis on praxis; 4) its different understanding of theological reflection in terms of a practical hermeneutics, a critical theory and a social theory. From a different perspective, Sharon D. Welch also argues that the rise of

liberation theologies exemplifies a major shift in Western knowledge, in *Communities of Resistance and Solidarity: A Feminist Theology of Liberation* (Maryknoll, N.Y.: Orbis, 1985). She claims that we are moving away from a model of knowledge which highlights science and historical teleology, and toward a model that emphasizes historical consciousness, political engagement, and societal transformation. Welch finds a striking convergence in the work of Michael Foucault and his analysis of the "insurrection of subjugated knowledges" and the concerns of liberation theologians. That is, suffering oppressed people, in opposition to the dominant theories of the theological establishment, highlight the limitations and shortcomings of the traditions upon which mainstream theologians rely. Welch asserts that liberation theologians contribute to the unearthing of suppressed traditions and cast new light on old ones. They do that by delving into the past and present experience of women, blacks, Hispanics, Indians, and other oppressed peoples.

28. Donald P. McNeill, Douglas A. Morrison, and Henri J. M. Nouwen, *Compassion: A Reflection on the Christian Life* (Garden City, N.J.: Doubleday, 1982), p. 4. This is a book of meditations which includes a moving story of oppression and compassion from Paraguay. See also Henri J. M. Nouwen, *Love in a Fearful Land: A Guatemalan Story* (Notre Dame, Ind.: Ave Maria Press, 1985). It tells the story of two North American parish priests in Central America as an eloquent testimony of compassion, solidarity, and social action in the midst of injustice and violence. Actually, this kind of testimony—which does not eschew alluding to the evil powers—is often more persuasive and prayer-, thought-, and action-provoking than many a radical tract embedded in revolutionary rhetoric.

29. Sobrino, *The True Church and the Poor*, p. 33.

30. Henri J. M. Nouwen, *Gracias!: A Latin American Journal* (San Francisco: Harper & Row, 1983), p. 183.

31. Jon Sobrino, "The 'Doctrinal Authority' of the People of God in Latin America," *Concilium* 180 (August 1985), p. 60.

32. This obviously presupposes a major change in terms of the legacy of Vatican II as appropriated by liberationists. It is the change of the traditional, dominant official Catholic model of the church as superintendent: the hierarchy teaches, theologians explain and defend the teaching, and the faithful listen and obey. See the whole volume of *Concilium* 180, under the title, "The Teaching Authority of the Believers." Editors Johannes B. Metz and Edward Schillebeeckx put forward "a theologically responsible and substantiated model of the way in which believers in the life of the church are not merely recipients of church doctrine, but living subjects . . . of a faith which they express in a theologically relevant manner" (p. ix). In connection with the possible tension between official hierarchical magisterium and poor people of God, Jon Sobrino states that "both bodies are required to be open to conversion: In the official hierarchical magisterium, this means examining itself to see whether it has really listened to the poor or ignored them; in the poor, it means openness to the corrections of the official hierarchical magisterium. In any case, at times of tension or impasse what is needed is historical patience and a conviction that in the final analysis . . . holiness . . . sooner or later, will turn the experience of faith into the experience of doctrine" (p. 61). And Leonardo Boff says:

"Laity and bishops alike may deviate. A mutual apprenticeship, in mutual openness, is the best means to avoid deviations on either side. Evangelization is a two-way street. The bishop evangelizes the people, and the people evangelize the bishop. Otherwise, who evangelizes the bishop? Who sees to his salvation?" (*Ecclesiogenesis: the Base Communities Reinvent the Church*, trans. Robert R. Barr [Maryknoll, N.Y.: Orbis, 1986], p. 40.)

33. Gregory Baum, "The Anabaptists: Teachers of the Churches," *The Mennonite Reporter* 5:16 (August 4, 1975), p. 5. Baum argues that the Anabaptist movement was inspired by a new imagination and new vision that had the virtue of anticipating developments which were to occur centuries later in the history of Christianity. Actually there is a striking parallel between the main contributions of the Radical Reformation and those of the BEC liberationist movement. Those contributions include, among other things: the prophetic critique of the social order (political-cultural as well as ecclesial), the development of base communities in terms of "free churches" by way of voluntary association as well as by repudiating the altar-throne marriage, the defense and promotion of religious freedom and the openness to ecumenical cooperation, and the understanding of Christian faith as discipleship and "orthopraxis." For a wider discussion of the Radical Reformation movement, including the Anabaptists and their legacy, and related Christian traditions, see George H. Williams, *The Radical Reformation* (Philadelphia: Westminster, 1962), and Donald F. Durnbaugh, *The Believers' Church: The History and Character of Radical Protestantism*, 2nd ed. (Scottsdale: Herald, 1985).

34. See Shaull, *Herald of a New Reformation*, pp. 76-85. Shaull discusses five theses about the view from below in light of his experience among the poor in South and North America as follows: 1) We need those who are underneath as our teachers if we hope to understand the world in which we live; 2) to the extent that we look at the world from below, space is created for the poor and the outcasts to affirm themselves and speak with their voice, for the enrichment of all; 3) Jesus, the poor Messiah, radically transforms our perception of what is happening in history; 4) the deprivation, exploitation, suffering, and death make the present intolerable for those underneath, especially if they are Christians whose expectations for another order are aroused by Jesus; 5) to look at the world from below, from the perspective of liberation, is to be guided by a utopian vision of life.

35. When the special nature and role of theological education is distinctively maintained or affirmed, it is possible to identify a number of principles and directions for theological education from a liberationist perspective. This in turn can substantially influence—both directly and indirectly—the foundations and training for the religious education ministry. Some of those principles have been alluded to in the previous chapter. See also *Theological Education* 16:1 (Autumn 1979), "Theological Education and Liberation Theology: A Symposium."

36. See F. Ross Kinsler, ed., *Ministry by the People: Theological Education by Extension* (Geneva: WCC Publications and Maryknoll, N.Y.: Orbis, 1983).

37. James Michael Lee, *The Flow of Religious Instruction* (Birmingham, Ala.: Religious Education Press, 1973), p. 20. Also, "The Authentic Source of Religious Instruction," in *Religious Education and Theology*, ed. Norma

H. Thompson (Birmingham, Ala.: Religious Education Press, 1982), pp. 100-197.

38. The theological task of whole church as belonging to the total faith community together with the affirmation of the leading role of the people as theological subjects have been recently underscored in Latin America and elsewhere. For example, Ian M. Fraser, in *Reinventing Theology as the People's Work* (London: USPG, 1983) argues for the reappropriation of theology by the whole community of the church. Says Fraser: "It is in the cards in our time, in a measure unexampled in history, that lay people, or rather the church as a whole, laity, and clergy together, may, by main force if need be, take into their own hands the theological task which is properly theirs. It is incumbent on those of us who are theological educators to encourage this to happen" (p. 35). Kim Young Bock, ed., *Minjung Theology: People as the Subjects of History* (Singapore: Christian Conference of Asia, 1981) supplies an Asian (Korean) perspective. This emphasis on grassroots participation is logically associated with the incarnational motif of contextualization. Liberation theologies assert not only that the gospel is a message of liberation from every kind of imperialism, domination, and alienation; they also assert that theology itself must be liberated from the biases of dominant cultures, classes, races, and political interest; theology must grow out of the people's struggle for liberation and justice. The Asian and African theologies insist that their agenda must be determined by Asian and African realities, interests, needs, and perspectives. In North America, black theology has exposed the racism and alienation of prevailing theologies, to rediscover its own rich heritage, and to contribute essential dimensions of God's revelation to the mainstream. Analogously, feminist theologians all over the world expose the male bias that has dominated church thought and practice through history, thus unveiling new relevance in God's revelation to and through women, and offering new perspectives and insights in theology as well as ministry. All of these liberationist movements converge to proclaim that all the people of God are called and empowered to participate in the theological vocation and the education ministry of the church.

39. Fray Betto, *Lo Que Son las Comunidades Eclesiales de Base* (Bogotá: Indo-American Press Service, 1981), pp. 24-28, 43-46.

40. James Michael Lee discusses this topic in "The Authentic Source of Religious Instruction," pp. 184-192.

41. John H. Westerhoff III, *Living the Faith Community: The Church that Makes a Difference* (Minneapolis: Winston, 1985), p. 83.

42. Walter Brueggemann, *The Creative Word: Canon as a Model for Biblical Education* (Philadelphia: Fortress, 1982), p. 50.

43. Craig Dykstra, "Education, the Gospel, and the Marginal," *The Princeton Seminary Bulletin* 5:1, New Series (1984), p. 20.

44. See for instance Barreiro, *Basic Ecclesial Communities*, p. 66.

45. Parker J. Palmer, *The Company of Strangers: Christians and the Renewal of America's Public Life* (New York: Crossroad, 1981), especially chap. 3.

46. Nouwen, *Gracias!*, pp. 187-188.

47. For a brief discussion of Christian base communities in Europe and the United States, see Cox, *Religion in the Secular City*, chapter 10. As a rule, these communities do not emerge from poor and working-class districts

but from middle-class ones. The combination of popular religiosity, grinding poverty, and political repression, characteristic of the Latin American scene, does not exist to the same extent in the North Atlantic. However, the North American and European base communities have common features observable also in the older and by far more numerous Latin American counterparts: fairly informal and participatory style of liturgical celebration, often led by lay people; Bible study and reflection; and some form of political engagement (disarmament and peace; hunger; ecology; imperialism and neo-colonialism; protection of refugees, etc.). It should be noted that in Latin America, the BECs are largely a Catholic phenomenon, although there are grassroots Protestant communities in some countries, such as Brazil and Guatemala, as well as a growing number of interdenominational and ecumenical BECs.

48. Cook, *The Expectation of the Poor*, pp. 2-3.
49. Betto, *Lo Que Son las Comunidades Eclesiales de Base*, p. 12.
50. Leonardo Boff, *Church, Charism and Power: Liberation Theology and the Institutional Church*, trans. John W. Dierksmeier (New York: Crossroads, 1985), p. 126. This book attempts to deal with the contradictions arising when theologians apply Roman Catholic social teaching to the social reality of the Roman Catholic Church itself. Its radical tone is derived from Boff's Latin American pastoral experience which has led him to believe that the church needs a dramatic and radical conversion. For Boff, in essence, the Holy Spirit's *charism* confronts the institutional church's hierarchical *power*. The book includes several ecclesiological theses for which the Vatican attempted to "silence" Boff: 1) The true Christian church is more than the Roman Catholic Church (i.e., the church cannot pretend to identify itself exclusively with the Church of Christ because the Church of Christ may also subsist in other Christian churches); 2) dogma is one key for the interpretation of the gospel, but its validity to a significant extent depends on a certain time and circumstance (i.e., the concept that the Catholic magisterium has received from God certain necessary, absolute, and infallible truths leads to dogmatism and intolerance); 3) the hope of the church lies in the "new model" provided by the church of the poor (i.e., the pyramidal, centralist structure of the Catholic church as an institution of power is superseded by the communal, participatory, "charismatic" reality of the gathered faithful); 4) the prophetic mission is possible only for a church that is born from the common people and becomes existentially aware of all forms of oppression and injustice (i.e., the church-institution tends to accommodate itself with existent regimes for the preservation of its own interests).
51. See William Cook, "Spirituality in the Struggles for Social Justice: A Brief Latin American Anthology," *Missiology: An International Review* 12:2 (April 1984), pp. 224-232. Some primary sources include: Leonardo Boff, *The Lord's Prayer: The Prayer of Integral Liberation,*, trans. Theodore Morrow (Maryknoll, N.Y.: Orbis, 1984); Dom Helder Camara, *The Desert is Fertile*, trans. Dinah Livingstone (Maryknoll, N.Y.: Orbis, 1976); Segundo Galilea, *Following Jesus*, trans. Helen Phillips (Maryknoll, N.Y.: Orbis, 1981) and *The Beatitudes: To Evangelize as Jesus Did*, trans. Robert R. Barr (Maryknoll, N.Y.: Orbis, 1984); Gustavo Gutiérrez, *We Drink from Our Own Wells: The Spiritual Journey of a People*, trans. Matthew J.

O'Connell (Maryknoll, N.Y.: Orbis, 1984); Joao B. Libanio, *Spiritual Discernment and Politics: Guidelines for Religious Communities*, trans. Theodore Morrow (Maryknoll, N.Y.: Orbis, 1982).

52. The notion that the BECs are in fact harbingers of a new Reformation is emphatically affirmed by Cox, *Religion in the Secular City* (especially chaps. 11 and 22) and Shaull, *Heralds of a New Reformation* (especially chap. 8). Johannes B. Metz also makes a strong case for a "second reformation" that will affect substantially, although in different ways, both Catholic and Protestant churches, in *The Emergent Church: The Future of Christianity in a Post-Bourgeois World*, trans. Peter Mann (New York: Crossroad, 1981). Together with the *Radical* (or "left wing") Reformation principles indicated above in note no. 33, other clear parallels with the sixteenth-century Protestant Reformation movement include the emphases of the BECs on creative protest (the so-called "Protestant principle"), the "priesthood of all believers," and the privileged place of the Bible for the church as hermeneutic community. It should be further noted that historically many of the Protestant churches that have become well-established institutions through a predictable sociological process can trace their origin to some kind of grassroots ecclesial community movement in Europe.

53. Several dimensions of the spirit and ramifications of Vatican II are noticeable in light of our discussion, such as these: ongoing reform and updating ("aggiornamento") of the Catholic church; ecumenical openness; collegiality among the bishops and at different levels of the Catholic church; legitimation of regional diversity; religious freedom; inculturation; some increase in the active participation of the laity; and involvement of the Catholic church in reshaping society at large.

54. See Boff, *Ecclesiogenesis*, chap. 1; and Cook, *The Expectation of the Poor*," chap. 4.

55. Barreiro, *Basic Ecclesial Communities*, p. 31.

56. Boff and Boff, *Cómo Hacer Teología de la Liberación*, chap. 2.

57. The transformational and revolutionary potential of these grassroots communities cannot be underestimated. However, their actual limitations as agents of social change are often overlooked. For example, W. E. Hewitt has analyzed the BECs "global improvement strategy," a principal means through which the communities instigate social change in Brazil in one specific locale. Five major problems were identified as facing the six BECs in the sample: lack of community recognition; interference from government officials; interference from the institutional church; religious traditionalism among the membership; and over-reliance on BEC leaders ("Strategies for Social Change Employed by Comunidades Eclesiais de Base (CEBs) in the Archidiocese of Sao Paulo," *Journal for the Scientific Study of Religion* 25:1; [March 1986], pp. 16-30).

58. Maurice L. Monette, "Justice, Peace, and the Pedagogy of the Grass Roots Christian Community," in Padraic O'Hare, ed., *Education for Peace and Justice* (San Francisco: Harper & Row, 1983), pp. 83-93.

59. This is actually Jon Sobrino's thesis in his *The True Church and the Poor*, namely that the church of the poor embodies and represents more fully than any other form of the church what might be called the basic substance of ecclesiality. See especially chapters 4 and 5.

60. Boff, *Teología Desde el Lugar del Pobre*, p. 32.

61. Boff, *Church, Charism and Power*, p. 126.

62. The Puebla Document (1979) already contains a strong warning "not to fall prey to the danger of organizational anarchy or narrow minded sectarian elitism" and refers to some "aspects of the whole problem of the 'people's church' . . . or of 'parallel magisteria.'" The bishops complain that the "official" or institutional Catholic church is accused of being "alienating." The bishops also castigate the seeming denial of the function of the hierarchy on the part of liberationists and supporters of the "people's church." (Eagleson and Sharper, eds., *Puebla and Beyond*, pp. 157-158). The Vatican "Instruction on Certain Aspects of the 'Theology of Liberation'" (1984) includes harsh criticism of the following: the supposedly required participation in the class struggle; the historical, political reductionism in the view of the faith; the "disastrous confusion between the poor and the proletariat of Marx"; the question of the "church of the poor" and "the church of the class that has become aware of the requirements of the revolutionary struggle as a step toward liberation and which celebrates this liberation in its liturgy. . . a church of the oppressed people whom it is necessary to 'conscientize' in the light of the organized struggle for freedom"; and the critique and challenge to the sacramental and hierarchical structure of the church (chap. ix: 7 to 13). We need to underscore, however, that this "Instruction" does not condemn or even criticize liberation theology as a movement or, for that matter, any specific liberation theology, but some aspects of some *unidentified* "theologies of liberation." The Vatican "Instruction on Christian Freedom and Liberation" (1986) includes a reference to the BECs in chapter iv ("Liberating Mission of the Church"). In connection with the evangelical love or preference for the poor, the document expresses that the BECs are to live in unity with the local and universal church and that their "fidelity to their mission will depend on how careful they are to educate their members in the fullness of the Christian faith through listening to the word of God, fidelity to the teaching of the magisterium, to the hierarchical order of the church, and to sacramental life. If this condition is fulfilled, their experience, rooted in a commitment to the complete liberation of man (sic), becomes a treasure for the whole church."

63. This analogy is taken from John H. Yoder, *The Original Revolution* (Scottdale, Pa.: Herald Press, 1971).

64. This discussion supplements the treatment of the messianic community in chapter 2.

65. Westerhoff, *Living the Faith Community*, p. 21.

66. Jack L. Seymour, "Approaches to Christian Education" and Charles R. Foster, "The Faith Community as a Guiding Image for Christian Education," in *Contemporary Approaches to Christian Education*, ed. Jack L. Seymour and Donald E. Miller (Nashville: Abingdon, 1982), pp. 11-34 and 53-71. See also Donald E. Miller, *Story and Context: An Introduction to Christian Education* (Nashville: Abingdon, 1987).

67. This discussion takes into account a number of liberationist sources concerning BEC ecclesiology and actual ecclesial experience and mainly the work of Leonardo Boff, *Church, Charism and Power* and *Ecclesiogenesis*. It also follows closely my discussion of persons in context principles in

Daniel S. Schipani, *Conscientization and Creativity: Paulo Freire and Christian Education* (Lanham, Md.: University Press of America, 1984), pp. 123-138.

68. See William B. Kennedy, "A Radical Challenge to Inherited Educational Patterns," *Religious Education* 74:5 (September-October 1979), pp. 491-495.

69. For further discussion on the direct connection between worship and religious education, the following books are recommended: Robert L. Browning and Roy A. Reed, *The Sacraments in Religious Education* (Birmingham, Ala.: Religious Education Press, 1985); John H. Westerhoff III, *A Pilgrim People: Learning Through the Church Year* (Minneapolis: Seabury, 1984); and John H. Westerhoff III and William H. Willimon, *Liturgy and Learning Through the Life Cycle* (Minneapolis: Seabury, 1980).

70. James E. Loder, "Negation and Transformation: A Study in Theology and Human Development," in *Toward Moral and Religious Maturity: The First International Conference on Moral and Religious Development*, ed. James Fowler and Antoine Vergote (Morristown: Silver Burdett, 1980), p. 191.

71. See Gwyneth Griffin, "Images of Interdependence: Learning/Teaching for Justice and Peace," *Religious Education* 79:3 (Summer 1984), pp. 340-352.

72. Boff, *Church, Charism and Power*, p. 128.

Epilogue

This book was written in the face of the seemingly major impact of liberation theology in the North American religious and theological scene.[1] In view of the need for a systematic and conclusive treatment of liberation thought with regard to religious education, one of the main purposes of this book has consistently been to provide a comprehensive and critical overview of Latin American liberation theology from the unique vantage point of religious education. We were especially interested in highlighting and appropriating major insights in light of the overall liberation thrust and spirit. Further, our intentention has been to participate in the larger dialogue on the relationship between religious education and theology, together with the germane and perennial question of practice and theory which is so central for the two fields. Thus, we aimed to devise constructive restatements of principles for religious education theory and practice in the context of its direct encounter with liberation theology.

At the conclusion of our endeavors to share a balanced view and a well-documented volume, it appears that our goals have been met. All major liberationist contributions, including critical assessments, have been discussed in terms of the five central tenets of liberation theology which set the overall agenda in each of the five chapters which comprise the book. Thus we have dealt with: 1) The process of conscientization as the practice of freedom and creativity (i.e., the Freirean background and inspiration of liberation theology); 2) the prophetic and utopian vision of the coming reign of God (i.e., the political-eschatological dimension of the gospel); 3) the praxis epistemology of obedience and the view of Christian faith as participation in God's creative and liberating activity for the world (i.e., knowing, discipleship, and the performative approach to faith); 4) critical interpretation for understanding and transformation (i.e., liberation hermeneutics as focal methodological perspective); and 5) the base Christian community and the place and role of the oppressed (i.e., the ecclesial context and the paradoxical contribution of the weak "other").

The unique viewpoint of religious education has allowed us to consistently discern and appraise the pedagogical structure and orientation of liberation theology, that is, its intrinsic educational thrust and interest. Among other things, our comprehensive and critical review further illumines the meaning and potential significance of key "guiding metaphors" that may be used in turn to define approaches and aims of Christian religious education. Thus, the metaphors of education and person, justice, meaning, and faith community[2] may be informed, respectively, by the contents of chapters 1, 2, and 3, 4, and 5 in specific ways. To the extent that those key metaphors help to identify and evaluate approaches to religious education, to that extent our discussion also helps to define and provide foundational material for complementary educational approaches to religious education, such as "instruction" and "development," "liberation," "interpretation," and "community of faith."[3]

The dialogical reading of liberation theology from the perspective of religious education highlights the significance of that theological movement for the task of religious education in several ways. For one thing, we have affirmed the very centrality of religious education in terms of what we have called the church's threefold reason for being, namely worship, community, and mission. For another thing, throughout the book we have suggested a redefinition of the religious education task in terms of categories and principles related to structural and substantive process content, to manifest substantive content, to goal and objectives, to timing, and persons in context. In other words, in its real-life encounter with religious education, liberation theology becomes indeed foundational for an overall theory or model.[4]

By way of summary we can briefly recapitulate the major emphases stemming from the encounter of religious education with liberation theology. Together with the general thrust which the educational ministry plays in discerning, sustaining, and enhancing the church's alternative consciousness and way of being God's community in the midst of history, we may reiterate the following: 1) "Conscientization" and critical awareness and reflection are underscored as major dimensions of the educational program and process, although subordinated to a holistic (i.e., comprehensive, multidimensional) lifestyle of discipleship. 2) The overall aim of "discipling" (i.e., formation, transformation, and empowerment on both personal and communal levels) is defined in terms of the utopia of God's coming reign of shalom (i.e., peace, with freedom and justice). Further, the appropriation of the gospel of the reign of God includes a twofold prophetic thrust involving denouncing, grieving, critique, (i.e., nonconformity) as well as announcing, imagining creative alternatives (i.e., Christ-inspired personal, communal, societal transformation). 3) Faith is redefined in terms of discipleship for the sake of the kingdom and the world (i.e., appropriation and participation in the Spirit-led movement for liberation and re-creation at all levels and in all dimensions of human life and the nonhuman environment). In other words, faithfulness is obedience and actual Christ-inspired praxis. 4) The hermeneutical-dialectical interplay engaging present historical situation and experience, scripture and ecclesial tradition, vision and hope, becomes a privileged educational process that assumes divine coparticipation (the Holy Spirit). 5) The church is viewed primarily as a base community (i.e., an efficacious sign—witness and service oriented—of the presence and reign of God in history) with a biased passion for the alienated, the poor and oppressed, the marginal, and the stranger.

It has been our thesis that in the encounter between liberation theology and religious education, mutual enlightenment can take place, provided that the integrity of the two fields is respected and maintained. In other words, the dialogical and critical interfacing must engage the two fields in their own respective terms, which amounts to a methodological stance essential for this kind of project. Thus we undertook the task required by the stated purposes by way of an "encounter" including the related connotations of meeting (i.e., interfacing, juxtaposition) and confronting (i.e., critical interplay). By focusing on key liberationist tenets, on the one hand, and on major categories and principles of religious education, on the other hand, in each chapter we have indicated various instances of reciprocal illumination as well as potential for the two fields to be advanced in their own terms.[5]

Liberation theology indeed informs Christian religious education as a dimension and form of ministry in specific ways in terms of the framework and viewpoint of religious education itself. In turn, religious education critically and constructively informs liberation theology seen as a relevant form of faith seeking understanding and transformation.

Our discussion throughout this book suggests that, together with being a partner in critical dialogue, liberation theology can provide the essential background and clue for religious education thus becoming pivotal for a theological restatement of the field at the present time.[6] Without implying of course that liberation theology is the sufficient theological foundation, the claim made is that it provides a necessary, indeed indispensable contribution for the educational ministry of the church in North America. The challenge for the Christian community to embrace a consistent commitment for shalom (peace, with freedom and justice) and social transformation certainly points in that direction.[7] That being the case, we must also affirm the need for further contextualization of the liberationist view of gospel and faith[8] and for further dialogue for complementarity and a mutually enriching and corrective service with other theological perspectives and traditions.[9] Finally, liberation theology must be engaged in a continuing conversation with religious education in search for a more comprehensive, effective, and pertinent educational ministry at the service of worship, community, and mission, and for the sake of the coming reign of God.[10]

Notes

1. Please review the Preface for a reminder on the background and the contours of this book.
2. The notion of key metaphors helpful to understand and assess approaches to religious education, together with suggested "metaphors," is taken from Jack L. Seymour, "Approaches to Christian Education," in Jack L. Seymour, Donald E. Miller et al., *Contemporary Approaches to Christian Education* (Nashville: Abingdon, 1982), pp. 11-34. The main idea is that key metaphors help to structure reflection on a given discipline and field from a certain perspective. Seymour also asserts that a better understanding of the perspectives by which Christian religious education is being organized will contribute to shaping a more coherent and comprehensive theory and practice.
3. Ibid. Those five approaches so identified are described in some detail in chapters 2 to 6 of the same book.
4. "Model" is here used with a connotation broader than "approach" or "perspective," that is, roughly equivalent to educational paradigm or vision. In other words, "Christian religious education in a liberation key" is a model which incorporates, reshapes, and integrates several approaches such as "interpretation," "community of faith," and so on.

5. To a certain extent, we are thus referring to religious education and liberation theology as "conversation partners" in a manner analogous to Craig Dykstra's suggestion in the case of religious education and faith development theory. ("Faith Development and Religious Education," in *Faith Development and Fowler*, ed. Craig Dykstra and Sharon Parks [Birmingham, Ala.: Religious Education Press, 1986], pp. 251-271). The analogy ends, however, at the point where we affirm the organic relationship between religious education as a major dimension of the educational ministry (theological education, for instance, being another dimension) and the Christian ecclesial community. In that context, the theological task plays an inherently normative role, for example regarding the very understanding of biblical faith itself.

6. We are alluding to the major questions raised by Randolph Crump Miller, Iris V. Cully, and Norma H. Thompson, as indicated in the Preface. Those and related questions are taken into consideration throughout the book and explicitly faced in the last major sections of chapters 2 and 3. We might add that liberation theology, almost by definition, appears to be more modest (or less "imperialistic") than other theological traditions and perspectives with regard to religious education in the sense that it underscores the necessary input of the social sciences (together with its own political interests) and insists on the secondary place of theological reflection per se.

7. See the incisive essay by Allen J. Moore, "Liberation and the Future of Christian Education," in *Contemporary Approaches to Christian Education*, pp. 103-122. From a Latin American perspective, see Matías Preiswerk, *Educating in the Living Word: A Theoretical Framework for Christian Education*, trans. Robert R. Barr (Maryknoll, N.Y.: Orbis, 1987).

8. See, for example, Frederick Herzog, *Justice Church: The New Function of the Church in North American Christianity* (Maryknoll, N.Y.: Orbis, 1980) and William K. Tabb, ed. *Churches in Struggle: Liberation Theologies and Social Change in North America* (New York: Monthly Review, 1986).

9. That dialogue and possible cooperation must include not only North American liberation theologies, such as black or feminist, but other differing views (e.g., process theology) as well, not to mention specific theological traditions (e.g., Reformed, Catholic, etc.). This is precisely one major challenge for further research.

10. Please review notes 72 and 73 in chapter 4. Undoubtedly, a special agenda for further discussion and research is the question of correlating the discipling work of religious education on the communal and personal levels. Our claim is that *discipling* (which involves formation, transformation, and empowerment) is essential in the threefold task of enabling for *worship*, equipping for *community*, and empowering for *mission*, on the one hand. On the other hand, we also claim (again in explicitly trinitarian fashion) that discipling is essential as a multidimensional process of formation for *vision*, transformation for *virtue*, and empowerment for *vocation* on the personal dimension.

Index of Names

Index of Subjects

Academic theology, 122, 158
Action-reflection paradigm, 140, 167
Alienation, 14, 24, 27, 29, 34, 36, 41, 80, 84, 85, 159
Anabaptists, 146, 225, 255
   see also Reformation, Radical

Base (Ecclesial/Christian) community, 4, 12, 38, 41, 44, 64, 78, 214, 227, 235-250, 256-257, 259, 261
   as focus for conscientization, 235-239
   as religious education context, 244-250
   see also Church
Base Education Movement, 38, 212
Bible (scriptures), 2, 41, 83, 95, 121, 161, 170-181, 186, 187, 197 204, 223, 232
   in Christian religious education, 186-187, 232
   liberation of, 170-181, 204
   see also Word
Black theology, 5, 59, 189, 209, 265
Brazil, 12, 26, 38, 162, 177, 179, 180, 197, 206, 212

Capitalism, 1, 111, 159, 198
Catholic action methodology, 162-170, 197, 238
   observing, 162-164
   judging, 164-167
   acting, 167-170
   see also Liberation theology—method
Central America, 1, 4, 212, 236
Christendom, 1, 104, 237
Christian realism, 101-102
Christian religious education, 3, 11, 47, 48, 51-55, 65-66, 96, 97-100, 134, 138-143, 148-149, 152, 154,

155, 169, 182-183, 184, 185-190, 190-194, 232, 244-250, 262-265
   agendas for, 96-100
   aim, overall objectives, 97-100, 139, 154, 192
   Bible in, 182-183, 186-187, 232
   faith community as context for, 244-250
   guiding metaphors, 100, 114, 262, 264
   guiding principle for, 94-97, 114, 139
   hermeneutical approach in, 185-187
   justice and peace in, 138-143, 152, 152-155, 239
   learning tasks in, 51-55, 67
   liberating learning in, 48, 51-55, 67
   liberating teaching in, 48-51
   timing principles for, 190-194
Christology of liberation, 32, 33, 69, 71-83, 102, 106-107
   christological reformulation in, 77-79
   critique of oppressive Christologies in, 72-76
   Freire's, 32-33
   limitations, weaknesses of, 79-81
Church, 2, 9, 10, 30, 31, 32, 36, 38, 42-46, 63, 78, 86, 92-93, 95-96, 100, 111-112, 131, 134, 139, 159, 240-244, 245-250, 257, 262, 263, 264
   as context for religious education, 244-250
   as contrast society, 93, 111-112
   as messianic community, 92-93, 111-112, 240-244
   prophetic, 9, 30, 42-46, 78, 86, 92-93, 95-96, 100, 111-112, 131, 134, 159, 240-244, 245-250, 257, 262, 263, 264

271